# California
# Preschool
# Learning
# Foundations

## Volume 1

Social-Emotional Development
Language and Literacy
English-Language Development
Mathematics

# Publishing Information

The *California Preschool Learning Foundations* (Volume 1) was developed by the Child Development Division, California Department of Education through a contract with WestEd. It was edited by Dixie Abbott, Janet Lundin, and Faye Ong, working in cooperation with Desiree Soto, Consultant, Child Development Division. It was prepared for printing by the staff of CDE Press: the cover and interior design were created and prepared by Cheryl McDonald; typesetting was done by Jeannette Reyes. It was published by the Department, 1430 N Street, Sacramento, CA 95814-5901. It was distributed under the provisions of the Library Distribution Act and *Government Code* Section 11096.

Reprinted in 2017.

ISBN 978-0-8011-1681-0

## Ordering Information

Copies of this publication are available for sale from the California Department of Education. For prices and ordering information, please visit the Department Web site at http://www.cde.ca.gov/re/pn or call the CDE Press Sales Office at (800) 995-4099. An illustrated *Educational Resources Catalog* describing publications, videos, and other instructional media available from the Department can be obtained without charge by writing to the CDE Press Sales Office, California Department of Education, 1430 N Street, Suite 3207, Sacramento, CA 95814-5901; FAX (916) 323-0823 or by calling the CDE Press Sales Office at the telephone number shown above.

## Notice

The guidance in *California Preschool Learning Foundations* (Volume 1) is not binding on local educational agencies or other entities. Except for the statutes, regulations, and court decisions that are referenced herein, the document is exemplary, and compliance with it is not mandatory. (See *Education Code* Section 33308.5.)

# Contents

# A Message from the State Superintendent of Public Instruction

I am delighted to present the *California Preschool Learning Foundations* (Volume 1), a publication that I believe will be instrumental in improving early learning and development for California's preschool children.

Young children are naturally eager to learn. However, not all of them are ready for school. All too often, children entering school for the first time as kindergarteners are already lagging behind their classmates, and this disadvantage can affect them socially and academically long past kindergarten. Children who have had the benefit of attending high-quality preschools are more comfortable in their surroundings, have been exposed to books, have learned how to play cooperatively, and are accustomed to learning with others.

Research shows that all children can benefit from participating in high-quality preschool programs. And a recent study by the RAND Corporation shows that closing the school "readiness" gap will help to close the achievement gap, in which far too many socioeconomically disadvantaged students and far too many African American and Latino children are lagging behind and achieving below their abilities. Not all preschool programs are equally effective, however. Those that strengthen children's school readiness operate with an in-depth understanding of what children need to learn before they start school.

With a goal of ensuring that all preschools in California offer such high-quality programs, the California Department of Education, during a three-year-long collaborative effort with leading early childhood educators, researchers, advocates, and parents, developed these preschool learning foundations.

The foundations outline key knowledge and skills that most children can achieve when provided with the kinds of interactions, instruction, and environments research has shown to promote early learning and development. The foundations can provide early childhood educators, parents, and the public with a clear understanding of the wide range of knowledge and skills that preschool children typically attain when given the benefits of a high-quality preschool program.

These foundations focus on four domains: social-emotional development, language and literacy, English-language development, and mathematics. They provide a comprehensive understanding of what children learn in these four domains.

It is my hope that these foundations will help guide and support all California preschools as they offer developmentally appropriate activities and instruction that are both purposeful and playful, instilling in our young children a love of learning that will last a lifetime.

*Jack O'Connell*

JACK O'CONNELL
*State Superintendent of Public Instruction*

# Acknowledgments

The development of the preschool learning foundations involved many people. The following groups contributed: (1) project leaders; (2) the Preschool Learning Foundations Research Consortium; (3) expanded research consortia; (4) lead researchers; (5) staff from the California Department of Education (CDE); (6) early childhood education stakeholder organizations; and (7) facilitators of public input sessions.

## Project Leaders

The developmental work involved the tireless work of dedicated staff. The following staff members are gratefully acknowledged for their many contributions: **Peter Mangione** and **Cathy Tsao**, WestEd; **Mark Wilson** and **Stephen Moore**, University of California, Berkeley.

## Preschool Learning Foundations Research Consortium

The development of the preschool learning foundations was guided by a research consortium composed of the following members:

**Melinda Brookshire,** WestEd

**Tzur Karelitz,** University of California, Berkeley

**Anne Kuschner,** Sonoma State University

**Peter Mangione,** WestEd

**Katie Monahan,** WestEd

**Stephen Moore,** University of California, Berkeley

**Maurine Ballard-Rosa,** California State University, Sacramento

**Kavita Seeratan,** University of California, Berkeley

**Janet Thompson,** University of California, Davis

**Ross Thompson,** University of California, Davis

**Cathy Tsao,** WestEd

**Ineko Tsuchida,** WestEd

**Rebeca Valdivia,** WestEd

**Ann Wakeley,** Sonoma State University

**Ann-Marie Wiese,** WestEd

**Mark Wilson,** University of California, Berkeley

**Hiro Yamada,** University of California, Berkeley

**Marlene Zepeda,** California State University, Los Angeles

**Osnat Zur,** WestEd

## Lead Researchers

Special thanks are extended to the following lead researchers for their expertise:

*Social-Emotional Development*

**Ross Thompson,** University of California, Davis

**Janet Thompson,** University of California, Davis

*Language and Literacy**

**Anne Cunningham,** University of California, Berkeley

**Christopher Lonigan,** Florida State University

*English-Language Development*

**Marlene Zepeda,** California State University, Los Angeles

*Mathematics*

**Doug Clements,** State University of New York

**Aki Murata,** Mills College and Stanford University

---

* **Susan Landry** and **Susan Gunnewig,** University of Texas, Houston, also made valuable contributions to early drafts.

## Expanded Research Consortia

Domain experts and their affiliations are listed as follows:

### Social-Emotional Development

**Oscar Barbarin,** University of North Carolina, Chapel Hill

**Susanne Denham,** George Mason University

**Michael Lopez,** National Center for Latino Child & Family Research, Washington D.C.

**Sandra Machida,** California State University, Chico

**Ross Thompson,** University of California, Davis

**Janet Thompson,** University of California, Davis

**Deborah Vandell,** University of California, Irvine

### Language and Literacy Development

**Sheila Arnold,** Orange County Department of Education

**Marilyn Astore,** Sacramento County Office of Education

**Janet Barnes,** Tehama County Office of Education

**Melinda Brookshire,** Sonoma State University

**Larry Champion,** Tehama County Office of Education

**Don Corrie,** Tehama County Office of Education

**Anne Cunningham,** University of California, Berkeley

**Jan Davis,** Sonoma State University

**Gary DeiRossi,** San Joaquin County Office of Education

**Karen Draney,** University of California, Berkeley

**Donna Elmore,** SETA Head Start

**Imelda Foley,** Los Angeles Unified School District

**Bertha Franco,** United Families, Inc.

**Magda Franco,** United Families, Inc.

**Susan Gunnewig,** University of Texas, Houston

**Rena Hallam,** University of Tennessee, Knoxville

**Whit Hayslip,** Los Angeles Unified School District

**Betsy Hiteshew,** University of California, Los Angeles Extension

**Carolyn Huie-Hofstetter,** University of California, Berkeley

**Deirdre Jackson,** San Bernardino City Unified School District

**Sarah Kania,** Tehama County Office of Education

**Linda Kroll,** Mills College

**Anne Kuschner,** Sonoma State University

**Susan Landry,** University of Texas, Houston

**Amy Lin Tan,** Sacramento City Unified School District

**Christopher Lonigan,** Florida State University

**Peter Mangione,** WestEd

**Rick McCallum,** University of California, Berkeley

**Daniel Meier,** San Francisco State University

**Deborah Montgomery Parrish,** American Institutes for Research

**Stephen Moore,** University of California, Berkeley

**Roberta Peck,** First 5 California

**Pat Phipps,** California Association for the Education of Young Children

**Eva Ponte,** University of California, Berkeley

**Lisa Sandberg,** Tehama County Office of Education

**Connie Tate,** San Joaquin County Office of Education

**Amy Wagner,** WestEd

**Mark Whitney,** Mira Costa College

**Mark Wilson,** University of California, Berkeley

**Frank Worrell,** University of California, Berkeley

**Joyce Wright,** Sacramento County Office of Education

### English-Language Development

**Barbara Flores,** California State University, San Bernardino

**Vera Gutierrez-Clellan,** San Diego State University

**Linda Espinosa,** University of Missouri, Columbia

**Celia Genishi,** Teachers College, Columbia University

**Alison Wishard Guerra,** University of California, San Diego

**RaMonda Horton-Ikard,** University of Tennessee, Knoxville

**Gisela Jia,** City University of New York

**Lisa Lopez,** University of South Florida

**Marlene Zepeda,** California State University, Los Angeles

### Mathematics

**Doug Clements,** State University of New York, Stony Brook

**Janet Barnes,** Tehama County Office of Education

**Melinda Brookshire,** Sonoma State University

**Larry Champion,** Tehama County Office of Education

**Don Corrie,** Tehama County Office of Education

**Jan Davis,** Sonoma State University

**Gary DeiRossi,** San Joaquin County Office of Education

**Karen Draney,** University of California, Berkeley

**Donna Elmore,** SETA Head Start

**Imelda Foley,** Los Angeles Unified School District

**Whit Hayslip,** Los Angeles Unified School District

**Carolyn Huie-Hofstetter,** University of California, Berkeley

**Deirdre Jackson,** San Bernardino City Unified School District

**Anne Kuschner,** Sonoma State University

**Peter Mangione,** WestEd

**Daniel Meier,** San Francisco State University

**Stephen Moore,** University of California, Berkeley

**Aki Murata,** Mills College and Stanford University

**Deborah Montgomery Parrish,** American Institutes for Research

**Roberta Peck,** First 5 California

**Pat Phipps,** California Association for the Education of Young Children

**Eva Ponte,** University of California, Berkeley

**Lisa Sandberg,** Tehama County Office of Education

**Ann Shannon,** University of California, Berkeley

**Eun Soo Shin,** University of California, Berkeley

**Amy Wagner,** WestEd

**Mark Whitney,** Mira Costa College

**Mark Wilson,** University of California, Berkeley

**Frank Worrell,** University of California, Berkeley

**Joyce Wright,** Sacramento County Office of Education

## California Department of Education

Thanks are also extended to the following staff members: **Gavin Payne,** Chief Deputy Superintendent; **Anthony Monreal,** Deputy Superintendent, Curriculum and Instruction Branch; and **Michael Jett,** Director, **Gwen Stephens,** Assistant Director, and **Desiree Soto,** Consultant, Child Development Division. During the lengthy development process, many CDE staff members were involved at various levels. Additional thanks are extended to **Sue Stickel,\* Meredith Cathcart, Barbara Metzuk,\* Sy Dang Nguyen, Mary Smithberger, Maria Trejo,** and **Charles Vail.**

*During the development of the foundations, these individuals worked for the California Department of Education.

## Early Childhood Education Stakeholder Organizations

Representatives from many statewide organizations provided perspectives affecting various aspects of the learning foundations:

Action Alliance for Children

Asian Pacific Islander Community Action Network

Association of California School Administrators

California Alliance Concerned with School-Age Parenting and Pregnancy Prevention

California Association for Bilingual Education

California Association for the Education of Young Children

California Association of Family Child Care

California Association of Professors of Early Childhood Special Education

California Child Care Coordinators Association

California Child Care Resource and Referral Network

California Child Development Administrators Association

California Child Development Corps

California Commission on Teacher Credentialing

California Community College Early Childhood Educators

California Community Colleges Chancellor's Office

California County Superintendents Educational Services Association

California Early Reading First Network

California Federation of Teachers

California Head Start Association

California Kindergarten Association

California National Even Start Association

California Preschool Instructional Network

California School Boards Association

California State Parent-Teacher Association

California State University Office of the Chancellor

California Teachers Association

California Tomorrow

Californians Together

Campaign for High Quality Early Learning Standards in California

Child Development Policy Institute

Child Development Policy Institute Education Fund

Children Now

Council for Exceptional Children/The California Division for Early Childhood

Council of CSU Campus Childcare

Curriculum and Instruction Steering Committee

Fight Crime, Invest in Kids California

First 5 Association of California

First 5 California Children and Families Commission

Infant Development Association of California

Learning Disabilities Association of California

Los Angeles Universal Preschool

Mexican American Legal Defense and Education Fund

Migrant Education Even Start

Migrant Head Start

National Black Child Development Institute

National Council of La Raza

Packard Foundation Children, Families, and Communities Program

Preschool California

Professional Association for Childhood Education

Special Education Local Plan Area Organization

University of California Child Care Directors

University of California, Office of the President

Zero to Three

## Public Input Sessions

Special thanks should also be extended to **Joyce Wright, Nancy Herota,** the regional leads of the California Preschool Instructional Network, and to **Melinda Brookshire** and **Jan Davis,** WestEd, for their contributions in facilitating 53 public input sessions on the draft foundations.

# Introduction

The preschool learning foundations are a critical step in the California Department of Education's efforts to strengthen preschool education and school readiness and to close the achievement gap in California. They describe competencies—knowledge and skills—that most children can be expected to exhibit in a high-quality program as they complete their first or second year of preschool. In other words, the foundations describe what all young children typically learn with appropriate support.

The support young children need to attain the competencies varies from child to child. Many children learn simply by participating in high-quality preschool programs. Such programs offer children environments and experiences that encourage active, playful exploration and experimentation. With play as an integral part of the curriculum, high-quality programs include purposeful teaching to help children gain knowledge and skills. In addition, many children in California's preschools benefit from specific support in learning English. Other children may have a special need that requires particular accommodations and adaptations. To serve all children, preschool programs must work to provide appropriate conditions for learning and individually assist each child to move along a pathway of healthy learning and development.

All 50 states either have developed preschool standards documents or are in the process of doing so. Many of them have sought to align early learning standards with their kindergarten content standards. In most cases these alignment efforts have focused on academic content areas, such as English–language arts or mathematics. In California priority has been placed on aligning expectations for preschool learning with the state's kindergarten academic content standards and complementing the content areas with attention to social-emotional development and English-language development. Like the learning in such domains as language and literacy and mathematics, the concepts in social-emotional development and English-language development also contribute significantly to young children's readiness for school (*From Neurons to Neighborhoods* 2000; *Eager to Learn* 2000; *Early Learning Standards* 2002). Because the focus on preschool learning in California includes the full range of domains, the term "foundations" is used rather than "standards." This term is intended to convey that learning in every domain affects young children's readiness for school.

The preschool learning foundations presented in this document cover the following domains:

- Social-Emotional Development
- Language and Literacy
- English-Language Development (for English learners)
- Mathematics

Together, these domains represent crucial areas of learning and development for young children. The foundations within a particular domain provide a thorough overview of development in that domain. Preschool children can be considered from the perspective of one domain, such as language and literacy or social-emotional development. Yet, when taking an in-depth look at one domain, one needs to keep in mind that, for young children, learning is usually an integrated experience. For example, a young child may be concentrating on mathematical reasoning, but at the same time, there may be linguistic aspects of the experience.

The foundations written for each of these domains are based on research and evidence and are enhanced with expert practitioners' suggestions and examples. Their purpose is to promote understanding of preschool children's learning and to guide instructional practice. It is anticipated that teachers, administrators, parents, and policymakers will use the foundations as a springboard to augment efforts to enable all young children to acquire the competencies that will prepare them for success in school.

## Overview of the Foundations

The strands for each of the domains discussed previously are listed in this section.

*Social-Emotional Development Domain.* The social-emotional development domain consists of the following three strands:

1. *Self,* which includes self-awareness and self-regulation, social and emotional understanding, empathy and caring, and initiative in learning

2. *Social Interaction,* which focuses on interactions with familiar adults, interactions with peers, group participation, and cooperation and responsibility

3. *Relationships,* which addresses attachments to parents, close relationships with teachers and caregivers, and friendships

The competencies covered by the social-emotional development foundations underscore the multiple ways in which young children's development in this domain influences their ability to adapt successfully to preschool and, later on, in school.

*Language and Literacy Domain.* The language and literacy foundations address a wide range of specific competencies that preschool children will need support to learn. These foundations focus on the following three strands:

1. *Listening and Speaking,* which includes language use and conventions, vocabulary, and grammar

2. *Reading,* which covers concepts about print, phonological awareness, alphabetics and word/print

recognition, comprehension and analysis of age-appropriate text, and literacy interest and response

3. *Writing,* which focuses on writing strategies, including the emergent use of writing and writing-like behaviors

The foundations that were written for this domain reflect the field's growing interest in and understanding of the knowledge and skills that foster children's language and literacy learning during the preschool years.

***English-Language Development Domain.*** The English-language development foundations are specifically designed for children entering preschool with a home language other than English. Some English learners will begin preschool already having had some experience with English. For other English learners, preschool will offer them their first meaningful exposure to English. No matter how much background English learners have with English before they enter preschool, they will be on a path of acquiring a second language. As the English-language development foundations indicate, the learning task for English learners is sequential and multifaceted. English learners will need support in developing knowledge and skills in the following four strands:

1. *Listening,* which includes understanding words, requests and directions, and basic and advanced concepts

2. *Speaking,* which focuses on using English to communicate needs, expand vocabulary, become skillful at engaging in conversations, use increasingly complex grammatical constructions when speaking, understand grammar,

ask questions, use social conventions, and tell personal stories

3. *Reading,* which covers appreciating and enjoying reading, understanding book reading, understanding print conventions, demonstrating awareness that print conveys meaning, developing awareness and recognition of letters, demonstrating phonological awareness, and manipulating sounds, such as rhyming

4. *Writing,* which includes understanding the communicative function of writing and engaging in simple writing and writing-like behaviors

Unlike the three other sets of foundations, in which the foundations are linked to age, the English-language development foundations are defined by three levels of development—Beginning, Middle, and Later. Depending on their prior experience with using their home language and English to communicate with others, preschool English learners will go through these levels at different paces. Once children reach the Later level, they will still need support to continue acquiring English and to apply their developing linguistic abilities in every domain.

***Mathematics Domain.*** Young children's development of mathematics knowledge and skills is receiving increasing attention in research and practice. The mathematics foundations cover the following five strands:

1. *Number Sense,* which includes understanding of counting, number relationships, and operations

2. *Algebra and Functions (Classification and Patterning),* which focuses on sorting and classifying objects

and recognizing and understanding simple, repeating patterns

3. *Measurement,* which includes comparison and ordering

4. *Geometry,* which focuses on properties of objects (shape, size, position) and the relation of objects in space

5. *Mathematical Reasoning,* which addresses how young children use mathematical thinking to solve everyday problems

Preschool programs can promote young children's learning in this domain by encouraging children to explore and manipulate materials that engage them in mathematical thinking and by introducing teacher-guided learning activities that focus on mathematical concepts.

## Organization of the Foundations

In the main body of this document, each strand is broken out into one or more substrands, and the foundations are organized under the substrands. Foundations are presented for children at around 48 months of age and at around 60 months of age. In some cases the difference between the foundations for 48 months and 60 months is more pronounced than for the other foundations. Even so, the foundations focus on 48 and 60 months of age because they correspond to the end of the first and second years of preschool. Of course, teachers need to know where each child is on a continuum of learning throughout the child's time in preschool. The Desired Results Developmental Profile-Revised (DRDP-R) is a teacher observation tool that is being aligned with the foundations.

The DRDP-R gives teachers a means to observe children's learning along a continuum of four developmental levels.

Finally, the examples listed under each foundation give a range of possible ways in which children can demonstrate a foundation. The examples suggest different kinds of contexts in which children may show the competencies reflected in the foundations. Examples highlight that children are learning while they are engaging in imaginative play, exploring the environment and materials, making discoveries, being inventive, or interacting with teachers or other adults. Although often illustrative of the diversity of young children's learning experiences, the examples listed under a foundation are not exhaustive. In fact, teachers often observe other ways in which young children demonstrate a foundation.

*Note:* The Appendix, "The Foundations," contains a listing of the foundations in each domain, without examples.

## Universal Design for Learning

The California preschool learning foundations are guides to support preschool programs in their efforts to foster the learning and development of all young children in California, including children who have disabilities. In some cases, children with disabilities will need to use alternate methods for demonstrating their development. It is important to provide opportunities to follow different pathways to learning in the preschool foundations in order to make them helpful for all of California's children. To that end, the California preschool learning foundations incorporate a concept known as universal design for learning.

Developed by the Center for Applied Special Technology (CAST), universal design for learning is based on the realization that children learn in different ways (CAST 2007). In today's diverse preschool settings and programs, the use of a curriculum accessible to all learners is critical to successful early learning. Universal design for learning is not a single approach that will accommodate everyone; rather, it refers to providing multiple approaches to learning in order to meet the needs of diverse learners. Universal design provides for multiple means of representation, multiple means of engagement, and multiple means of expression (CAST 2007). Multiple means of representation refers to providing information in a variety of ways so the learning needs of all of the children are met. Multiple means of expression refers to allowing children to use alternative methods to demonstrate what they know or what they are feeling. Multiple means of engagement refers to providing choices for activities within the setting or program that facilitate learning by building on children's interests.

The examples given in the preschool learning foundations have been worded in such a way as to incorporate multiple means of receiving and expressing. This has been accomplished by the inclusion of a variety of examples for each foundation and the use of words that are inclusive rather than exclusive, as follows:

- The terms "communicates" and "responds" are often used rather than the term "says." "Communicates" and "responds" are inclusive of any language and any form of communication, including speaking, sign language, finger spelling, pictures, electronic communication devices, eye-pointing, gesturing, and so forth.
- The terms "identifies" and "indicates or points to" are often used to represent multiple means of indicating objects, people, or events in the environment. Examples include, among other means of indicating, the use of gestures, eye-pointing, nodding, or responding "yes" or "no" when another points to or touches an object.

Teachers should read each foundation and the accompanying examples, then consider the means by which a child with a disability might best acquire information and demonstrate competence in these areas. A child's special education teacher, parents, or related service provider may be contacted for consultation and suggestions.

## The Foundations and Preschool Learning in California

The foundations are at the heart of the CDE's approach to promoting preschool learning. Teachers use best practices, curricular strategies, and instructional techniques that assist children in learning the knowledge and skills described in the preschool learning foundations. The "how to's" of teaching young children include setting up environments, supporting children's self-initiated play, selecting appropriate materials, and planning and implementing teacher-guided learning activities. Two major considerations underlie the "how to's" of teaching. First, teachers can effectively foster early learning by thoughtfully considering the preschool learning foundations as they plan environments and activities. And second, during every step in the planning for young children's learning, teachers have an opportunity to tap into the prominent role of play. Teachers can best support young children both by encouraging the rich learning that occurs in children's self-initiated play and by introducing purposeful instructional activities that playfully engage preschoolers in learning.

Professional development is a key component in fostering preschool learning. The foundations can become a unifying element for both preservice and in-service professional development. Preschool program directors and teachers can use the foundations to facilitate curriculum planning and implementation. At the center of the CDE's evolving system for supporting young children during the preschool years, the foundations are designed to help teachers be intentional and focus their efforts on the knowledge and skills that all young children need to acquire for success in preschool and, later on, in school.

## References

Center for Applied Special Technology (CAST). 2007. *Universal design for learning.* http://www.cast.org/udl/ (accessed June 8, 2007).

*Eager to Learn: Educating Our Preschoolers.* 2000. Edited by B. T. Bowman, M. S. Donovan, and M. S. Burns. Washington, DC: National Academy Press.

*Early Learning Standards: Creating the Conditions for Success.* 2002. Washington, DC: National Association for the Education of Young Children.

*From Neurons to Neighborhoods: The Science of Early Childhood Development.* 2000. Edited by J. P. Shonkoff and D. A. Phillips. Washington, DC: National Academy Press.

Scott-Little, C.; S. L. Kagan; and V. S. Frelow. 2006. "Conceptualization of Readiness and the Content of Early Learning Standards: The Intersection of Policy and Research?" *Early Childhood Research Quarterly,* Vol. 21, 153–73.

FOUNDATIONS IN
# Social-Emotional Development

This section describes foundations for the behavior of preschool children in the domain of social-emotional development. The goal of the California Department of Education (CDE) in developing these foundations was to *describe the behaviors that are typical of preschool children who are making good progress toward readiness for kindergarten.* The research focus was, in particular, on behavior reflecting age-appropriate competency for children in the 40- to 47-month age span and children in the 52- to 59-month age span.

These competencies are included as foundations for children "at around 48 months of age" and "at around 60 months of age," respectively. In focusing on the social and emotional foundations of school readiness, a central assumption—well supported by developmental and educational research—was that *school readiness consists of social-emotional competencies as well as other cognitive and motivational competencies required for success in school.* The foundations of social and emotional development described here—including the growth of self-awareness, self-regulation, cooperation and responsibility, social and emotional understanding, empathy and

caring, interactions with peers, friendship, group participation (such as in the classroom), initiative in learning, attachments to parents, close relationships with teachers and caregivers, and interactions with familiar adults— are each predictive of children's adaptation to school and their academic success. Research literature highlighting the social-emotional foundations of early school success has been published, and relevant studies from that literature are cited in the bibliographic listings at the end of this section.

---

*School readiness consists of social-emotional competencies as well as other cognitive and motivational competencies required for success in school.*

---

The CDE's endeavor to describe the behaviors typical of preschool children who are on course for school readiness involved three additional assumptions. *The first was the assumption that young children have access to the appropriate kinds of social interactions, experiences, and environments that normally support healthy development.* Young children growing up in markedly deprived settings experience

1

greater challenges to healthy development because they are more likely to lack those supports; consequently, their readiness to begin school is hindered. *The second assumption was that the purpose of these foundations is to describe typical development rather than to articulate aspirational expectations for children's behavior under the best possible conditions or for the behaviors to be instilled in children.* In order for these foundations to be useful, they must describe what can typically be expected of young children growing up in conditions appropriate for healthy development. *The third assumption was that these foundations, especially the behavioral examples for each foundation, are not meant to be assessment items; rather, they are meant to be guidelines and teaching tools.* Those who use these foundations should not try to measure the children they observe against the specific examples included in each domain. This is because the examples given are meant to be general illustrations of the competencies described rather than essential criteria for age-appropriate development. Children are different from one another and will vary in the extent to which their behaviors match those given in the examples.

---

*The third assumption was that these foundations, especially the behavioral examples for each foundation, are not meant to be assessment items; rather, they are meant to be guidelines and teaching tools.*

---

Educators, early childhood specialists, and others involved in any effort to describe the behaviors typical of children at around 48 months of age compared with children at around

60 months of age will find themselves humbled by the realization that the developmental changes apparent over the course of a single year (albeit a duration that is one-quarter of the child's lifetime to date) can be subtle. In other words, one should not expect extensive changes in the behavior of preschool children during a 12-month period. Indeed, individual differences in the characteristics and behavior of children of any age can be greater than the average behavioral changes they will experience over the course of a year of development. The purpose of these foundations, however, is to highlight the developmental differences that are most common between typical children at around 48 and 60 months of age. Although the differences between children of each age can be subtle, there are some consistent themes that run throughout the social-emotional domain. Compared with younger children, for example, children at around 60 months of age are more behaviorally competent and take greater active initiative in social interactions and learning; they have an enhanced psychological awareness of themselves and others; they have a greater capacity for self-control; and their social relationships are more reciprocal in quality. In general, these differences should be apparent in various ways across different social and emotional areas.

Children are a remarkably diverse population, even when children of comparable ages are considered. They vary in their temperamental qualities and personality, family background, cultural heritage and values, and other features that make the application of these foundations (and the behavioral examples included in each) a challenging task. This is another reason the examples should be used *for illustrative purposes only.* Indeed, the variability in children's temperamental qualities, for instance, means that different children will display skills relevant to each social-emotional foundation in individual ways, thus requiring care and sensitivity in the application of these foundations. It is important that the individual characteristics of a child, the child's family, and their background be considered seriously in determining how the foundations relate to the child.

---

*Indeed, the variability in children's temperamental qualities, for instance, means that different children will display skills relevant to each social-emotional foundation in individual ways, thus requiring care and sensitivity in the application of these foundations.*

---

Children in California are particularly diverse in their culture of origin. Culture is associated with family values and practices, language, and other characteristics that are directly related to the meaning of these foundations and their application to individual children, especially children who are from underrepresented groups, English learners, or from special populations. Although the developmental research literature is rich in studies of English-speaking, middle-class European-American children, there is, unfortunately, a dearth of studies focusing on children who speak other languages and have other backgrounds. The few studies that do exist are often so specific to children from particular backgrounds or circumstances as to be of limited generalizability. With culture

in mind, a number of important studies were enlisted in the preparation of these foundations (e.g., Cabrera and Garcia-Coll 2004; Fitzgerald and others 2003; Hughes and Chen 1999; Hughes and others 2006; Johnson 2005; and Johnson and others 2003). But it is clear that much more study is needed.

The lack of adequate research literature on the social-emotional development of preschoolers who are English learners or from backgrounds other than European-American should be considered when using these foundations because they may be of uncertain applicability to such children. The use of language as an indicator of social or emotional competency, for example, may be very different as applied to English learners, especially when they are observed in play groups with predominantly English-speaking children or are being observed by an English-speaking teacher. The range of social relationships on which children can depend may be influenced by the cultural context of the child's development as well as the dominant language of the adults and children at home. For some children, language can be socially isolating. Certain social and emotional themes in this section, such as "Initiative in Learning," may be limited in application to children from cultural backgrounds that discourage the kind of assertiveness typical of middle-class, English-speaking children in the same preschool program or setting. It is important, then, to acknowledge that the research literature providing a basis for these foundations draws on populations of children that vary widely in their diversity and, thus, must be considered carefully.

Likewise, these foundations must be used carefully for children with special needs. Children who have physical or mental challenges, neuro-developmental disorders, or other special needs proceed developmentally in ways that are similar to, but also different from, more typically developing children. Again, the research literature is limited regarding the documentation of age-related changes in social and emotional competencies. Furthermore, because the examples illustrating each of these competencies are written with typically developing children in mind, they may not be consistently relevant to children with special needs. Caregivers and teachers will be relied on for the insight needed to understand how these foundations can be applied to the children in their care.

*It is important, then, to acknowledge that the research literature providing a basis for these foundations draws on populations of children that vary widely in their diversity and, thus, must be considered carefully.*

Young children acquire social and emotional competencies in ways that are often different from how they acquire competence in the naming of letters or numbers. As illustrated in this section, social-emotional skills emerge through children's experience in close relationships and the varied activities that occur in relational experience, such as shared conversation, warm nurturance, and guided assistance in learning capacities for sociability, responsibility, and self-control. Social and emotional skills also develop through the shared activities of a developmentally appropriate,

well-designed preschool environment. In such settings (and at home) and under the guidance of sensitive teachers, young children develop an understanding of other people's feelings and needs, are encouraged to feel empathy and caring, learn to manage their own behavior as responsible group members, and acquire a variety of other capabilities that will be directly relevant to their success in managing the classroom environment of kindergarten or the primary grades.

Last, but perhaps most important, play is a central context for social and emotional development in early childhood. Although these foundations focus specifically on developmental changes in only one kind of play (specifically, pretend play), it is apparent that many kinds of play contribute to social-emotional competence in preschoolers, including social play with caregivers and peers, play with toys and other objects, structured group activities, and even games with rules. One conclusion to be derived from this observation is that play is an essential cornerstone of healthy social and emotional development in early childhood and contributes to the skills necessary for adjustment to and success in school. This conclusion is reflected in the fact that one-third of the examples illustrating these competencies are based on children's experience in play.

*Play is a central context for social and emotional development in early childhood.*

The preparation of these foundations enlisted many sources, including documents from the CDE detailing developmental expectations in relevant domains for older and younger children.

In addition, early childhood standards from a number of other states were consulted.[1] Moreover, general sources on early childhood development (e.g., Berk 2006; Hohmann and Weikart 1995; Shaffer 2004), culture and development (e.g., Rogoff 1990, 2003), and early learning (Committee on Early Childhood Pedagogy 2001; Committee on Developments in the Science of Learning 2000) were consulted. In addition, a number of well-validated assessment tools for preschoolers were relied on, including those developed by Bricker and others (1999); Dichtelmiller and others (2001); High/Scope Educational Research Foundation (2003); Meisels and others (2003); and Squires, Brickner, and Twombly (2003).

The most important source for preparing these foundations was the research literature in developmental and educational psychology concerning early social and emotional development. A reference list is included at the end of this section. Detailed bibliographic notes for reference materials consulted for this domain also appear later in this section. The bibliographic notes include useful background information for individuals who may wish to learn more about the research basis for these foundations.

---

[1]Early childhood standards from the following states were examined in the preparation of the foundations: Alaska, Florida, Georgia, Hawaii, Illinois, Massachusetts, Rhode Island, Texas, and Washington.

# Self

## 1.0 Self-Awareness

| *At around 48 months of age* | *At around 60 months of age* |
| --- | --- |
| **1.1** Describe their physical characteristics, behavior, and abilities positively. | **1.1** Compare their characteristics with those of others and display a growing awareness of their psychological characteristics, such as thoughts and feelings. |
| Children view their characteristics and abilities positively, enjoy demonstrating them, and assert their own preferences and desires. Children also want to be viewed positively by adults who matter to them. | Children are confident in their abilities and characteristics, sometimes (depending on cultural values) comparing them favorably with those of others. Children also regard themselves in terms of their past abilities and remain sensitive to how they are viewed by adults, peers, and other people whose opinions matter to them. |
| **Examples** | **Examples** |
| • Seeks to do things by himself, sometimes refusing an adult's assistance, and communicates, "Do it myself." <br><br> • Communicates, "I like rice!" or "See my picture!" or "I don't like getting wet" or "Look what I did!" <br><br> • Shows a painting or demonstrates an accomplishment to elicit the acknowledgment of the teacher or parent and smiles when the adult responds. <br><br> • Communicates, "My skin is brown," in a positive manner. <br><br> • Seems dismayed and withdraws after her behavior is disapproved of by an adult. <br><br> • Communicates, "I did it!" or "Yea!" after finishing a puzzle. <br><br> • Communicates, "Mine!" when claiming a preferred toy. <br><br> • Expects success in a game or task, even when he has just failed at the same task. | • Communicates, "I can ride a bike, but my baby sister doesn't." <br><br> • Smiles with delight at accomplishing something that was difficult to do and looks to the teacher for acknowledgment. <br><br> • Communicates, "I couldn't do that when I was little." <br><br> • Communicates, "Sometimes I just want to be by myself." <br><br> • Seems disappointed if a drawing or demonstration of physical skill does not elicit the expected acknowledgement from an adult. <br><br> • Tries new things, even those that may be too difficult. <br><br> • While using her wheelchair, communicates, "I can go faster than you!" <br><br> • Asks for help after several attempts to solve a problem. <br><br> • Communicates, "I can speak Spanish and English." <br><br> • Watches a peer demonstrate a skill, then tries to do the same thing. |

## 2.0 Self-Regulation

| At around 48 months of age | At around 60 months of age |
|---|---|
| **2.1** Need adult guidance in managing their attention, feelings, and impulses and show some effort at self-control. | **2.1** Regulate their attention, thoughts, feelings, and impulses more consistently, although adult guidance is sometimes necessary. |
| Children follow simple rules and routines, seek to cooperate, manage classroom transitions, and make efforts at self-control (such as self-soothing and waiting) with adult guidance. Children also easily lose control of their attention, feelings, and behavior. | Children anticipate routines, cooperate with fewer reminders, can focus attention on the task at hand, and manage transitions. They are more capable of emotional and behavioral self-regulation but sometimes require adult guidance. |

| Examples | Examples |
|---|---|
| • Jumps up and down on the couch but stops when asked to do so by a parent or teacher. | • May anticipate cleanup after play time and begin cleaning up without being prompted to do so. |
| • Manages transitions in the classroom routine (such as moving from play time to cleanup) when helped to anticipate them or provided some choice. | • Puts away books where they belong without being prompted by an adult. |
| • When asked by a teacher to share with another child, may initially resist but eventually cooperates. | • Is more capable of focusing attention on a task in a busy classroom and is less distractible than a three-year old. |
| • Knows to put away his coat and boots after arriving at the classroom. | • Spontaneously tells the teacher she has broken something. |
| • Is distracted by other children when working at a table or easel. | • Tells another child about how to treat the classroom pet. |
| • Accepts a teacher's comfort when distressed and calms readily. | • Suggests that he can share the blocks with another child. |
| • Reacts strongly when a peer takes away a valued toy. | • With a teacher's prompt, remembers to use words to convey strong feelings (e.g., "It makes me mad when you push!"). |
| • Has difficulty following instructions when too many directions are provided at once. | • Tries to control her distress after falling off a tricycle. |
| • Covers her eyes when seeing something that is upsetting. | • Asks for a teacher's help when another child will not share. |
| • Turns away instead of hitting another child. | • Can be overheard saying when scared by a story, "It's just pretend" or "That's not real, right?" |
| • Has difficulty waiting an extended period for a desired object. | • Has strategies for waiting (such as distracting herself or not looking at the desired object). |
| • Is learning to act differently in different settings (e.g., speaking loudly outside rather than in the classroom), although often has to be reminded to do so. | • Deliberately slows down her movements in a game such as "Red Light – Green Light." |
| | • Explains the reasons for a behavioral rule (e.g., "We walk inside so we don't bump into other people"). |

## 3.0    Social and Emotional Understanding

| *At around 48 months of age* | *At around 60 months of age* |
|---|---|
| **3.1** Seek to understand people's feelings and behavior, notice diversity in human characteristics, and are interested in how people are similar and different. | **3.1** Begin to comprehend the mental and psychological reasons people act as they do and how they contribute to differences between people. |
| Children are interested in people's feelings and the reasons they feel that way. They can describe familiar routines, inquire about the causes and consequences of behavior, and notice how people are similar and different, although their understanding is limited. | Children have a better understanding of people's thoughts and feelings as well as their own. They comprehend that another's ideas can be mistaken. They are also beginning to understand differences in personality, temperament, and background (e.g., culture) and their importance. |

| Examples | Examples |
|---|---|
| • Communicates, "Marco's crying. He fell down." <br><br> • Conveys a range of feelings, including happy, sad, and mad and describes simple situations that evoke them. <br><br> • Describes what happens at circle time. <br><br> • Shows interest in how another child's appearance or eating habits are different from his own. <br><br> • Enacts in pretend play everyday situations involving people's emotions and needs (e.g., the baby doll is crying because she is hungry). <br><br> • Understands that another child might be mad because she couldn't do what she desired (e.g., her block tower keeps falling down). <br><br> • Comments on differences in behavior or appearance between boys and girls. <br><br> • Wants to ride in Johnny's wheelchair or use Sara's walker. <br><br> • Begins to understand how people's feelings can be alike and, on other occasions, be very different. | • Tells a teacher, "Jorge was sad because he *thought* his mommy wasn't coming." <br><br> • Tries to hide how she is feeling or to "mask" her feelings with a different emotional expression (e.g., appearing calm and unafraid when encountering a big dog). <br><br> • Communicates about a peer, "Emma's really shy." <br><br> • Has a growing vocabulary for identifying emotions and can describe more complex emotional situations that might evoke different feelings. <br><br> • Explores more complex feelings, desires, and concepts in pretend play. <br><br> • Deliberately does not communicate truthfully about inappropriate behavior. <br><br> • Describes which peers are friendly, aggressive, or have other qualities. <br><br> • Tends to play in same-sex groups. <br><br> • Notices a child with a physical disability and responds with questions or curiosity. |

## 4.0 Empathy and Caring

| At around 48 months of age | At around 60 months of age |
| --- | --- |
| **4.1** Demonstrate concern for the needs of others and people in distress. | **4.1** Respond to another's distress and needs with sympathetic caring and are more likely to assist. |
| Children respond with concern when a child or adult is distressed, strive to understand why, and may display simple efforts to assist the other person. | Children respond sympathetically to a distressed person and are more competent at responding helpfully. |
| **Examples** | **Examples** |
| • Asks a teacher, "Why is Jessie crying?" and/or asks the teacher to help.<br><br>• Watches another child crying loudly and makes a sad face.<br><br>• Communicates about an infant nearby, "Jacob's scared of that loud noise."<br><br>• Gets a toy for a distressed peer and may communicate, "Do you feel better?"<br><br>• Brings a carrot to school for the class guinea pig. | • Asks a younger child, "Why are you crying?" and when told that she misses her mommy, communicates, "Don't worry—your mommy will come back soon."<br><br>• May communicate, "That's not fair!" in response to another child being excluded from the group.<br><br>• Helps a friend rebuild a fallen block tower.<br><br>• Offers a friend her favorite book when she looks or acts sad.<br><br>• May come to the defense of a friend who is teased by a peer.<br><br>• Asks a teacher for bandages after a peer has fallen and scraped his knee.<br><br>• Asks, "Want some water?" of a friend who is coughing. |

## 5.0   Initiative in Learning

| At around 48 months of age | At around 60 months of age |
| --- | --- |
| **5.1**  Enjoy learning and are confident in their abilities to make new discoveries although may not persist at solving difficult problems. | **5.1**  Take greater initiative in making new discoveries, identifying new solutions, and persisting in trying to figure things out. |
| Children become engaged in learning opportunities, approach learning with enthusiasm, and have confidence in their capacities to learn more. But they may give up when facing difficult problem-solving challenges. | Children are self-confident learners who become actively involved in formal and informal learning opportunities by asking questions, proposing new ways of doing things, and offering their own ideas and theories. |
| **Examples** | **Examples** |
| • Shows interest in many different activities in the classroom.<br>• Responds positively to a teacher's invitation to try a new activity.<br>• Moves away after working on a puzzle that he has been unable to solve.<br>• Asks, "Why?" when faced with a perplexing discovery.<br>• Notices when a new science display has been prepared by the teacher.<br>• Starts many challenging puzzles but may finish few. | • Communicates, "Here's a different way!"<br>• Asks "why" questions fairly often out of real curiosity (e.g., "Why is the worm doing that?").<br>• Suggests another way of creating a castle at the sand table.<br>• Wants to try again when failing in his initial efforts to solve a problem.<br>• Offers information about animals that she has learned at home.<br>• Initiates a conversation with an adult about a class activity.<br>• Works hard on a project that has captured her interest.<br>• Communicates, "I'm going to play with blocks and then go to the science table." |

# Social Interaction

## 1.0 Interactions with Familiar Adults

| *At around 48 months of age* | *At around 60 months of age* |
|---|---|
| **1.1** Interact with familiar adults comfortably and competently, especially in familiar settings. | **1.1** Participate in longer and more reciprocal interactions with familiar adults and take greater initiative in social interaction. |
| Children comfortably interact with familiar adults in play or problem solving, ask questions or communicate about their experiences, cooperate with instructions, or demonstrate skills to the familiar adult, especially in familiar settings. | Children take increasing initiative in interacting with familiar adults through conversation, suggesting a shared activity or asking for the adult's assistance, and cooperate readily. |
| **Examples** | **Examples** |
| • Participates in pretend play or storytelling with a familiar preschool teacher. <br><br> • Shares a brief conversation initiated by a familiar adult or initiates such a conversation. <br><br> • Shows a familiar adult a picture she has drawn. <br><br> • Responds appropriately to a request or question by a teacher, although perhaps with delay. <br><br> • Seeks assistance of a familiar adult, often with nonverbal cues. <br><br> • Stays close to a familiar adult when faced with adult strangers or in an unfamiliar setting. | • Asks a specific teacher to help build a road in the sandbox and interacts cooperatively with the teacher for a sustained period. <br><br> • Communicates to a weekly volunteer, "Guess what I did!" and continues conversing with the visitor about it. <br><br> • Answers a teacher's question, then asks the teacher another question. <br><br> • Communicates, "What?" or "Huh?" when the teacher asks a question that the child does not understand. |

SOCIAL-EMOTIONAL DEVELOPMENT

SOCIAL-EMOTIONAL DEVELOPMENT

## 2.0    Interactions with Peers

| *At around 48 months of age* | *At around 60 months of age* |
|---|---|
| **2.1**  Interact easily with peers in shared activities that occasionally become cooperative efforts. | **2.1**  More actively and intentionally cooperate with each other. |
| Children interact comfortably with one or two playmates, although sociability is still basic. Children sometimes share materials and communicate together, occasionally working cooperatively on a mutual goal or project, especially with adult support. | Children initiate and participate in more complex, cooperative activity with peers. This may involve working together in groups to achieve a shared goal or communicating about how to share materials so all can use them. |
| **Examples** | **Examples** |
| • After watching another child dig in the sandbox, begins to dig alongside in a similar fashion; eventually the two children are digging together.<br>• Paints with other children on easels side by side, with the children looking at each other's pictures, occasionally conflicting over the sharing of paints, and commenting about their own painting.<br>• Uses rhythm instruments together with several other children.<br>• With adult prompting, shares the blocks she is using or participates in turn-taking with another child. | • Invites several children to help dig a hole in the sandbox.<br>• Suggests taking turns riding the tricycle.<br>• Responds appropriately to another child's ideas about how to build a better car track on the floor.<br>• Shares play dough so another child can make something.<br>• Talks for several minutes with another child about how they are dressing up in adult clothes for pretend play.<br>• Joins several other children to create a train track, using blocks on the floor.<br>• Holds the bubble wand for another child so she can blow bubbles.<br>• Sets the table with another child, communicating about what is needed next. |
| **2.2**  Participate in simple sequences of pretend play.* | **2.2**  Create more complex sequences of pretend play that involve planning, coordination of roles, and cooperation. |
| Children play imaginative, complementary roles (such as parent and child) in pretend play but without much planning or a well-developed story line. | Children develop longer, more complex pretend play narratives involving a shared script, coordination of child-selected roles, and mutual correction within those roles as they play. |
| **Examples** | **Examples** |
| • Communicates to another child, "I'll be the tiger!" when they are playing outside.<br>• Leaps into the air in pretend "flying," and other children join in and do the same. | • Creates with a small group of children an extended imaginary story with a beginning, a middle, and an end (e.g., a story of sickness and healing that involves a doctor's visit, a trip to the hospital, an operation, and the patient's recovery). |

* Children may "play" whether or not they are communicating orally, narrating the play, or motorically engaging in activities. For example, they may ask an adult or peer to assist in the motor aspects of play.

## 2.0    Interactions with Peers (Continued)

| At around 48 months of age | At around 60 months of age |
|---|---|
| *Examples (Continued)* | *Examples (Continued)* |
| • Begins roaring like a scary monster; as other children notice, they run away in mock terror or become monsters, too.<br>• Pretends with another child to make a birthday cake, then the two sing "Happy Birthday."<br>• Acts out a story with peers as a teacher is reading it to them. | • Communicates to another child, "You can't say that! You're the baby, remember?"<br>• While playing with other children, communicates, "I'm sick," to which another child responds, "Really?" and he responds, "No, just pretend."<br>• Communicates to another child, "Let's say this is a secret cave, OK?" and the other children in the group respond, "OK!" |
| **2.3**  Seek assistance in resolving peer conflict, especially when disagreements have escalated into physical aggression. | **2.3**  Negotiate with each other, seeking adult assistance when needed, and increasingly use words to respond to conflict. Disagreements may be expressed with verbal taunting in addition to physical aggression. |
| Children seek adult help when experiencing conflict with another child. Peer disagreements (such as those regarding the sharing of toys) can escalate into physical aggression, although not as readily as happens with children of younger ages. | Children can suggest simple conflict resolution strategies as well as respond to adult suggestions for resolving peer disputes. Children may taunt or tease another child rather than hitting and may also retaliate when provoked. |
| **Examples** | **Examples** |
| • Pulls another child off the tricycle he wants to ride, then the other child cries and runs to the teacher for help.<br>• At the block area, communicates to the teacher, "She won't share!" when another child takes all the blocks.<br>• Immediately begins to cry when another child knocks down the block structure he was building, then looks for adult assistance. | • Communicates at the water table where other children are playing, "When can it be my turn?"<br>• Excludes another child from the group, communicating, "You can't play with us."<br>• Communicates to another child in the block area, "I'm playing with these; you play with those," or suggests taking turns.<br>• Communicates, "I don't like it when you push me!" without a prompt from the teacher.<br>• Pushes another child who shoved her in line, to which other children respond, "Stop that!" |

SOCIAL-EMOTIONAL DEVELOPMENT

## 3.0 Group Participation

| *At around 48 months of age* | *At around 60 months of age* |
|---|---|
| **3.1** Participate in group activities and are beginning to understand and cooperate with social expectations, group rules, and roles. | **3.1** Participate positively and cooperatively as group members. |
| Children enjoy participating in group activities and are beginning to understand social expectations and group rules and their application. Children may have difficulty, however, coordinating their interests with those of the group. | Children participate in group activities with the ability to anticipate familiar routines and contribute to shared projects more competently as group members. |

| **Examples** | **Examples** |
|---|---|
| • Enjoys playing simple games, such as "Duck-Duck-Goose" or "Follow the Leader," with adult help. | • Anticipates the predictable routines of the day, such as initiating hand washing without being prompted when snack time arrives. |
| • Stays with the group for a nature walk. | • Actively explores social roles in imaginative play. |
| • Notices when other children are missing from class. | • Is more capable of sustained attention and remaining engaged in group activities, such as putting a puzzle together cooperatively. |
| • Responds appropriately when a teacher announces circle time or cleanup, although may need guidance in what to do. | • Applies game rules more consistently for simple games. |
| • Is interested in playing games but often deviates from the rules. | • Knows the procedure for leaving the setting to go to the bathroom or to another room and corrects children who do not follow the procedure. |
| • Attention often wanders after a brief period of group activity, especially if it is not personally engaging, which may result in inappropriate behavior or nonparticipation. | • Anticipates and begins preparing for an activity, such as a painting project. |
| • Begins to explore social roles (e.g., mother, teacher) in pretend play. | • Sometimes shares spontaneously and thinks of turn-taking without adult prompting. |
| • Responds appropriately to verbal prompts in songs or stories during circle time (e.g., "Hokey Pokey," "Head, Shoulders, Knees, and Toes," "Itsy Bitsy Spider"). | |
| • Needs help remembering how to prepare for an activity, such as getting ready to paint at an easel. | |
| • With adult prompting, can share toys or wait for a turn. | |

## 4.0    Cooperation and Responsibility

| At around 48 months of age | At around 60 months of age |
|---|---|
| **4.1**  Seek to cooperate with adult instructions but their capacities for self-control are limited, especially when they are frustrated or upset. | **4.1**  Have growing capacities for self-control and are motivated to cooperate in order to receive adult approval and think approvingly of themselves. |
| Children strive to follow adult instructions to maintain a good relationship with the parent or teacher and because of incentives and rules. Children often become dismayed or distressed when corrected. Children have more difficulty complying with instructions when without adult support or when distressed or frustrated. | Children's cooperation with adult instructions is more reliable because of better capacities for self-control. Children are motivated by adult approval and by a desire to view themselves approvingly for their good conduct, reflecting their acceptance of adult standards for themselves. |

| Examples | Examples |
|---|---|
| • Plays gently with the classroom rabbit when reminded to do so by the teacher but may play more roughly on other occasions.<br><br>• Seems sad and hides after the teacher comments on inappropriate behavior.<br><br>• Smiles when the teacher comments on the child's cooperative behavior while setting the table for lunch.<br><br>• Hits another child when frustrated, then looks at the teacher.<br><br>• Shouts angrily at another child, but looks confused or upset when the other child begins to cry.<br><br>• Participates in classroom routines, such as cleanup. | • Tells another child to be gentle with the classroom guinea pig.<br><br>• Suggests taking turns with another child who wants to ride the tricycle.<br><br>• Spontaneously communicates, "I'm a good helper!"<br><br>• Accidentally spills paint on another child's art-work, then communicates, "I'm sorry," or gets another piece of paper for the other child.<br><br>• Communicates, "uh-oh," and begins to pick up the pieces of a puzzle she has knocked off a shelf.<br><br>• Works cooperatively with a friend to wipe off the table with sponges after lunch.<br><br>• Responds cooperatively when his behavior is corrected by a teacher. |

SOCIAL-EMOTIONAL DEVELOPMENT

# Relationships

## 1.0 Attachments to Parents

| At around 48 months of age | At around 60 months of age |
| --- | --- |
| **1.1** Seek security and support from their primary family attachment figures. | **1.1** Take greater initiative in seeking support from their primary family attachment figures. |
| Children use their family caregivers (e.g., mother, father, grandparent, other adult raising the child) as sources of security and support, especially in challenging circumstances, by obtaining comfort, requesting help, and communicating about feelings. | Children seek the support of their family caregivers, especially in difficult situations, by requesting help in resolving conflicts with others, initiating cooperative problem solving, or seeking comfort when distressed. |
| **Examples** | **Examples** |
| • Plays comfortably on the other side of the room or the yard while the parent talks to the teacher, but cries to the parent to be consoled if hurt or frustrated and readily calms when comforted. <br>• Asks for the parent's help with a task (e.g., putting on shoes) and may cooperate with the parent's assistance. <br>• Responds positively to the parent's arrival after an absence. <br>• Runs over to his parent to tell about having bumped his head and asks for a hug. | • Seeks the parent's help in a conflict with a sibling. <br>• With assistance from the parent, describes her feelings about a recent upsetting experience. <br>• Seeks the parent's help with a difficult task (e.g., zipping a coat, folding a note) and cooperates readily. |
| **1.2** Contribute to maintaining positive relationships with their primary family attachment figures. | **1.2** Contribute to positive mutual cooperation with their primary family attachment figures. |
| Children prefer interacting with their family caregivers, choosing them for sharing activities, providing assistance, and displaying discoveries or achievements. | Children demonstrate an awareness of the mutuality of close relationships in their efforts to be helpful, showing interest in the family caregiver's feelings, preferences, or well-being and sharing activities. |
| **Examples** | **Examples** |
| • Asks the parent to watch something the child has learned to do. <br>• Prefers the parent's company or assistance to that of other adults who may be equally available. <br>• Responds positively when the mother initiates a conversation about a shared experience, although will not contribute much to the conversation at this age. | • Wants to make a birthday card for the parent while at school. <br>• Wants to help the parent care for a baby sibling or a pet or work together with the parent on a task at home (as reported by the parent). <br>• Communicates feelings to the mother, sometimes taking the initiative in doing so. |

**1.0    Attachments to Parents (Continued)**

| *At around 48 months of age* | *At around 60 months of age* |
|---|---|
| *Examples (Continued)* <br>• Shows the parent a drawing she has made at school that day. <br>• Shares information about parents with a teacher (e.g., "My dad caught a fish!"). | *Examples (Continued)* <br>• Reports to the teacher about helping with a chore at home. <br>• Shows the attachment figure what she has been working on at school. |
| **1.3** After experience with out-of-home care, manage departures and separations from primary family attachment figures with the teacher's assistance. | **1.3** After experience with out-of-home care, comfortably depart from primary family attachment figures. Also maintain well-being while apart from primary family attachment figures during the day. |
| Children show affection to the family caregiver when the adult departs at the beginning of the day but may need the assistance of a teacher in coping with separation. | Children are eager to begin the day in preschool. They respond affectionately to the family caregiver as the adult departs and have little difficulty being separated. |
| **Examples** | **Examples** |
| • Gives the father a hug and kiss and lingers near him as he prepares to leave the child at preschool in the morning. <br>• Begins to fuss as the mother departs but soothes easily with the primary caregiver at school. <br>• After a distressing fall, cries for the mother but is reassured when reminded that the mother will return at the end of the day. <br>• Manages his feelings after the parent leaves by playing with favorite objects, carrying personal objects around the room, and so forth. <br>• Switches to the language typically used at home when the parent arrives. | • Runs into the preschool at arrival to greet friends, then runs back to the mother for a hug and kiss as she departs. <br>• Eagerly waves good-bye to the father as he leaves, then turns to a favorite activity. <br>• Greets the parent with conversation in the home language at the end of the day. |

SOCIAL-EMOTIONAL DEVELOPMENT

## 2.0 Close Relationships with Teachers and Caregivers

| *At around 48 months of age* | *At around 60 months of age* |
|---|---|
| **2.1** Seek security and support from their primary teachers and caregivers. | **2.1** Take greater initiative in seeking the support of their primary teachers and caregivers. |
| Children use their primary teachers and caregivers as sources of security and support, especially in challenging circumstances, by obtaining comfort, requesting help, and communicating about feelings. | Children seek the support of their primary teachers and caregivers, especially when they are in difficult situations, by requesting the adult's help in resolving conflicts with others, initiating cooperative problem solving, or seeking comfort when distressed. |
| **Examples** | **Examples** |
| • Plays comfortably at a distance from the teacher, but cries to the teacher for help if hurt or frustrated and readily calms when comforted.<br>• Prefers a particular teacher's company or assistance to that of other teachers who may be equally available.<br>• Seeks to be near the primary teacher if distressed by peer conflict or frightened by an unfamiliar adult.<br>• Talks about the primary teacher at home (as reported by the parent). | • Seeks the teacher's help in a conflict with another child.<br>• Seeks the teacher's assistance when confronted with a difficult task (e.g., challenging puzzle, new skill to master).<br>• Upon returning from outdoors, looks for the primary teacher and asks to play a game together.<br>• With assistance from the primary caregiver, can describe his own feelings about a recent upsetting experience. |
| **2.2** Contribute to maintaining positive relationships with primary teachers and caregivers. | **2.2** Contribute to positive mutual cooperation with primary teachers and caregivers. |
| Children prefer interacting with their primary teachers and caregivers, choosing them for sharing activities, seeking comfort and assistance, and displaying discoveries or achievements. | Children demonstrate an awareness of the mutuality of close relationships in their efforts to be helpful, showing interest in the teacher's feelings, preferences, or well-being and sharing personal experiences with the teacher. |
| **Examples** | **Examples** |
| • Completes a puzzle and proudly shows it to the primary teacher.<br>• Rebuffs another adult's attempts to help when the child is hurt and looks around to locate the primary teacher or caregiver.<br>• Responds with pleasure when the primary teacher talks about a project done together with the child; may not, however, contribute much to the conversation at this age. | • Responds with interest when the primary teacher communicates, "Yesterday I got a new dog!" and continues the conversation about dogs.<br>• Proudly displays a drawing or discovery to the primary teacher for a positive response.<br>• Contributes to classroom cleanup at the primary teacher's request and, sometimes, initiates the cleanup of her own project, then shows the teacher what she has done.<br>• Volunteers to help when the primary teacher is setting up a new activity. |

## 2.0    Close Relationships with Teachers and Caregivers (Continued)

| At around 48 months of age | At around 60 months of age |
|---|---|
| *Examples (Continued)* | *Examples (Continued)* |
| • Communicates, "Good morning, teacher!" or uses another term of respect when prompted by the parent after arriving at preschool.<br>• Imitates the behavior of the primary teacher. | • Cooperates when asked to do so by the primary teacher.<br>• Refers to the primary teacher by the proper name when doing so is consistent with the family's cultural values.<br>• Physically greets the primary teacher or uses other culturally appropriate means of greeting. |

SOCIAL-EMOTIONAL DEVELOPMENT

SOCIAL-EMOTIONAL DEVELOPMENT

## 3.0  Friendships

| *At around 48 months of age* | *At around 60 months of age* |
|---|---|
| **3.1**  Choose to play with one or two special peers whom they identify as friends. | **3.1**  Friendships are more reciprocal, exclusive, and enduring. |
| Children play with many peers but also seek the company of one or two specific children whom they identify as friends. Children are more cooperative and share more complex play with friends than with other children. | Children seek to share activities with special friends who, in return, seek their company. Friends act more positively toward each other but may also experience greater conflict. Children respond with enhanced efforts at conflict resolution. |
| **Examples** | **Examples** |
| • Plays with the same friend regularly.<br>• Plays more complex, imaginative roles with a friend than with other peers.<br>• Seeks out a favorite peer when entering the room.<br>• Sits next to a friend at circle time or mealtime.<br>• Notices when a friend is absent.<br>• Can identify a friend by name (e.g., "Sara is my friend!").<br>• Offers a toy to a friend to play with. | • Sits regularly with one or two special friends at lunch.<br>• Seeks to play exclusively with one or more friends, even to the extent of excluding other children from the play group.<br>• Communicates, "We're friends, right?" when seeking to play with a special peer.<br>• Comes to the defense of a friend who is teased by a peer.<br>• Engages in recurrent, familiar, and cooperative role-play activities with one or more favorite friends in the setting.<br>• Shares about experiences in the family with a special friend.<br>• Laughs with a friend about an experience they have shared. |

# Bibliographic Notes

## Self

### Self-Awareness

There has been recent, considerable research interest in the development of self-awareness in young children, particularly because of the realization that older preschoolers are capable of significantly greater depth and psychological insight into their conceptions of themselves. The period of time addressed by these foundations is, therefore, an important transitional period. This period starts with the very simple, rudimentary self-awareness of the younger child, focusing on physical self-recognition (such as in a mirror image) and dispositional self-attributions (e.g., "Me big!") and progressing to a more fully realized form of the psychological self-awareness of the early-grade-schooler. For general reviews of this research literature, consult Harter (1999, 2006) and Thompson (2006), who offer somewhat different portrayals of the emergence of self-awareness during the preschool period. Self-awareness is an important component of early school success because young children's self-confidence shapes their interest, motivation, and persistence in academic work, and their success in the classroom reciprocally influences their sense of pride and accomplishment.

Research revealing young children's (unrealistically) optimistic self-regard has often used Harter's Self-Perception Scale for Children (Harter and Pike 1984); see also studies by Stipek (1984; Stipek and Hoffman 1980; Stipek and Mac Iver 1989; Stipek, Roberts, and Sanborn 1984). The sensitivity of preschool children to adults' evaluative judgments of their performance is also well documented by Stipek's research (1995; Stipek, Recchia, and McClintic 1992). A number of studies have revealed the emerging awareness of internal, psychological characteristics in the self-awareness of older four-year-olds; see Eder (1989, 1990), Measelle and others (1998), and the work of Marsh and his colleagues (Marsh, Craven, and Debus 1998; Marsh, Ellis, and Craven 2002). This work challenges earlier, traditional views that preschoolers are focused exclusively on observable appearance and behavior in their self-perceptions and shows that when developmentally appropriate research methods are used, even four-year-olds reveal a dawning understanding of their psychological selves.

---

*Self-awareness is an important component of early school success because young children's self-confidence shapes their interest, motivation, and persistence in academic work . . .*

---

Povinelli's creative research studies have shown that older preschoolers are also capable of perceiving themselves in a more extended temporal context, including the past and future (Povinelli 2001; Povinelli, Landau, and Perilloux 1996; Povinelli and others 1999; Povinelli and Simon 1998). That capability is relevant to both autobiographical memory development and self-awareness. Finally, by the time they reach kindergarten, young children are already becoming experts in the use and interpretation of social comparison information, a skill that will continue to develop throughout the primary school years (Pomerantz and others 1995). Older preschoolers are just beginning to incorporate social comparison information into their self-perceptions.

## Self-Regulation

The development of self-regulation involves emerging capacities to suppress a dominant response and to perform, instead, a subdominant response. It is also associated with the self-control of impulsivity and the development of more deliberate, intentional activity throughout early and middle childhood. Self-regulation is relevant to the management of emotions and emotion-related behavior, attention, cognitive activity, and social behavior (such as impulses to act aggressively when provoked). The significant growth in self-regulation in early childhood is revealed through the contrast between the impulsivity of a toddler and the capacities for more careful, deliberate behavior of a child preparing to enter kindergarten (although these capacities are not, of course, consistently exercised). Bronson (2000) has written a valuable overview of research and practical knowledge on this topic (see also Brazelton and Sparrow 2001; Knitzer 2000; Committee on Integrating the Science of Early Childhood Development 2000). The relevance of self-regulation to young children's school readiness is widely acknowledged because of the importance of cognitive, behavioral,

and emotional self-control to learning and classroom conduct (see Kopp 2002; Thompson 2002; Thompson [in press]). Several research teams have found that differences in aspects of self-regulation predict children's reading and mathematics achievement in the early primary grades (Alexander, Entwisle, and Dauber 1993; Howse and others 2003; NICHD Early Child Care Research Network 2003a).

---

*Self-regulation is relevant to the management of emotions and emotion-related behavior, attention, cognitive activity, and social behavior (such as impulses to act aggressively when provoked).*

---

The development of self-regulation has been a topic of long-standing interest to developmental scholars (see reviews of this research: Kopp 1982; Kopp and Wyer 1994). This topic has recently gained renewed attention under the concepts of "effortful control" and "executive function." Although effortful control is often studied as a component of emergent personality, developmental researchers, including Eisenberg (Eisenberg and others 2004; Liew, Eisenberg, and Reiser 2004) and Kochanska (Kochanska and Knaack 2003; Kochanska, Murray, and Harlan 2000), have documented important developmental changes in young children's capacities for effortful control. Their research has revealed not only significant increases in children's capacities for self-regulated conduct throughout early and middle childhood, but also a consistent association between individual differences in effortful control and independent measures of social competence, emotion regulation, conscience development, and psychological adjustment. Higher effortful control is, in short, a benefit for young children's deliberate and socialized conduct.

The research on executive function seeks to explain young children's problem-solving behavior in regard to their ability to regulate their attentional and cognitive processes, another aspect of self-regulation (see Zelazo and others 2003). This research identifies the period of three to five years of age as an especially important developmental period for executive function, which may be associated with concurrent changes in brain functioning (Bunge and Zelazo 2006; Diamond and Taylor 1996; Gerstadt, Hong, and Diamond 1994).

Among the various capacities young children gradually acquire for self-control, emotion regulation has been of particular interest to developmental scientists because of its relevance to social competence and psychological adjustment. Thompson, Meyer, and Jochem (in press) have written several reviews of theory and research on this topic, summarizing an expanding body of research literature.

## Social and Emotional Understanding

Over the past several decades, there has been an enormous amount of research interest in the early development of social and emotional understanding. This interest has arisen from the realization that, contrary to traditional ideas, toddlers and preschoolers are not egocentric but are, instead, very interested in others' beliefs and how those beliefs compare with their own (see Dunn 1988; Saarni 1999). Further exploration of this topic has also been motivated by the realization that early differences in social and emotional understanding are associated with individual differences in social competence. Preschoolers who are more socially and emotionally perceptive are capable of greater success in their relationships with peers and adults (see Denham and others 2003; Denham and others 2002a; Denham and others 2002b; Denham and others 2001; and see reviews by Denham 1998, 2006; Denham and Weissberg 2004; Halberstadt, Denham, and Dunsmore 2001), which is relevant to school readiness. Young children who are more competent in understanding others' feelings have been found, for example, to become more academically competent in the primary grades, which may arise from the more successful peer relationships to which they contribute (Izard 2002; Izard and others 2001; see also Dowsett and Huston 2005; Raver 2002; Raver and Knitzer 2002).

*Preschoolers who are more socially and emotionally perceptive are capable of greater success in their relationships with peers and adults . . .*

In recent years, research in this area has grown under the idea that young children develop a progressively more complex "theory of mind," by which they explain people's behavior with respect to internal mental states. They gradually come to understand internal mental states more and more fully. Research on developing theory of mind has focused on the ages of three to five years, the period during which young children advance from a theory of mind that is focused primarily on comprehending others' intentions, desires, and feelings as motivators of behavior, to a more advanced theory of mind in which they also understand the nature of people's thoughts and beliefs as motivators of behavior. One of the central features of this conceptual advance is the four-year-old's emerging understanding that people's beliefs can be mistaken; thus, others can be misled or fooled, and the child's own feelings can be hidden or masked. The research literature on developing theory of mind is vast; recent summaries can be found in Wellman (2002) and Harris (2006).

Although young children's understanding of the internal determinants of behavior remains rudimentary, there is evidence that they are already beginning to comprehend the concept of personality characteristics and their association with enduring behavioral characteristics in others. This emerging understanding parallels similar advances in their ability to perceive themselves in terms of psychological characteristics as well, as is discussed in the bibliographic note on self-awareness. Research by Heyman and her colleagues shows that by the later preschool years, children are beginning to derive personality-like generalizations about the behavior of others (see Giles and Heyman 2005a, 2005b; Heyman, Gee, and Giles 2003; Heyman and Gelman 2000).

---

*One of the central features of this conceptual advance is the four-year-old's emerging understanding that people's beliefs can be mistaken . . .*

---

There is also vigorous research literature on young children's developing emotion understanding, an aspect of theory of mind that is especially important to social competence. This research shows that from three to five years of age, young children become increasingly capable of identifying a broader range of emotions and describing prototypical situations in which these emotions might be elicited. They also become capable of explaining the causes of these emotions and their consequences in ways that reveal a greater understanding of the psychological bases of emotional experience (e.g., frustrated goals with respect to anger). This is consistent, of course, with broader characteristics of their developing theory of mind. The research on developing emotion understanding is reviewed by Denham (1998, 2006), Harris (1989), Lagattuta and Thompson (2007), Saarni and others (2006), and Thompson (in press; Thompson 2006; Thompson, Goodvin, and Meyer 2006; Thompson and Lagattuta 2006).

The later preschool years also witness growth in event knowledge—that is, the capacity to comprehend and predict everyday routines—which is an important component of social understanding. Young preschool children can describe the sequence of events that characterize everyday routines and experiences in their lives (e.g., a trip to the grocery store), and older preschool children have more comprehensive knowledge of these events (see Hudson 1993; *Narratives from the Crib* 1989; Nelson 1993).

Finally, the preschool years also witness young children's growing awareness of and response to diversity in gender, culture, and ethnicity, particularly as these are apparent in differences in people's appearance and behavior. This is complex research literature, particularly because of the multiple origins (e.g., social learning, conceptual development, direct exposure to diversity) of young children's responses to human diversity in their experience; see Aboud (2005, 2003).

## Empathy and Caring

Young children's capacities to respond sympathetically and helpfully to others in distress have been of long-standing interest to parents, professionals, and researchers. These capacities build on children's developing social and emotional understanding and contribute to their ability to cooperate successfully with others in group learning environments.

In understanding the development of caring, it is important to distinguish a young child's emotional response to another's distress, which emerges very early, from the behavioral capacity to help the distressed person. Knowing how to aid a peer in distress is a complex challenge to a young child (it is an even greater conceptual challenge to figure out how to assist a distressed adult); therefore, genuine helping behavior emerges later in the preschool years than does a child's emotional response to another's upset. The period of three to four years of age is a crucial one. From before the age of three, young children respond with concerned attention to the distress of another and are interested in finding out why the person is upset. But it is not until later in the preschool years that children can accompany their empathic response with assistance

(although this does not necessarily occur reliably). For recent reviews of this research, consult Eisenberg, Spinrad, and Sadovsky (2006), Thompson (1998), and Zahn-Waxler and Robinson (1995).

## Initiative in Learning

How children approach new learning and problem-solving challenges is a critical feature of their academic success. "Approaches to learning" is an important predictor of classroom achievement in kindergarten and the primary grades, with the term "approaches to learning" defined as teacher ratings of children's classroom engagement, motivation, and participation (Alexander, Entwisle, and Dauber 1993; Duncan, Claessens, and Engel 2005). Young children's natural curiosity, interest, and self-confidence that they can discover the answers to their questions are a central component of their capacities to benefit from learning opportunities (Thompson 2002).

Beginning in early childhood, there are significant differences in the enthusiasm, motivation, and self-confidence that children bring to new learning situations. The work of Dweck and her colleagues has demonstrated that from relatively early in childhood, children develop distinctly different learning styles that influence their initiative in learning and their persistence when faced with difficult challenges (see Burhans and Dweck 1995; Dweck 2002; Dweck and Leggett 1988). Children with a "performance orientation" focus on efforts in learning situations that elicit positive evaluations from others and avoid negative judgments. As a consequence, these children may avoid situations that are likely to result in failure and they may not persist in circumstances in which they are unlikely to succeed. This orientation can, under some circumstances, result in a learned helplessness orientation in which children tend to give up after failing because they do not have confidence in their ability to succeed. In contrast, children with a "learning (or mastery) orientation" focus on efforts that increase their ability. These children will be more likely to tackle difficult challenges if they can foster new learning (even if their initial efforts result in failure) and are more likely to persist until they are successful. This is the kind of learning orientation that best predicts classroom achievement. These differences in learning orientation are readily observed among primary grade students, but there is evidence that they are present among older preschoolers as well (see Burhans and Dweck 1995; Smiley and Dweck 1994). Research by Dweck and her colleagues indicates that these differences arise from many influences, including the kinds of reactions by parents and teachers to children's achievement successes and failures that emphasize the child's intrinsic ability and strong effort.

The research on learning orientations focuses on individual differences among children of a given age. But there are also developmental differences in preschool children's initiative in learning, with younger children being more likely to approach new

*Young children's natural curiosity, interest, and self-confidence that they can discover the answers to their questions are a central component of their capacities to benefit from learning opportunities.*

learning situations with enthusiasm and self-confidence but not necessarily with persistence in confronting difficult problem-solving situations. In contrast, older children are more active learners who are more persistent but who are also more likely to be creative problem solvers, proposing their own ideas and approaching new learning opportunities with initiative and involvement (see Committee on Early Childhood Pedagogy 2001; *The Role of Interest in Learning and Development* 1992; Renninger and Wozniak 1985; Flavell, Miller, and Miller 2001).

# Social Interaction

## Interactions with Familiar Adults

Young children regularly interact with familiar adults in preschool and other early childhood settings. Although these adults are not attachment figures, and children's relationships with them are not necessarily sources of security and support, a child's ability to interact competently with familiar adults is important to social competence and the ability to obtain the assistance the child needs. The ability to interact with other adults is important also to school success because children in kindergarten and the primary grades must interact with many adults other than their teachers.

With the primary focus of developmental research on young children's establishment and maintenance of close relationships, scientists have devoted considerably less attention to the growth of social skills relevant to interacting with familiar adults (see Durkin 1995 for a general source). The relevant research offers a portrayal that is consistent with conclusions from other foundations. Older three-year-olds have developed a number of social skills for interacting competently with familiar adults—including developing abilities to engage in simple conversations, enjoy other shared activities, and cooperate with requests or instructions—and they can exercise these skills particularly in familiar and comfortable settings. Older four-year-olds are not only more advanced in most of these social skills but also take greater active initiative in interacting with familiar adults. Based on these conclusions, most children are becoming prepared for the variety of social encounters that will characterize their experience in kindergarten and the primary grades.

## Interactions with Peers

It was not so long ago that developmental researchers and practitioners underestimated the peer social skills of young children, interpreting episodes of conflict to reflect preschoolers' egocentrism and limited social interest. With the growing experience of young children in preschool and early childhood settings, researchers have rethought peer interactions and have discovered that they are far more complex, sophisticated, and multifaceted than earlier believed. This discovery is consistent with the developmental accomplishments described in the other foundations. As preschoolers achieve considerable insights into others' thoughts and feelings through their growth in "theory of mind," for example, they are capable of greater cooperation with other children and more adept at using conflict resolution strategies.

The development of social skills with peers is also important to the growth of school readiness. A number of studies have shown that the peer experiences of children in kindergarten and the primary grades are an important predictor of children's academic success and school adjustment. Children who experience greater peer acceptance and positive peer relationships tend to feel more positively about coming to school, participate more in classroom activities, and achieve more in the classroom (Buhs and Ladd 2001; Ladd, Birch, and Buhs 1999; Ladd, Kochenderfer, and Coleman 1996, 1997; O'Neil and others 1997).

The period of ages three to five years is a particularly significant one for the growth of social skills with peers, and these foundations illustrate the multifaceted ways in which peer relationships evolve during this time (see reviews of this research by Rubin, Bukowski, and Parker [2006] and Rubin and others [2005]). Young children initially acquire greater skill and confidence in interacting with other children in playgroups of two or three; later, they do so in larger, well-coordinated peer groups. Among the important achievements of the later preschool period is the ability to initiate peer sociability and smoothly join others in play; to cooperatively and spontaneously share with others; to coordinate one's behavior with that of one or more other children; to communicate in ways that other children can understand; and to spontaneously enlist procedures (such as turn-taking) that reduce the chance of peer conflict (Howes 1987, 1988; Vandell, Nenide, and Van Winkle 2006).

Children's play with peers changes significantly during the later preschool period. Preschoolers become capable of greater cooperation and coordination in their shared activity, playing interactively rather than just side by side. In addition, imaginative or pretend play—one of the hallmarks of preschool play activity—develops significantly in complexity and sophistication. Young children proceed from simple sequences of pretend activity to well-coordinated, complex episodes of imaginative play that involve planning, coordination of roles, and mutual correction as the story line is enacted (Goncu 1993; Howes 1987, 1988, 1992; Howes and Matheson 1992). The remarkable ability of older preschool children to competently enact pretend roles, coordinate their activity with that of other children in pretend roles, and monitor the unfolding of the sociodramatic play script is consistent with—and helps to confirm—much of what we know about their social understanding and capacities for cooperation, self-awareness, and self-regulation during this period.

Peer interactions do not always proceed happily, of course. There are significant developmental changes during this period in how young children express their hostility when disagreements arise. Younger preschool children are more likely to respond with physical aggression, while older preschool children are more capable of expressing their hostility in more socially acceptable

*Imaginative or pretend play—one of the hallmarks of preschool play activity—develops significantly in complexity and sophistication.*

ways and are more likely to use verbal taunts and teasing rather than hitting (Tremblay 2000). Fortunately, there are also developmental changes in children's capacities for conflict negotiation, such that by the later preschool years, children are capable of spontaneously suggesting simple conflict resolution strategies (such as proposing alternative play materials or taking turns) and enlisting negotiation over aggression (Howes 1987, 1988; Rubin and others 2005; Rubin, Bukowski, and Parker 2006; Vandell, Nenide, and Van Winkle 2006). These conflict resolution strategies will develop further in the elementary grades, of course, but differences in the capacities of preschoolers to spontaneously enlist conflict resolution strategies are an important basis for their social competence with peers at this age.

## Group Participation

The ability to participate cooperatively and constructively in group activity is an essential skill in any group learning activity; thus, it is a critical component of school readiness. This substrand integrates the developmental achievements described in other social-emotional foundations and applies them to the young child's competency as a group member (see *Developmentally Appropriate Practice in Early Childhood Programs* 1997; Landy 2002). These developmental achievements (described in detail in other foundations) include:

- Developing capacities for self-regulation and self-control, which enable the older preschool child to remember the rules for classroom behavior, games, and other activities; apply the rules to his or her own behav-

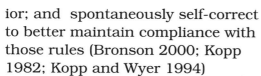

ior; and spontaneously self-correct to better maintain compliance with those rules (Bronson 2000; Kopp 1982; Kopp and Wyer 1994)

- Developing skills for behavioral and attentional self-control, which enable preschool children to gradually attain a greater ability to deliberately focus attention; sit still for longer periods; manage transitions in the daily routine more easily; cooperate in games that require specific responses at particular times (e.g., "Hokey Pokey"); and be less fidgety and distractible (Zelazo and others 2003)

- Developing capacities for cooperation and a sense of responsibility in relation to others, which cause older preschoolers to have a more conscientious commitment to complying with group procedures (sometimes, spontaneously correcting other children who fail to comply), often anticipating the procedures before being reminded by the teacher, and acting in a manner that helps the group to function better (Kochanska and Thompson 1997; Thompson and others 2006)

- Developing event knowledge, which enables the older child to understand and predict the ordinary routines of the classroom schedule; manage transitions in the routine well; and cooperate with new activities when they are initiated by the teacher, especially when preparatory tasks for the activity are required (e.g., getting ready to paint at an easel) (Hudson 1993; *Narratives from the Crib* 1989; Nelson 1993).

- Developing social and emotional understanding, which enables older children (with a more advanced "theory of mind") to better coordi-

nate their own desires, needs, and interests with those of others, which, in turn, facilitates older children's capacities to collaborate on group activities as well as to play harmoniously with peers (Harris 2006; Thompson 2006)

- Developing self-awareness, which enables preschool children to identify themselves not just as individuals in a classroom but also as members of a group, and prompts older preschoolers to strive to make the group work better in shared activities (Harter 1999, 2006; Thompson 2006)

The purpose of delineating a new substrand for group participation, therefore, is to indicate how these different developmental achievements assemble in a manner that enables older preschool children, because of this developing constellation of skills, to be more constructive group participants than are younger children. In this respect, therefore, the whole (of these advances for classroom conduct) is truly greater than the sum of the developmental parts.

## Cooperation and Responsibility

Because of the moral development theories of Piaget (1965) and Kohlberg (1969), young children were, for many years, believed to be motivated primarily by rewards and punishments in their cooperation with adult standards. This belief was consistent with the traditional view that young children are egocentric in considering the needs of others in relation to their own. During the past several decades, however, a new view of the early growth of cooperation and responsibility—studied under the term "conscience development"—has emerged. It emphasizes that in addition to responding to the incentives and punishments of adults, young children are motivated to cooperate by their emotional attachments to those adults and their desire to maintain positive relationships with them. Children cooperate in order to maintain relationships of mutual cooperation with the adults who care for them. Furthermore, young children are also motivated by the feelings of others to act in ways that do not cause others distress. Moreover, as they reach the end of the preschool years, children are also motivated to cooperate and act responsibly because in doing so, they think more approvingly of themselves. This reflects that young children have proceeded from a primarily "external" view of adults' expectations and standards—in other words, cooperating because this is what adults expect—to an "internalized" acceptance of adult standards as their goal. The desire to perceive themselves as cooperative, helpful, and "good" emerges at this time and will remain an important, lifelong motivator of moral conduct.

These conclusions about the development of cooperation and responsibility emerge from a large body of research literature, to which Kochanska has made major contributions (e.g., see Kochanska 1997, 2002; Kochanska and Thompson 1997). A review of this research literature can be found in Thompson, Meyer, and McGinley (2006). The development of capacities for cooperation and responsibility is important to early school success. A number of research teams have found that individual differences in children's cooperation capacities are directly associated with children's academic achievement in the early primary grades (Alexander, Entwisle, and Dauber 1993; McClelland, Morrison, and Holmes 2000; Yen, Konold, and McDermott 2004). Children who show greater cooperative compliance with their teachers are capable of getting along better in the classroom and achieve more than do children who are less cooperative.

*During the past several decades, however, a new view of the early growth of cooperation and responsibility—studied under the term "conscience development"— has emerged.*

Developmental changes in children's motivated cooperation and their growing sense of responsibility build on developmental accomplishments in other social and emotional areas. In particular, these changes build on children's developing capacities for self-regulation and changes in self-awareness that enable older preschoolers to perceive themselves as positive and approvable. In this respect, as in others, growth in the later preschool period is integrated and consistent across different areas of development.

# Relationships

## Attachments to Parents

One of the central conclusions of developmental research is the extent to which young children rely on their close relationships with caregivers for emotional security and well-being. Decades of research on parent-child attachment relationships in infancy and early childhood have established the importance of the security of these relationships and their long-term importance for a child's self-concept, relationships with others, and understanding of what people are like (see reviews by Thompson 2006; Thompson and others 2005; and Waters and others 1991). At the same time, developmental researchers realized that the caregivers on whom children are emotionally reliant are not always biological parents. Sometimes they are grandparents or other adults who assume a regular caregiving role in the child's life—they are, in a sense, "psychological parents" to the child. This is true when nonparents are substitute parents (such as when grandparents are providing full-time care instead of a parent who is incapacitated or absent) and when nonparents are co-parents along with the child's biological parents. In each case, these adult caregivers assume a parenting function in the child's life and are usually attachment figures. This substrand is labeled "Attachments to Parents," although the foundations refer to "primary family attachment figures" to acknowledge the diversity of adults who are attachment figures to young children.

Consistent with their psychological importance to young children, parent-child attachments have also been found to be important to the development of school readiness. Many studies have found that the quality of the parent-child relationship in the preschool years, especially its quality in terms of warmth and support to the child, predicts children's subsequent

---

*Children with more secure, supportive family relationships also show fewer conduct problems and have better work habits.*

---

academic success in kindergarten and the early primary grades as well as their social competence in the classroom. Children with more secure, supportive family relationships also show fewer conduct problems and have better work habits (Burchinal and others 2002; Estrada and others 1987; Morrison, Rimm-Kauffman, and Pianta 2003; NICHD Early Child Care Research Network 2003b, 2003c, 2005; Pianta, Nimetz, and Bennett 1997).

The behavioral indications of parent-child attachment in preschoolers are well established (Marvin and Britner 1999), and the indicators of attachment relationships incorporated into this foundation are drawn from the extensive research literature as well as validated assessment instruments for assessing parent-child attachment quality (see Solomon and George 1999; Waters 2006). In contrast to the dependence of infants and toddlers on physical proximity to their caregivers, preschool children are more independent socially yet are still very emotionally reliant on their attachment figures. The indicators included here focus on how preschoolers seek security and support from their attachment figures in age-appropriate ways as well as their capacities to maintain positive relationships with their attachment figures through their own initiative (Maccoby 1984). An important developmental change in attachment relationships during this period is the greater initiative of older preschoolers in both seeking support and maintaining a relationship of positive mutual cooperation with their attachment figures, which is an outgrowth of their greater psychological understanding of the adult and of the relationship they share. As with younger children, preschoolers exhibit their trust in attachment figures through their preference to be with the adult; the adult's capacity to assist and comfort them when others cannot; their efforts to attract the attachment figure's positive regard (and avoid criticism by this person); their pleasure in shared activity with the adult; and the greater ease with which they can disclose and discuss troubling topics (such as distressing experiences) with the attachment figure.

All of the behavioral indicators included in this foundation should be readily observed of children interacting with their family attachment figures while in a preschool or early childhood setting. An additional indicator concerns preschoolers' success in coping with departing from the attachment figure at the beginning of the day and with separation throughout the day, for which younger preschool children require greater assistance than do older preschool children. This difference arises from the greater ability of older preschoolers to maintain a satisfying mental representation of the attachment figure and their relationship with that person to sustain them; their greater self-regulatory capacities; and their enhanced involvement with peer relationships and the activities of the setting.

## Close Relationships with Teachers and Caregivers

Just as researchers have acknowledged the importance of nonparental caregivers within the family to the emotional well-being of young children, they have also recognized the importance of caregivers outside the home. Preschoolers develop strong emotional bonds with their teachers and caregivers in early childhood settings, and although there is some debate about whether these should be considered "attachments" as the term is applied to primary family caregivers (parents or other adults raising the child), it is apparent that these close family caregiver relationships function very much like attachment relationships for children in early childhood settings (Berlin and Cassidy 1999; Dunn 1993; Howes 1999). Young children rely on their primary teachers or caregivers in early childhood settings in much the same manner that they rely on their family caregivers at home. Although these relationships are not interchangeable, and close relationships outside the home do not diminish the strength of the young child's attachments to the parents, it is apparent that both kinds of relationships are developmentally important.

Young children's close relationships with preschool teachers and caregivers are also important to their development of school readiness. A number of studies have found that the warmth and security of the preschool child's relationship with a preschool teacher are predictive of the child's subsequent classroom performance, attentional skills, and social competence in the kindergarten and primary grade classroom (Peisner-Feinberg and others 2001; Pianta, Nimetz, and Bennett 1997; see Committee on Early Childhood Pedagogy 2001 and Lamb 1998 for reviews). The importance of close relationships outside the home extends to children's adaptation to school. Several studies have confirmed that young children's success in kindergarten and the primary grades is significantly influenced by the quality of the teacher-child relationship and that conflict in the relationship is a predictor of children's poorer academic performance and greater behavior problems, sometimes years later (Birch and Ladd 1997; Hamre and Pianta 2001; La Paro and Pianta 2000; Pianta, Steinberg, and Rollins 1995; Pianta and Stuhlman 2004a, 2004b). In a manner similar to the way in which successful peer relationships in the classroom contribute to children's enthusiasm for learning and classroom success, so is the teacher-child relationship a significant contributor—both before school entry and afterward.

The indicators of young children's close relationships with preschool teachers and caregivers are remarkably consistent with the behavioral indicators of children's attachments to their family caregivers. In both cases, the significant features are the extent to which children seek security and support from their primary preschool teachers and caregivers and the extent to which they contribute to maintaining positive relationships with those adults. Preschoolers exhibit their reliance on their primary preschool teachers through their preference to be with the adult; the adult's capacity to assist and comfort them when others cannot; their efforts to attract the teacher's positive regard (and avoid criticism by

*Although these relationships are not interchangeable, and close relationships outside the home do not diminish the strength of the young child's attachments to the parents, it is apparent that both kinds of relationships are developmentally important.*

*Several studies have confirmed that young children's success in kindergarten and the primary grades is significantly influenced by the quality of the teacher-child relationship and that conflict in the relationship is a predictor of children's poorer academic performance and greater behavior problems, sometimes years later.*

this person); their pleasure in shared activity with the adult; and the greater ease with which they can disclose and discuss troubling topics (such as distressing experiences) with the primary preschool teacher or caregiver. Although this similarity in behavioral indicators should not be taken to indicate that young children's relationships with their parents are identical to their relationships with their primary preschool teachers and caregivers in early childhood settings—clearly, they are not—it is important to recognize that children derive security and support from their close relationships in these settings comparable to the confidence they derive from attachment relationships at home.

## Friendships

Our understanding of preschool children's friendships has advanced in concert with our knowledge of peer interactions, both of which reveal children's skill and sophistication in peer sociability to be greater than was earlier believed. Friendships are important to children's adaptation to school and their academic success for the same reason that successful peer interactions are important: they cause kindergarteners and elementary grade children to look forward to coming to school, to have a more positive classroom experience, and to achieve more as students (Ladd, Kochenderfer, and Coleman 1996, 1997; Ladd, Birch, and Buhs 1999).

Research on the friendships of preschool children reveals that close relationships between peers tend to be stable over time; but with the children's increasing age, these friendships become more reciprocal, more exclusive (i.e., children are more likely to exclude other children from the activities they share with friends), and friends become more psychologically aware of the relationship they share (see reviews by Gottman 1983; Parker and Gottman 1989; Rubin and others

---

*Friendships become characterized by more complex play between friends and more positive and affectionate behavior. But, somewhat surprisingly, there can be greater conflict between friends than in interactions with nonfriends.*

---

2005; Rubin, Bukowski, and Parker 2006; Vandell, Nenide, and Van Winkle 2006). Friendships become characterized by more complex play between friends and more positive and affectionate behavior. But, somewhat surprisingly, there can be greater conflict between friends than in interactions with nonfriends. The greater incidence of conflict may derive both from the greater frequency of friendship interaction and the greater emotional investment in these interactions. However, toward the end of the preschool years, friends are more likely to negotiate with each other, to disengage from disagreements before conflict worsens, and to find other ways of maintaining their friendship beyond the disagreement (Gottman 1983; Hartup 1996; Howes, Droege, and Matheson 1994; Parker and Gottman 1989). In these ways, then, broader features of developing social and emotional competences in early childhood contribute to the maintenance of friendship in older preschoolers and their greater endurance over time.

# Glossary

**approaches to learning.** Children's classroom engagement, motivation, and participation

**attachment figures.** Caregivers on whom children are emotionally reliant, such as a parent, grandparent, or nonparental caregiver; adults who assume a parenting function

**caregiver.** An adult with responsibility for children in a family child care home, or an adult who provides family, friend, or neighbor care

**family caregiver.** A mother, father, grandparent, or other adult raising the child

**early childhood setting.** Any setting in which preschool children receive education and care

**teacher.** An adult with responsibility for the education and care of children in a preschool program

**theory of mind.** Children's developing ability to explain people's behavior with respect to internal mental states

# References and Source Material

Aboud, Frances E. 2005. "The Development of Prejudice in Childhood and Adolescence," in *On the Nature of Prejudice: Fifty Years After Allport.* Edited by J. F. Dovidio; P. Glick; and L. A. Rudman. Malden, MA: Blackwell.

Aboud, Frances E. 2003. "The Formation of In-Group Favoritism and Out-Group Prejudice in Young Children: Are They Distinct Attitudes?" *Developmental Psychology,* Vol. 39, No. 1, 48–60.

Alexander, Karl L.; Doris R. Entwisle; and Susan L. Dauber. 1993. "First Grade Classroom Behavior: Its Short- and Long-Term Consequences for School Performance," *Child Development,* Vol. 64, 801–14.

Berk, L. E. 2006. *Child Development* (Seventh edition). Boston: Pearson.

Berlin, Lisa J., and Jude Cassidy. 1999. "Relations Among Relationships: Contributions from Attachment Theory and Research," in *Handbook of Attachment: Theory, Research and Clinical Applications.* Edited by Jude Cassidy and Phillip Shaver. New York: Guilford.

Birch, Sondra H., and Gary W. Ladd. 1997. "The Teacher-Child Relationship and Children's Early School Adjustment," *Journal of School Psychology,* Vol. 35, No. 1, 61–79.

Brazelton, T. B., and Joshua D. Sparrow. 2001. *Touchpoints Three to Six: Your Child's Emotional and Behavioral Development.* Cambridge, MA: Perseus.

Bricker, Diane, and others. 1999. *Ages & Stages Questionnaires (ASQ): A Parent-Completed, Child-Monitoring System* (Second edition). Baltimore: Paul H. Brookes Publishing.

Bronson, Martha B. 2000. *Self-Regulation in Early Childhood: Nature and Nurture.* New York: Guilford.

Buhs, Eric S., and Gary W. Ladd. 2001. "Peer Rejection as an Antecedent of Young Children's School Adjustment: An Examination of Mediating Processes," *Developmental Psychology,* Vol. 37, No. 4, 550–60.

Bunge, Silvia A., and Philip D. Zelazo. 2006. "A Brain-Based Account of the Development of Rule Use in Childhood," *Current Directions in Psychological Science,* Vol. 15, No. 3, 118–21.

Burchinal, Margaret R., and others. 2002. "Development of Academic Skills from Preschool Through Second Grade: Family and Classroom Predictors of Developmental Trajectories," *Journal of School Psychology,* Vol. 40, No. 5, 415–36.

Burhans, Karen K., and Carol S. Dweck, 1995. "Helplessness in Early Childhood: The Role of Contingent Worth," *Child Development,* Vol. 66, 1719–38.

Cabrera, N. J., and C. Garcia-Coll. 2004. "Latino Fathers: Uncharted Territory in Need of Much Exploration," in *The Role of the Father in Child Development* (Fourth edition). Edited by Michael E. Lamb. Hoboken, NJ: Wiley.

Committee on Developments in the Science of Learning, National Research Council. 2000. *How People Learn: Brain, Mind, Experience, and School.* Edited by John D. Bransford, Ann L. Brown, and Rodney R. Cocking. Washington, DC: National Academy Press.

Committee on Early Childhood Pedagogy, National Research Council. 2001. *Eager to Learn: Educating Our Preschoolers.* Edited by Barbara T. Bowman, M. S. Donovan, and M. S. Burns. Washington, DC: National Academy Press.

Committee on Integrating the Science of Early Childhood Development, National Research Council and Institute of Medicine. 2000. *From Neurons to Neighborhoods: The Science of Early*

*Childhood Development.* Edited by Jack P. Shonkoff and Deborah A. Phillips. Washington, DC: National Academy Press.

Denham, Susanne. 1998. *Emotional Development in Young Children.* New York: Guilford.

Denham, Susanne, 2006. "The Emotional Basis of Learning and Development in Early Childhood Education," in *Handbook of Research on the Education of Young Children* (Second edition). Edited by Bernard Spodek and Olivia N. Saracho. Mahwah, NJ: Erlbaum.

Denham, Susanne, and Roger P. Weissberg. 2004. "Social-Emotional Learning in Early Childhood: What We Know and Where to Go From Here?" in *A Blueprint for the Promotion of Prosocial Behavior in Early Childhood.* Edited by Elda Chesebrough and others. New York: Kluwer Academic/Plenum Publishers.

Denham, Susanne, and others. 2001. "Preschoolers at Play: Co-Socialisers of Emotional and Social Competence," *International Journal of Behavioral Development,* Vol. 25, No. 4, 290–301.

Denham, Susanne, and others. 2002a. "Compromised Emotional Competence: Seeds of Violence Sown Early?" *American Journal of Orthopsychiatry,* Vol. 72, No. 1, 70–82.

Denham, Susanne, and others. 2002b. "Preschool Understanding of Emotions: Contributions to Classroom Anger and Aggression," *Journal of Child Psychology & Psychiatry,* Vol. 43, No. 7, 901–16.

Denham, Susanne, and others. 2003. "Preschool Emotional Competence: Pathway to Social Competence," *Child Development,* Vol. 74, No. 1, 238–56.

*Developmentally Appropriate Practice in Early Childhood Programs* (Revised edition). 1997. Edited by Sue Bredekamp and Carol Copple. Washington, DC: National Association for the Education of Young Children.

Diamond, Adele, and Colleen Taylor. 1996. "Development of an Aspect of Executive Control: Development of the Abilities to Remember What I Said and to 'Do as I Say, Not as I Do,'" *Developmental Psychobiology,* Vol. 29, No. 4, 315–34.

Dichtelmiller, Margo L., and others. 2001. *The Work Sampling System Omnibus Guidelines, Preschool Through Third Grade* (Fourth edition). Ann Arbor, MI: Rebus.

Dowsett, C., and A. Huston. 2005. "The Role of Social-Emotional Behavior in School Readiness." In G. Duncan (Chair), *Hard Skills and Socioemotional Behavior at School Entry: What Matters Most for Subsequent Achievement?* Symposium presented to the biennial meeting of the Society for Research in Child Development, Atlanta, Georgia, April 2005.

Duncan, G. J.; A. Claessens; and M. Engel. 2005. "The Contributions of Hard Skills and Socioemotional Behavior to School Readiness in the ECLS-K." In G. Duncan (Chair), *Hard Skills and Socioemotional Behavior at School Entry: What Matters Most for Subsequent Achievement?* Symposium presented to the biennial meeting of the Society for Research in Child Development, Atlanta, Georgia, April 2005.

Dunn, Judy. 1993. *Young Children's Close Relationships: Beyond Attachment.* Newbury Park, CA: Sage.

Dunn, Judy. 1998. *The Beginnings of Social Understanding.* Cambridge, MA: Harvard University Press.

Durkin, Kevin. 1995. *Developmental Social Psychology: From Infancy to Old Age.* Oxford, UK: Blackwell.

Dweck, Carol S. 2002. "The Development of Ability Conceptions," in *Development of Achievement Motivation.* Edited by Allan Wigfield and Jacquelynne S. Eccles. San Diego, CA: Academic Press.

Dweck, Carol S., and Ellen L. Leggett. 1988. "A Social-Cognitive Approach to

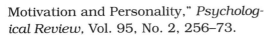
Motivation and Personality," *Psychological Review*, Vol. 95, No. 2, 256–73.

Eder, Rebecca. 1989. "The Emergent Personologist: The Structure and Content of 3 1/2-, 5 1/2-, and 7 1/2-Year-Olds' Concepts of Themselves and Other Persons," *Child Development*, Vol. 60, No. 5, 1218–28.

Eder, Rebecca. 1989. "Uncovering Young Children's Psychological Selves: Individual and Developmental Differences," *Child Development*, Vol. 61, No. 3, 849–63.

Eisenberg, Nancy; Tracy L. Spinrad; and Adrienne Sadovsky. 2006. "Empathy-Related Responding in Children," in *Handbook of Moral Development.* Edited by Melanie Killen and Judith G. Smetana. Mahwah, NJ: Erlbaum.

Eisenberg, Nancy, and others. 2004. "The Relations of Effortful Control and Impulsivity to Children's Resiliency and Adjustment," *Child Development*, Vol. 75, No. 1, 25–46.

Estrada, Peggy, and others. 1987. "Affective Quality of the Mother-Child Relationship: Longitudinal Consequences for Children's School-Relevant Cognitive Functioning," *Developmental Psychology*, Vol. 23, No. 2, 210–15.

Fitzgerald, H., and others. 2003. "Diversity in Caregiving Contexts," in *Handbook of Psychology,* Vol. 6. *Developmental Psychology,* Edited by I. B. Weiner and others. Hoboken, NJ: Wiley.

Flavell, J. H.; P. H. Miller; and S. A. Miller. 2001. *Cognitive Development* (Fourth edition). New York: Prentice Hall.

Gerstadt, Cherie; Yoon Joo Hong; and Adele Diamond. 1994. "The Relationship Between Cognition and Action: Performance of Children 3½–7 Years Old on a Stroop-Like Day-Night Test," *Cognition*, Vol. 53, No. 2, 129–53.

Giles, Jessica W., and Gail D. Heyman. 2005a. "Preschoolers Use Trait-Relevant Information to Evaluate the Appropriateness of an Aggressive Response," *Aggressive Behavior,* Vol. 31, No. 5, 498–509.

Giles, Jessica W., and Gail D. Heyman. 2005b. "Young Children's Beliefs About the Relationship Between Gender and Aggressive Behavior," *Child Development*, Vol. 76, No. 1, 107–21.

Goncu, Artin. 1993. "Development of Intersubjectivity in the Dyadic Play of Preschoolers," *Early Childhood Research Quarterly*, Vol. 8, No. 1, 99–116.

Gottman, J. M. 1983. "How Children Become Friends," *Monographs of the Society for Research in Child Development*, Vol. 48, No. 3 (Serial no. 201).

Halberstadt, Amy G.; Susanne A. Denham; and Julie C. Dunsmore. 2001. "Affective Social Competence," *Social Development*, Vol. 10, No. 1, 79–119.

Hamre, B. K., and R. C. Pianta. 2001. "Early Teacher-Child Relationships and the Trajectory of Children's School Outcomes Through Eighth Grade," *Child Development*, Vol. 72, 625–38.

Harris, Paul. 1989. *Children and Emotion: The Development of Psychological Understanding.* Oxford: Blackwell.

Harris, Paul. 2006. "Social Cognition," in *Handbook of Child Psychology* (Sixth edition), Vol. 2. *Cognition, Perception, and Language.* Edited by William Damon and others. New York: Wiley.

Harter, Susan. 1999. *The Construction of the Self: A Developmental Perspective.* New York: Guilford.

Harter, Susan. 2006. "The Self," in *Handbook of Child Psychology* (Sixth edition), Vol. 3. *Social, Emotional, and Personality Development.* Edited by William Damon, Richard M. Lerner, and Nancy Eisenberg. New York: Wiley.

Harter, Susan, and Robin Pike. 1984. "The Pictorial Scale of Perceived Competence and Social Acceptance for Young Children," *Child Development*, Vol. 55, 1969–82.

Hartup, Willard W. 1996. "The Company They Keep: Friendships and Their Developmental Significance," *Child Development*, Vol. 67, 1–13.

Heyman, Gail D.; Caroline L. Gee; and Jessica W. Giles. 2003. "Preschool Children's Reasoning About Ability," *Child Development*, Vol. 74, No. 2, 516–34.

Heyman, Gail D., and Susan A. Gelman. 2000. "Preschool Children's Use of Trait Labels to Make Inductive Inferences," *Journal of Experimental Child Psychology*, Vol. 77, 1–19.

High/Scope Educational Research Foundation. 2003. *Preschool Child Observation Record: Observation Items* (Second edition). Ypsilanti, MI: High/Scope Press.

Hohmann, Mary, and David P. Weikart. 1995. *Educating Young Children.* Ypsilanti, MI: High/Scope Press.

Howes, Carollee. 1987. "Social Competence with Peers in Young Children: Developmental Sequences," *Developmental Review*, Vol. 7, 252–72.

Howes, Carollee. 1988. "Peer Interaction of Young Children." *Monographs of the Society for Research in Child Development*, Vol. 53 (Serial no. 217).

Howes, Carollee. 1992. *The Collaborative Construction of Pretend.* Albany: State University of New York Press.

Howes, Carollee. 1999. "Attachment Relationships in the Context of Multiple Caregivers," in *Handbook of Attachment: Theory, Research and Clinical Applications.* Edited by Jude Cassidy and Phillip Shaver. New York: Guilford.

Howes, Carollee; Kristin Droege; and Catherine C. Matheson.1994. "Play and Communicative Processes Within Long-Term and Short-Term Friendship Dyads," *Journal of Social and Personal Relationships*, Vol. 11, 401–10.

Howes, Carollee, and Catherine C. Matheson. 1992. "Sequences in the Development of Competent Play with Peers: Social and Social Pretend Play," *Developmental Psychology*, Vol. 28, No. 5, 961–74.

Howse, Robin B., and others. 2003. "Motivation and Self-Regulation as Predictors of Achievement in Economically Disadvantaged Young Children," *The Journal of Experimental Education*, Vol. 71, No. 2, 151–74.

Hudson, Judith. 1993. "Understanding Events: The Development of Script Knowledge," in *The Child as Psychologist: An Introduction to the Development of Social Cognition.* Edited by M. Bennett. New York: Harvester Wheatsheaf.

Hughes, Diane, and Lisa Chen. 1999. "The Nature of Parents' Race-Related Communications to Children: A Developmental Perspective," in *Child Psychology: A Handbook of Contemporary Issues.* Edited by L. Balter and C. S. Tamis-LeMonda. New York: Psychology Press.

Hughes, Diane, and others. 2006. "Parents' Ethnic-Racial Socialization Practices: A Review of Research and Directions for Future Study," *Developmental Psychology*, Vol. 42, No. 5, 747–70.

Izard, Carroll E. 2002. "Emotion Knowledge and Emotion Utilization Facilitate School Readiness," *Social Policy Report*, Vol. 16, 7.

Izard, Carroll, and others. 2001. "Emotion Knowledge as a Predictor of Social Behavior and Academic Competence in Children at Risk," *Psychological Science*, Vol. 12, No. 1, 18–23.

Johnson, Deborah J. 2005. "The Ecology of Children's Racial Coping: Family, School, and Community Influences," in *Discovering Successful Pathways in Children's Development: Mixed Methods in the Study of Childhood and Family Life.* Edited by T. S. Weisner. Chicago: University of Chicago Press.

Johnson, Deborah J., and others. 2003. "Studying the Effects of Early Child Care Experiences on the Development of Children of Color in the United States: Toward a More Inclusive Research Agenda," *Child Development*, Vol. 74, No. 5, 1227–44.

Knitzer, J. 2000. *Using Mental Health Strategies to Move the Early Childhood*

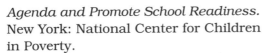

*Agenda and Promote School Readiness.* New York: National Center for Children in Poverty.

Kochanska, Grazyna. 1997. "Mutually Responsive Orientation Between Mothers and Their Young Children: Implications for Early Socialization," *Child Development,* Vol. 68, No. 1, 94–112.

Kochanska, Grazyna. 2002. "Committed Compliance, Moral Self, and Internalization: A Mediated Model," *Developmental Psychology,* Vol. 38, No. 3, 339–51.

Kochanska, Grazyna, and A. Knaack. 2003. "Effortful Control as a Personality Characteristic of Young Children: Antecedents, Correlates, and Consequences," *Journal of Personality,* Vol. 71, No. 6, 1087–1112.

Kochanska, Grazyna; Kathleen T. Murray; and Elena T. Harlan. 2000. "Effortful Control in Early Childhood: Continuity and Change, Antecedents, and Implications for Social Development," *Developmental Psychology,* Vol. 36, No. 2, 220–32.

Kochanska, Grazyna, and Ross A. Thompson. 1997. "The Emergence and Development of Conscience in Toddlerhood and Early Childhood," in *Parenting and Children's Internalization of Values.* Edited by J. Grusec and L. Kuczynski. New York: Wiley.

Kohlberg, L. 1969. "Stage and Sequence: The Cognitive-Developmental Approach to Socialization," in *Handbook of Socialization Theory and Research.* Edited by D. A. Goslin. Skokie, IL: Rand McNally.

Kopp, Claire B. 1982. "Antecedents of Self-Regulation: A Developmental Perspective," *Developmental Psychology,* Vol. 18, No. 2, 199–214.

Kopp, Claire B. 2002. "School Readiness and Regulatory Processes," in *Social Policy Report,* Vol. 16, No. 3, 11.

Kopp, Claire B., and Natalie Wyer. 1994. "Self-Regulation in Normal and Atypical Development," in *Disorders and Dysfunctions of the Self* (Rochester

Symposium on Developmental Psychopathology), Vol. 5. Edited by D. Cicchetti and S. L. Toth. Rochester, NY: University of Rochester Press.

Ladd, Gary W.; Sondra H. Birch; and Eric S. Buhs. 1999. "Children's Social and Scholastic Lives in Kindergarten: Related Spheres of Influence?" *Child Development,* Vol. 70, No. 6, 1373–1400.

Ladd, Gary W.; Becky J. Kochenderfer; and Cynthia C. Coleman. 1996. "Friendship Quality as a Predictor of Young Children's Early School Adjustment," *Child Development,* Vol. 67, 1103–18.

Ladd, Gary W.; Becky J. Kochenderfer; and Cynthia C. Coleman. 1997. "Classroom Peer Acceptance, Friendship, and Victimization: Distinct Relational Systems That Contribute Uniquely to Children's School Adjustment?" *Child Development,* Vol. 68, No. 6, 1181–97.

Lagattuta, K., and R. A. Thompson. 2007. "The Development of Self-Conscious Emotions: Cognitive Processes and Social Influences," in *Self-Conscious Emotions: Theory and Research* (Second edition). Edited by R. W. Robins, J. Tracy, and J. P. Tangney. New York: Guilford.

Lamb, M. E. 1998. "Nonparental Child Care: Context, Quality, Correlates, and Consequences," in *Handbook of Child Psychology* (Fifth edition), Vol. 4. *Child Psychology in Practice.* Edited by W. Damon, I. E. Sigel, and K. A. Renninger. New York: Wiley.

Landy, Sarah. 2002. *Pathways to Competence: Encouraging Healthy Social and Emotional Development in Young Children.* Baltimore: Paul H. Brooks Publishing Co.

La Paro, Karen M., and R. C. Pianta. 2000. "Predicting Children's Competence in the Early School Years: A Meta-Analytic Review," *Review of Educational Research,* Vol. 70, No. 4, 443–84.

Liew, Jeffrey; Nancy Eisenberg; and Mark Reiser. 2004. "Preschoolers' Effortful

Control and Negative Emotionality, Immediate Reactions to Disappointment, and Quality of Social Functioning," *Journal of Experimental Child Psychology,* Vol. 89, No. 4, 298–319.

Maccoby, E. E. 1984. "Socialization and Developmental Change," *Child Development,* Vol. 55, 317–28.

Marsh, Herbert; Rhonda Craven; and Raymond Debus. 1998. "Structure, Stability, and Development of Young Children's Self-Concepts: A Multicohort-Multioccasion Study," *Child Development,* Vol. 69, No. 4, 1030–53.

Marsh, Herbert; Louise Ellis; and Rhonda Craven. 2002. "How Do Preschool Children Feel About Themselves? Unraveling Measurement and Multidimensional Self-Concept Structure," *Developmental Psychology,* Vol. 38, No. 3, 376–93.

Marvin, Robert S., and Preston A. Britner. 1999. "Normative Development: The Ontogeny of Attachment," in *Handbook of Attachment: Theory, Research, and Clinical Applications.* Edited by Jude Cassidy and Phillip R. Shaver. New York: Guilford.

McClelland, Megan M.; Frederick J. Morrison; and Deborah L. Holmes. 2000. "Children at Risk for Early Academic Problems: The Role of Learning-Related Social Skills," *Early Childhood Research Quarterly,* Vol. 15, No. 3, 307–29.

Measelle, Jeffrey, and others. 1998. "Assessing Young Children's Views of Their Academic, Social, and Emotional Lives: An Evaluation of the Self-Perception Scales of the Berkeley Puppet Interview," *Child Development,* Vol. 69, No. 6, 1556–76.

Meisels, S. J., and others. 2003. *The Ounce Scale: Standards for the Developmental Profiles, Birth–42 Months.* New York: Pearson Early Learning.

Morrison, Emily F.; Sara Rimm-Kauffman; and Robert C. Pianta. 2003. "A Longitudinal Study of Mother-Child Interactions at School Entry and Social and Academic Outcomes in Middle School," *Journal of School Psychology,* Vol. 41, 185–200.

*Narratives from the Crib.* 1989. Edited by Katherine Nelson. Cambridge: Harvard University Press.

Nelson, Katherine. 1993. "Events, Narratives, Memory: What Develops?" In *Memory and Affect in Development* (Minnesota Symposia on Child Psychology), Vol. 26. Edited by C. Nelson. Hillsdale, NJ: Erlbaum.

NICHD Early Child Care Research Network. 2003a. "Do Children's Attention Processes Mediate the Link Between Family Predictors and School Readiness?" *Developmental Psychology,* Vol. 39, No. 3, 581–93.

NICHD Early Child Care Research Network. 2003b. "Social Functioning in First Grade: Associations with Earlier Home and Child Care Predictors and with Current Classroom Experiences," *Child Development,* Vol. 74, No. 6, 1639–62.

NICHD Early Child Care Research Network. 2003c. "Does the Amount of Time Spent in Child Care Predict Socioemotional Adjustment During the Transition to Kindergarten?" *Child Development,* Vol. 74, No. 4, 976–1005.

NICHD Early Child Care Research Network. 2005. "Predicting Individual Differences in Attention, Memory, and Planning in First Graders from Experiences at Home, Child Care, and School," *Developmental Psychology,* Vol. 41, No. 1, 99–114.

O'Neil, Robin, and others. 1997. "A Longitudinal Assessment of the Academic Correlates of Early Acceptance and Rejection," *Journal of Clinical Child Psychology,* Vol. 26, No. 3, 290–303.

Parker, J. G., and J. M. Gottman. 1989. "Social and Emotional Development in a Relational Context: Friendship Interaction from Early Childhood to Adolescence," in *Peer Relationships in Child*

*Development.* Edited by T. J. Berndt and G. W. Ladd. New York: Wiley.

Peisner-Feinberg, Ellen S., and others. 2001. "The Relation of Preschool Child-Care Quality to Children's Cognitive and Social Developmental Trajectories Through Second Grade," *Child Development,* Vol. 72, No. 5, 1534–53.

Piaget, J. 1965. *The Moral Judgment of the Child.* New York: Free Press.

Pianta, Robert C.; Sheri L. Nimetz; and Elizabeth Bennett. 1997. "Mother-Child Relationships, Teacher-Child Relationships, and School Outcomes in Preschool and Kindergarten," *Early Childhood Research Quarterly,* Vol. 12, 263–80.

Pianta, Robert C.; Michael S. Steinberg; and Kristin B. Rollins. 1995. "The First Two Years of School: Teacher-Child Relationships and Deflections in Children's Classroom Adjustment," *Development & Psychopathology,* Vol. 7, 295–312.

Pianta, Robert C., and Megan W. Stuhlman. 2004a. "Teacher-Child Relationships and Children's Success in the First Years of School. *School Psychology Review,* Vol. 33, No. 3, 444–58.

Pianta, Robert C., and Megan W. Stuhlman. 2004b. "Conceptualizing Risk in Relational Terms: Associations Among the Quality of Child-Adult Relationships Prior to School Entry and Children's Developmental Outcomes in First Grade," *Educational & Child Psychology,* Vol. 21, No. 1, 32–45.

Pomerantz, Eva M., and others. 1995. "Meeting Goals and Confronting Conflict: Children's Changing Perceptions of Social Comparison," *Child Development,* Vol. 66, 723–38.

Povinelli, Daniel. 2001. "The Self: Elevated in Consciousness and Extended in Time," in *The Self in Time.* Edited by C. Moore and K. Lemmon. Mahwah, NJ: Erlbaum.

Povinelli, Daniel; Keli Landau; and Helen Perilloux. 1996. "Self-Recognition in Young Children Using Delayed versus Live Feedback: Evidence of a Developmental Asynchrony," *Child Development,* Vol. 67, 1540–54.

Povinelli, Daniel, and Bridgett Simon. 1998. "Young Children's Understanding of Briefly versus Extremely Delayed Images of the Self: Emergence of the Autobiographical Stance," *Developmental Psychology,* Vol. 34, No. 1, 188–94.

Povinelli, Daniel, and others. 1999. "Development of Young Children's Understanding that the Recent Past Is Causally Bound to the Present," *Developmental Psychology,* Vol. 35, No. 6, 1426–39.

Raver, C. C. 2002. "Emotions Matter: Making the Case for the Role of Young Children's Emotional Development for Early School Readiness," *Social Policy Report,* Vol. 16, No. 3, 3–18.

Raver, C. C., and Jane Knitzer. 2002. *Ready to Enter: What Research Tells Policymakers About Strategies to Promote Social and Emotional School Readiness Among Three- and Four-Year-Old Children.* New York: National Center for Children in Poverty.

Renninger, K. A., and Robert H. Wozniak. 1985. "Effect of Interest on Attentional Shift, Recognition, and Recall in Young Children," *Developmental Psychology,* Vol. 21, No. 4, 624–32.

Rogoff, Barbara. 1990. *Apprenticeship in Thinking: Cognitive Development in Social Context.* New York: Oxford University Press.

Rogoff, Barbara. 2003. *The Cultural Nature of Human Development.* New York: Oxford University Press.

*The Role of Interest in Learning and Development.* 1992. Edited by K. A. Renninger, Suzanne Hidi, and Andreas Krapp. Hillsdale, NJ: Erlbaum.

Rubin, Kenneth H.; William M. Bukowski; and Jeffrey G. Parker. 2006. "Peer Interactions, Relationships, and Groups," in *Handbook of Child Psychology* (Sixth edition), Vol. 3. *Social, Emo-*

tional, and Personality Development. Edited by William Damon, Richard M. Lerner, and Nancy Eisenberg. New York: Wiley.

Rubin, Kenneth H., and others. 2005. "Peer Relationships in Childhood," in Developmental Science: An Advanced Textbook (Fifth edition). Edited by M. H. Bornstein and M. E. Lamb. Mahwah, NJ: Erlbaum.

Saarni, Carolyn. 1999. The Development of Emotional Competence. New York: Guilford.

Saarni, Carolyn, and others. 2006. "Emotional Development: Action, Communication, and Understanding," in Handbook of Child Psychology (Sixth edition), Vol. 3. Social, Emotional, and Personality Development. Edited by William Damon, Richard M. Lerner, and Nancy Eisenberg. New York: Wiley.

Shaffer, David R. 2004. Social and Personality Development (Fifth edition). Belmont, CA: Thomson Wadsworth.

Smiley, Patricia A., and Carol S. Dweck. 1994. "Individual Differences in Achievement Goals Among Young Children," Child Development, Vol. 65, 1723–43.

Solomon, Judith, and Carol George. 1999. "The Measurement of Attachment Security in Infancy and Childhood," in Handbook of Attachment: Theory, Research and Clinical Applications. Edited by Jude Cassidy and Phillip Shaver. New York: Guilford.

Squires, J.; D. Brickner; and E. Twombly. 2003. The ASQ: SE User's Guide for the Ages & Stages Questionnaires: Social-Emotional. Baltimore: Paul H. Brookes Publishing Co.

Stipek, Deborah. 1984. "Young Children's Performance Expectations: Logical Analysis or Wishful Thinking?" in Advances in Achievement Motivation: The Development of Achievement Motivation, Vol. 3. Edited by John G. Nicholls. Greenwich, CT: JAI Press.

Stipek, Deborah. 1995. "The Development of Pride and Shame in Toddlers," in Self-Conscious Emotions: The Psychology of Shame, Guilt, Embarrassment and Pride. Edited by June P. Tangney and Kurt W. Fischer. New York: Guilford.

Stipek, Deborah, and Joel Hoffman. 1980. "Development of Children's Performance-Related Judgments," Child Development, Vol. 51, 912–14.

Stipek, Deborah, and Douglas Mac Iver. 1989. "Developmental Change in Children's Assessment of Intellectual Competence," Child Development, Vol. 60, 521–38.

Stipek, Deborah; Susan Recchia; and Susan McClintic. 1992. "Self-Evaluation in Young Children," Monographs of the Society for Research in Child Development, Vol. 57, No. 1 (Serial no. 226).

Stipek, Deborah; Theresa A. Roberts; and Mary E. Sanborn. 1984. "Preschool-Age Children's Performance Expectations for Themselves and Another Child as a Function of the Incentive Value of Success and the Salience of Past Performance," Child Development, Vol. 55, 1983–89.

Stipek, Deborah, and others.1995. "Effects of Different Instructional Approaches on Young Children's Achievement and Motivation," Child Development, Vol. 66, 209–23.

Thompson, Ross A. 1990. "Emotion and Self-Regulation," in Socioemotional Development (Nebraska Symposium on Motivation), Vol. 36. Edited by Ross A. Thompson. Lincoln, NE: University of Nebraska Press.

Thompson, Ross A. 1994. "Emotion Regulation: A Theme in Search of Definition," in The Development of Emotion Regulation and Dysregulation: Biological and Behavioral Aspects. Edited by N. A. Fox. Monographs of the Society for Research in Child Development, Vol. 59, No. 2–3 (Serial no. 240).

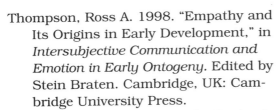
Thompson, Ross A. 1998. "Empathy and Its Origins in Early Development," in *Intersubjective Communication and Emotion in Early Ontogeny*. Edited by Stein Braten. Cambridge, UK: Cambridge University Press.

Thompson, Ross A. 2002. "The Roots of School Readiness in Social and Emotional Development," *The Kauffman Early Education Exchange*, Vol. 1, 8–29.

Thompson, Ross A. 2006. "The Development of the Person: Social Understanding, Relationships, Conscience, Self," in *Handbook of Child Psychology* (Sixth edition), Vol. 3. *Social, Emotional, and Personality Development*. Edited by William Damon, Richard M. Lerner, Nancy Eisenberg. New York: Wiley.

Thompson, Ross A. In press. "Emotional Development," in *The Chicago Companion to the Child*. Edited by R. A. Schweder. Chicago: University of Chicago Press.

Thompson, Ross A., and Rebecca Goodvin. 2007. "Taming the Tempest in the Teapot: Emotion Regulation in Toddlers," in *Socioemotional Development in the Toddler Years: Transitions and Transformations*. Edited by C. A. Brownell and C. B. Kopp. New York: Guilford.

Thompson, Ross A.; Rebecca Goodvin; and Sara Meyer. 2006. "Social Development: Psychological Understanding, Self Understanding, and Relationships," in *Handbook of Preschool Mental Health: Development, Disorders and Treatment*. Edited by Joan Luby. New York: Guilford.

Thompson, Ross A., and Kristin Lagatutta. 2006. "Feeling and Understanding: Early Emotional Development," in *The Blackwell Handbook of Early Childhood Development*. Edited by Kathleen McCartney and Deborah Phillips. Oxford, UK: Blackwell.

Thompson, Ross A; Sara Meyer; and R. Jochem. In press. "Emotion Regulation," in *Encyclopedia of Infant and Early Childhood Development*. Oxford, UK: Elsevier.

Thompson, Ross A.; Sara Meyer; and Meredith McGinley. 2006. "Understanding Values in Relationship: The Development of Conscience," in *Handbook of Moral Development*. Edited by M. Killen and J. Smetana. Mahwah, NJ: Erlbaum.

Thompson, Ross A., and H. A. Raikes. 2007. "The Social and Emotional Foundations of School Readiness," in *Social and Emotional Health in Early Childhood: Building Bridges Between Services and Systems*. Edited by J. Knitzer, R. Kaufmann, and D. Perry. Baltimore, MD: Paul H. Brookes Publishing Co.

Thompson, Ross A., and others. 2005. "Early Social Attachment and Its Consequences: The Dynamics of a Developing Relationship," in *Attachment and Bonding: A New Synthesis* (Dahlem Workshop Report 92). Edited by C. S. Carter and others. Cambridge, MA: The MIT Press.

Tremblay, Robert E. 2000. "The Development of Aggressive Behaviour During Childhood: What Have We Learned in the Past Century?" *International Journal of Behavioral Development*, Vol. 24, No. 2, 129–41.

Vandell, Deborah L.; Lana Nenide; and Sara J. Van Winkle. 2006. "Peer Relationships in Early Childhood," in *Blackwell Handbook of Early Childhood Development*. Edited by Kathleen McCartney and Deborah Phillips. Oxford, UK: Blackwell.

Waters, E. *Attachment Q-set* (Version 3). 2006. http://www.johnbowlby.com (accessed November 1, 2006).

Waters, E., and others. 1991. "Learning to Love: Mechanisms and Milestones," in *Self Processes and Development* (Minnesota Symposia on Child Psychology), Vol. 23. Edited by M. Gunnar and L. Sroufe. Hillsdale, NJ: Erlbaum.

Wellman, Henry. 2002. "Understanding the Psychological World: Developing a Theory of Mind," in *Handbook of Childhood Cognitive Development.* Edited by Usha Goswami. Oxford: Blackwell.

Yen, Cherng-Jyh; Timothy R. Konold; and Paul A. McDermott. 2004. "Does Learning Behavior Augment Cognitive Ability as an Indicator of Academic Achievement?" *Journal of School Psychology,* Vol. 42, 157–69.

Zahn-Waxler, Carolyn, and Joann Robinson. 1995. "Empathy and Guilt: Early Origins of Feelings of Responsibility," in *Self-Conscious Emotions.* Edited by June Price Tangney and Kurt Fischer. New York: Guilford.

Zelazo, P. D., and others. 2003. "The Development of Executive Function," *Monographs of the Society for Research in Child Development,* Vol. 68.

FOUNDATIONS IN

# Language and Literacy

## Purpose of the Language and Literacy Preschool Learning Foundations

This section presents preschool learning foundations for preschool children in the central domain of language and literacy learning and development. Based on research, these preschool learning foundations identify key competencies typical of children who are making progress toward being ready for kindergarten and becoming fluent communicators and readers. The foundations describe age-appropriate knowledge and skills expected of older three-year-olds (i.e., at around 48 months of age) and of older four-year-olds (i.e., at around 60 months of age). In other words, the focus of these foundations is on the language and literacy competencies of young children near the time when they are three years old going on four years old and four years old going on five years old. Although an in-depth consideration of children's language and literacy competencies during the preschool years is fundamentally important, attention to this domain is best understood in the broad context of early learning and development. Language and literacy learning depends on children's functioning in the other domains, including social-emotional development, physical development, and for English learners, English-language development. Many such complementary and mutually supporting aspects of the child's overall learning and development are addressed in the learning foundations for the other domains, such as those for social-emotional development and mathematics learning.

An assumption underlying the language and literacy foundations is that children should experience the kinds of interactions, relationships, activities, and play that research has shown to support successful learning and development. Like the foundations for the other domains, the language and literacy foundations describe learning and development that would typically be expected with appropriate support rather than presenting aspirational expectations that would be expected only under the best possible conditions. The foundations are not intended to be assessment items. This publication is meant to be a resource and a guide to support preschool programs in their efforts to foster learning in all young children.

# Organization of the Language and Literacy Foundations

The preschool learning foundations in language and literacy are organized into three developmental strands to align with the strands for listening and speaking, reading, and writing in the California Department of Education's English–language arts content standards for kindergarten. The first strand, listening and speaking, relates primarily to language development. This strand includes the substrands of language use and conventions, vocabulary, and grammar. The other two strands relate to literacy development. The reading strand consists of the substrands of concepts about print, phonological awareness, alphabetics and word/print recognition, comprehension and analysis of age-appropriate text, and literacy interest and response. The writing strand has one substrand: writing strategies.

Within each substrand, individual foundations specify distinct competencies. Each substrand is divided into two columns: The column on the left-hand side focuses on children at around 48 months of age, and the column on the right-hand side focuses on children at around 60 months of age. The substrand descriptions for children at around 60 months of age detail more sophisticated and advanced competencies than do those for children at around 48 months of age. In some cases the difference between the foundations for the two age ranges is more pronounced than for the other foundations. Although two points of a developmental progression (at around 48 months of age and at around 60 months of age) are specified within each strand, the order in which the strands are presented is not meant to indicate a developmental progression from strand to strand. Nor is the order of presentation of the substrands within a strand meant to indicate a developmental progression from substrand to substrand.

Both substrands and foundations are numbered sequentially. For example, if a substrand is numbered 1.0, the foundations under that substrand are 1.1, 1.2, and so on for both age levels; likewise, if a substrand is numbered 2.0, the foundations under that substrand are 2.1, 2.2, and so on, again for both age levels. While both substrands and foundations are numbered sequentially, the order of presentation does not represent a developmental progression.

Each foundation is accompanied by examples that further illustrate the meaning of the foundation. They provide behavioral illustrations of how a child might demonstrate a competency described in a given foundation. In some instances the examples may also clarify the meaning of a foundation. However, the examples are not exhaustive checklists or assessment items and should be used for illustrative purposes only.

Following the foundations, a review of the relevant research for each strand is presented to indicate the research basis for the foundations in that strand. This section provides the reader with a more complete explanation of each strand. At the end of this section, a selected bibliography of research citations is provided for the entire set of language and literacy foundations. Brief explanations of the main points within the strands are provided next.

## Listening and Speaking— Language Use and Conventions, Vocabulary, and Grammar

The rate of children's early language growth and later language outcomes is directly related to the verbal input that children receive when communicating with adults and other children. Detailed within the three substrands is the sequential progression of children's developing understanding of language use and conventions, vocabulary, and grammar.

***Language Use and Conventions.*** The substrand of language use and conventions covers a broad range of knowledge and skills, including using language to communicate for a variety of purposes, using accepted language and style when communicating with adults and children, understanding and using language to communicate effectively with others, and constructing narratives with language. In preschool, children are developing the ability to use language for a range of purposes, such as describing, requesting, commenting, greeting, reasoning, problem solving, seeking new information, and predicting. Children nearing four years of age are expected to generate an appropriate response to at least one comment made during a conversation, and those nearing five years of age are expected to maintain a conversation for several turns.

Another development in the area of language use and conventions is learning to use accepted language and style during communication. It is important to note that accepted language or behavior is that which commonly occurs in the child's environment or community. For example, in some environments people make eye contact when they speak, while in other communities they do not. At around 48 months of age, children typically can make themselves understood when they communicate with familiar adults and children. At this age they may make pronunciation errors or sometimes use words in unusual ways that are understood by people who know them, but not by people who are unfamiliar with them. As children develop, they increasingly speak in ways that most familiar and unfamiliar adults and children can understand. This development pertains to the articulation of specific words and the expression of specific sounds rather than to the overall way in which children speak or whether they speak with an accent.

At this age children also begin constructing narrative by engaging in extended monologues that communicate to the listener an experience, a story, or something desired in the future. As children get older, such stories become more detailed, linear, and geared toward the perspective of the listener. When children are about 48 months of age, their narratives may consist of several unrelated ideas, characters, or events. Children near five years of age begin to produce narratives that convey a causal or temporal sequence of events (e.g., "After naptime we woke up. Then we had a snack and went outside. Then . . . "). For children at the older age, the narratives tend to be longer, make more sense, and provide more information than those of younger children. Teachers can support young children in the area of language use and conventions by repeating and extending what children say in conversations. Teachers can also provide opportunities for chil-

LANGUAGE AND LITERACY

dren to use language for a broad range of purposes, including encouraging children to repeat or tell stories.

***Vocabulary.*** The vocabulary substrand represents an important tool for accessing background knowledge, expressing ideas, and acquiring new concepts. Children with large vocabularies can acquire new words more easily, are more effective readers, and are more proficient in reading comprehension. Multiple experiences with words across a variety of contexts are critical for children's acquisition and extension of vocabulary. An important element of vocabulary development is the attainment of an increasing variety and specificity of accepted words (words that are commonly used in the children's environment or community) for objects, actions, and attributes used in both real and symbolic contexts. For example, many children nearing the age of four would call all dinosaurs "dinosaurs." By the time children are approaching the age of five, they refer to dinosaurs with greater specificity, pointing to an Apatosaurus and saying, "Apatosaurus," or pointing to a Tyrannosaurus and saying, "Tyrannosaurus."

Vocabulary development also consists of understanding and using accepted words for categories of objects. At around 48 months of age, children understand and use category names they encounter frequently, such as *toys, food, clothes,* or *animals.* As children near the age of 60 months, their understanding and use of verbal categories expands to ones they encounter less often, such as *reptiles, vehicles, fruits, vegetables,* and *furniture.* Another important aspect of vocabulary development during the preschool years is the understanding and use of words that describe relations between objects. For example, as children near 48 months of age, they use such words as *under, in,* and *different.* Children at around 60 months of age continue to use simple words to describe relations between objects and add complex relational words to their vocabulary, for example, *smaller, bigger, next to,* and *in front of.* During the preschool years, children begin to use the comparative *-er* and the superlative *-est* (*big, bigger, biggest; long, longer, longest*) to discriminate among the sizes of objects.

Often, to promote children's vocabulary development, adults' language must be contextualized, or supported by the immediate context. Children can understand and express more decontextualized language as their concepts of vocabulary and language expand. They can describe concepts without the support of the immediate context and increasingly communicate about events and actions in the past and in the future. This movement from concrete and contextualized language to abstract and decontextualized language plays a critical role in children's growing comprehension of abstract ideas. Children learn much of their vocabulary and basic language concepts indirectly through their interaction with others. They also acquire vocabulary through teacher-guided instructional activities.

***Grammar.*** The third substrand of listening and speaking, grammar, refers to the ways in which words, phrases, and sentences are structured and marked to make meaning in language. In preschool, children take important steps toward acquiring grammar. Preschoolers learn the rules of making basic sentences, joining phrases and clauses to make language into more complex sentences, joining adjectives to nouns, and using verb tenses, adverbs, and other parts of speech. At around 48 months of age, children tend to convey their thoughts by using simple, short phrases that communicate only one main idea (e.g., "I'm hungry!" or "Almost bedtime!") Over time, preschool children begin producing increasingly longer compound sentences (e.g., "It's almost bedtime and I am still hungry!") by connecting clauses (using words such as *and* and *but*). They also begin to generate more complex sentences (e.g., "Because I haven't eaten yet, I am still hungry") that combine multiple phrases or concepts to communicate more sophisticated and interrelated ideas (using words such as *if* and *because*). As children develop their comprehension and use of verb markers, such as *-ed*, they tend to make errors (e.g., "I wented," "He hitted"). Errors among preschoolers in the use of pronouns are very common (e.g., "Her did it," "It's hims"). Children's use of basic negative sentences between two and three years of age (e.g., "no go," "no want") becomes increasingly precise during the preschool years (e.g., "I don't want any" or "You are not going"). Some errors in negation will be observed during the preschool years (e.g., "I not want to do that!"), but these errors occur less frequently as children near 60 months of age.

As with the development of children's vocabulary and basic language concepts, children's ability to use increasingly sophisticated language structures allows them to make greater use of "decontextualized language"—language that requires little reliance on the immediate context for it to be understood. Children's development of grammatical sophistication is greatly enhanced by the teacher's modeling of correct forms and providing support in play and through teacher-guided instructional activities.

## Reading—Concepts About Print, Phonological Awareness, Alphabetics and Word/Print Recognition, Comprehension and Analysis of Age-Appropriate Text, Literacy Interest and Response

**Concepts About Print.** Children develop concepts about print through seeing print in the environment and observing people using print for various purposes. Central to an understanding of the nature and role of reading and writing is a child's understanding of "intentionality," i.e., that intentional meaning is encoded in print and print conveys a message. Children's understanding that print carries meaning often begins earlier than at preschool age, but the concept becomes increasingly sophisticated during the preschool years, and it depends largely on exposure to print and interaction with it in preschool. Preschoolers begin to use print to communicate, to understand the way print is organized in text and in books, to recite the alphabet, and to recognize some letters and words in print. They develop sophisticated knowledge about print conventions—how print is organized and how this organization changes to fit various purposes and genres. Preschool children's understanding of print conventions supports their knowledge of the alphabet and letter recognition. The print

LANGUAGE AND LITERACY

conventions preschoolers learn include directionality (e.g., the left-to-right and top-to-bottom organization of print in books and other print media in English), the way books are organized (title, author, front and back), and the way books are handled. Preschoolers develop an understanding of the functions of print—that it serves a number of purposes related to social and cultural contexts. In the preschool setting, children are beginning to understand and operate within the routines and contexts where literacy instruction occurs, contexts such as reading a page and a story, writing, and drawing. This knowledge extends to routines governing the use of literacy in the classroom or home, such as reading stories, making lists, and writing letters. Preschool-age children also gain an understanding that print forms (e.g., words, letters, and other print units) have distinct names and are used in specific, organized ways. Knowing that the word is the basic unit of meaning in the reading and writing process is a critical transition point in children's literacy development. Adults can encourage children's engagement with print by explicitly focusing children's attention on print forms and functions.

***Phonological Awareness.*** Spoken language is made up of various phonological units that include words, syllables, subsyllabic units (onsets, rimes), and sounds (phonemes). "Phonological awareness" is generally defined as an individual's sensitivity to the sound (or phonological) structure of spoken language. It is an oral language skill that does not involve print. Unlike the foundations for all the other substrands, those for phonological awareness are written only for children between four

and five years of age. The focus is on this age group because research indicates that children younger than four tend not to demonstrate this ability in reliable ways that can be readily observed. At age four, however, children begin to develop phonological awareness along a developmental progression from sensitivity to large units of sound, such as phrases and words, to small units of sound, such as syllables and phonemes. Phonological awareness is an important area of early and later reading instruction. It plays a direct role in several components of reading, such as understanding the alphabetic principle, decoding printed words, and spelling—and an indirect but important role in reading comprehension through its direct role in facilitating decoding.

Children demonstrate phonological awareness in three ways—detection (matching similar sounds), synthesis (combining smaller segments into syllables and words), and analysis (segmenting words or syllables into smaller units). Children usually develop detection skills first, then synthesis skills, followed by analysis skills. But children do not have to master one skill before they begin to acquire the next. In the foundations for phonological awareness, there is a progression from the ability to detect and blend words to the ability to segment at the onset-rime level. Preschoolers' development of phonological awareness depends to a great extent on the amount and kind of support provided by the teacher. For example, when asking children to delete the onset of a word, teachers can help children remember the word by showing pictures. The foundations for phonological awareness indicate which skills are most likely to be demonstrated in the context of such teacher support, i.e., when the teacher uses pictures, props, objects, and so forth in activities intended to support phonological awareness.

**Alphabetics and Word/Print Recognition.** Knowing the letters of the alphabet at preschool age is related to both short- and long-term reading proficiency. Knowledge of letter names facilitates children's ability to decode text and to apply the alphabetic principle to word recognition. For most children letter names help them connect the sounds in words and letters in print. Preschool children tend to learn first the letters that are most familiar to them, such as the letters in their own names and the letters that occur earlier in the alphabet string. As children become aware of letter names, they also start to identify printed words. Word recognition at the preschool age is mainly prealphabetic (i.e., the recognition of words by sight and by reliance on familiar cues). Children can recognize some words, but rarely can they examine the alphabetic or phonetic structures of the word to arrive at its meaning. Preschool children are able to recognize some words in the environment (e.g., Stop, Exit, and some brand names) but usually only in a familiar context. Typically, four-year-olds develop their knowledge of the alphabet and letter-sound correspondences. Coupled with their improving phonological awareness, those children may read at partial alphabetic levels during the preschool years. They may be able to look at some unknown words and use letters and their corresponding sounds to decode the printed word. For instance, seeing the word *Thomas* in a book, the child may use some alphabetic information (e.g., the first letter *T* and its corresponding letter sound) to make a good guess at what it says.

**Comprehension and Analysis of Age-Appropriate Text.** Preschoolers' development of narrative thinking goes through a series of stages that ultimately lead to their making sense of stories and the world around them. At the earliest stage, preschoolers construct narrative scripts, or primitive accounts of story plots that focus on familiar events and routine activities. In the next stage, children construct narrative schemas, which include knowledge about the main elements of stories (such as characters and settings) and about the sequence of events (such as time, order, and causal progression). Then preschoolers come to understand and relate to characters' internal responses, such as their mental processes and experiences. Ultimately, children recognize both the external and internal features of narrative. Preschoolers' competence with narratives can be greatly expanded through instructional activities guided by teachers. Exposure to wordless picture books provides instructional opportunities for children and, for teachers, a window into children's learning processes. The efforts of children to make sense of the pictures when they are reading wordless picture books form the foundation for reading comprehension and making meaning. Storybook reading, both of wordless picture books and regular books, when combined with interactive language activities, such as active discussion of stories, before, during, and after reading, enhances children's understanding and recall of stories. Shared reading activities allow teach-

LANGUAGE AND LITERACY

ers to model key components of the reading task and enable children to begin discovering the components of reading themselves. Interaction during shared reading creates opportunities for cognitive processing and problem solving.

**Literacy Interest and Response.** Interest in books and a positive regard for reading are important developmental accomplishments for preschool-age children. Participation in such literacy activities as handling books and listening to stories leads to continuing engagement with text and to motivation and persistence in challenging reading tasks. These experiences are necessary for children to become able readers and lifelong literacy learners. An emerging body of research shows that motivation is an important factor in the development of early literacy in preschool and later reading achievement. Increasing engagement in literacy and expanding reading activities are tied to increases in motivation, which, in turn, facilitates comprehension and recall of information. Children's active engagement in text-related activities, such as turning pages in a book, is related to knowledge of print concepts at around four years of age. Opportunities for reading are related to children's interest in reading at home and at school. Children who are read to more frequently and from an earlier age tend to have greater interest in literacy, exhibit superior literacy skills during the preschool and school years, choose reading more frequently, initiate reading sessions on their own, and show greater engagement during reading sessions. Adult-child storybook reading promotes children's interest in

reading and leads to increased exposure and engagement with text.

## Writing—Writing Strategies

**Writing Strategies.** Learning to write involves cognitive, social, and physical development. Children from a very young age notice writing in their surroundings. They begin to understand that signs in the environment represent words for ideas or concepts. By age three they begin to differentiate between writing and other kinds of visual representation, such as drawing. With this realization comes differentiation between tools for writing and tools for drawing ("I need to get a pencil to write my name"). Their writing starts to look different from their drawing—more linear than circular. Young children become involved with written text by being read to, examining books, and observing others writing. Preschoolers begin to experiment with writing by pretending to write and by learning to write their names. Initially, children demonstrate a global form of writing. They tend to use drawings as writing or use idiosyncratic scribbles (i.e., markings that have only personal meaning). Later, children use letter-like forms that resemble some of the characteristics of real writing (e.g., longer words are represented by longer strings of letter-like symbols). Children in the next phase start using actual letters to write, but with little or no connection to the actual spelling of what they want to write (i.e., nonphonetic strings of letters). This phase is followed by attempts at phonetic spelling, also called "invented spelling." In this phase, children use letters to match letter sounds to parts of words they hear, but from a phonological rather than an orthographic perspective.

Children may recognize that writing the word they are thinking of requires more than one or two symbols and that the same symbols may be in different words or in different places in the same word, but they have not yet mastered the alphabetic principle. Even so, invented spelling is an effective vehicle through which many children begin to understand the alphabetic principle. It also helps children realize that writing carries meaning, that other people should be able to read what they write, and that people write for different purposes. Children who have the physical experience of writing in this way begin to develop ways of handling writing implements, but they need support from adults in learning to do so.

LANGUAGE AND LITERACY

# Listening and Speaking

## 1.0 Language Use and Conventions

| At around 48 months of age | At around 60 months of age |
|---|---|
| **Children understand and use language to communicate with others effectively.** | **Children extend their understanding and usage of language to communicate with others effectively.** |
| **1.1** Use language to communicate with others in familiar social situations for a variety of basic purposes, including describing, requesting, commenting, acknowledging, greeting, and rejecting. | **1.1** Use language to communicate with others in both familiar and unfamiliar social situations for a variety of basic and advanced purposes, including reasoning, predicting, problem solving, and seeking new information. |
| **Examples** | **Examples** |
| *Describing*<br>• The child says, "It was big and green and scary."<br><br>*Requesting*<br>• The child asks, "Can I have more play dough?" while in the art area.<br><br>*Commenting*<br>• The child says, "This is my blanket."<br><br>*Acknowledging*<br>• The child indicates, "Me too."<br><br>*Greeting*<br>• The child says, "Hi, Mrs. Franklin," when entering the room.<br><br>*Rejecting*<br>• The child says, "I don't want to clean up blocks" during clean-up time. | *Reasoning*<br>• The child says, "I think we can go outside because it's sunny now" or "I don't need my coat because it's not windy."<br><br>*Predicting*<br>• The child says, "I think that bear's going to get lost!" or "If it keeps raining I think the worms will come out."<br><br>*Problem solving*<br>• The child says, "Maybe we can put the milk in here and then it will be cookie dough."<br><br>*Seeking new information*<br>• The child asks, "Why isn't Jerome at school?" or "Why are you dressed up? Where are you going?" |
| **1.2** Speak clearly enough to be understood by familiar adults and children. | **1.2** Speak clearly enough to be understood by both familiar and unfamiliar adults and children. |
| **Examples** | **Examples** |
| • The child's speech may contain pronunciation errors that are understood by familiar adults and children, but those errors would be difficult for a visitor to the classroom to understand.<br>• The child may speak using some idiosyncratic words that are understood by familiar adults and peers but not by unfamiliar adults (e.g., Bryan calls his blanket a "wobie"). | • The child generally speaks with correct pronunciation, although some continuing speech errors are age-appropriate.<br>• Most of the child's speech is free of speech errors. Most listeners do not have to ask the child to repeat himself or herself by asking, "What did you say?" |

## 1.0 Language Use and Conventions (Continued)

| At around 48 months of age | At around 60 months of age |
|---|---|
| **1.3** Use accepted language and style during communication with familiar adults and children. | **1.3** Use accepted language and style during communication with both familiar and unfamiliar adults and children. |

| Examples | Examples |
|---|---|
| • The child responds on the topic for at least one turn in a conversation. For example, the child responds, "Me too. I got new shoes," following a peer's comment, "I got new shoes," while playing in the dress-up area.<br><br>• The child adjusts the form and style of language use according to the listener's status or competence. For example, asks the teacher, "Can I please have that paintbrush," but tells peer, "Give me that paintbrush," or speaks slowly and deliberately to a younger child.<br><br>• The child often uses appropriate nonverbal standards in conversation with others (e.g., eye contact, distance to conversational partner, facial expressions).<br><br>• The child often uses polite forms of communication as appropriate (e.g., says thank you, please, addresses adults as Mr., Mrs., or Ms.).<br><br>• The child often uses volume and intonation appropriate for a situation when speaking. For example, speaks quietly to the teacher while the other children are napping or speaks in a slower and quieter tone while expressing regret (e.g., "I'm sorry I broke it"). | • The child responds on topic across several turns in conversation. For example, during dramatic play, the child says, "I'm the baby and I'm hungry." A friend responds, "Okay, I'll cook you breakfast." The child responds, "Then you're the mommy and you're cooking the breakfast." A friend responds, "I'm going to make pancakes."<br><br>• The child adjusts the form and style of language use according to the listener's status, competence, or knowledge. For example, during a field trip to the fire station, tells a firefighter, "Wow! That's neat. Can I hold it?" but tells a peer, "I want to see!" While talking with older brother, prefaces the description of the fire truck and equipment by stating that the class went on a field trip to the fire station that day.<br><br>• The child consistently uses appropriate nonverbal standards in conversation with others (e.g., eye contact, distance to conversational partner, facial expressions).<br><br>• The child typically uses polite forms of communication as appropriate (e.g., says thank you, please, addresses adults as Mr., Mrs., or Ms.).<br><br>• The child typically uses volume and intonation appropriate for a situation when speaking. For example, uses a quieter voice inside the classroom than on the playground. |

LANGUAGE AND LITERACY

**1.0    Language Use and Conventions (Continued)**

| *At around 48 months of age* | *At around 60 months of age* |
|---|---|
| **1.4**  Use language to construct short narratives that are real or fictional.* | **1.4**  Use language to construct extended narratives that are real or fictional.* |
| **Examples** | **Examples** |
| • The child draws attention or points to pictures on the wall of a special class event: "The mama bird built a nest in our toy box. The baby birds flew away." | • The child tells a brief story that unfolds over time: "I went to the park with my mommy, and we played in the sandbox. Then we had a picnic. After that, we went to the store." |
| • The child describes an unfolding event at snack time: "I want to put peanut butter on my bread. I'm going to put jelly on, too." | • The child tells about activities of interest to him or her that day: "First we come to school and sit on the carpet. Then we have our circle time. And then we do the centers. And then it's time for lunch." |
| • The child relays events from the day's morning: "My daddy's truck broke down. We walked to school. It was a long way." | • The child retells the major events of a favorite story: "The boy wrote to the zoo, and they kept sending him animals. But he doesn't like them. So, then he gets a puppy, and he keeps it. He was happy then." |

* Producing narratives may vary at these ages for children who are communicating with sign language or alternative communication systems. As is true for all children, teachers can support young children's communication knowledge and skills by repeating and extending what children communicate in conversations. Teachers can also provide opportunities for children to repeat or tell stories as a way to encourage them to produce narratives.

LANGUAGE AND LITERACY

## 2.0 Vocabulary

| *At around 48 months of age* | *At around 60 months of age* |
|---|---|
| **Children develop age-appropriate vocabulary.** | **Children develop age-appropriate vocabulary.** |
| **2.1** Understand and use accepted words for objects, actions, and attributes encountered frequently in both real and symbolic contexts. | **2.1** Understand and use an increasing variety and specificity of accepted words for objects, actions, and attributes encountered in both real and symbolic contexts. |
| **Examples\*** | **Examples\*** |

*Nouns/Objects*

* The child hands a friend the trucks when the friend says, "I want to play with those *trucks*" during play.
* While reading a book about spiders, the child answers, *"spiders,"* when the teacher asks, "What are these?"

*Verbs/Actions*

* When the child is playing with tools in the dramatic play area, the child responds, "the stove," when a friend asks, "What needs to be *fixed*?"
* The child says to a parent volunteer, "I have a story. Can you *do* it on the computer for me?"

*Attributes*

* During a cooking project, the child gives the teacher the big bowl when the teacher says, "Hand me the *big* bowl."
* While in the block area, the child says to a friend, "Look at what I made. It's *tall*."

*Nouns/Objects*

* The child hands a friend the *fire truck*, the *dump truck*, and the *semitruck* when the friend says, "I want to play with the fire truck, dump truck, and semi" during play.
* While reading a book about dinosaurs, the child answers, "That's a *Apatosaurus* and that's a *Tyrannosaurus*," when the teacher asks, "What are these?"

*Verbs/Actions*

* When the child is playing with tools in the dramatic play area, the child responds, "the stove," when a friend asks, "What needs to be *repaired*?"
* The child says to a parent volunteer, "I have a story. Can you *type* it on the computer for me?"

*Attributes*

* During a cooking project, the child gives the teacher the plastic fork when the teacher says, "Hand me the *plastic* one."
* During dramatic play, the child says to a friend, "Look at my necklace. It's *shiny*."

\* Key word forms in the examples are italicized.

LANGUAGE AND LITERACY

**2.0 Vocabulary (Continued)**

| *At around 48 months of age* | *At around 60 months of age* |
|---|---|
| **2.2** Understand and use accepted words for categories of objects encountered and used frequently in everyday life. | **2.2** Understand and use accepted words for categories of objects encountered in everyday life. |
| **Examples*** | **Examples*** |
| • When painting at the easel, Min paints a picture of a doll and a dollhouse and says, "This is my doll and her dollhouse. They're my favorite *toys*."<br><br>• While playing store, Peter tells Judy, "I want to buy some *food*," and Judy says, "OK. We have milk, bread, and corn."<br><br>• Frieda puts some hats on the shelf and puts some dresses in a box when the teacher asks, "Can you please put the dress-up *clothes* away?"<br><br>• During play Lorenzo brings an elephant, a giraffe, a goat, a hippopotamus, and a lion to the table and says to Miguel and Larry, "Here are the *animals* for our zoo." | • After reading a book about reptiles, the child points to pictures of a snake, a lizard, and a turtle when the teacher asks the children to find the pictures of *reptiles*.<br><br>• When the children and teacher are making a pretend city, the teacher says, "Now, we need some *vehicles*," and Sammy brings a car, a truck, a tractor, and a motorcycle.<br><br>• During play the child puts the apple, banana, and pear into one bowl and puts the broccoli, carrots, and corn into another bowl and says to a friend, "These are the *fruits* and these are the *vegetables*."<br><br>• During play Anne tells Cathy, "You go get the *furniture* for the house. We need a chair, a table, a sofa, a desk, and a dresser." |
| **2.3** Understand and use simple words that describe the relations between objects. | **2.3** Understand and use both simple and complex words that describe the relations between objects. |
| **Examples*** | **Examples*** |
| • While playing a game, the child is able to collect all the circles when the teacher says, "Find all the things that are the *same* shape as this" (while showing a picture of a circle).<br><br>• During play Alice tells Mary, "Ortiz is *under* the table."<br><br>• The child puts all the marbles *in* the box when a peer says, "Now let's put them all *in* the box."<br><br>• During story time the child points to pictures of a dog and a cat and says, "These are *different* animals." | • After reading a story about the zoo, the teacher asks, "What animals are *smaller* than an elephant?" The child correctly identifies a lion, a tiger, a bear, and a zebra.<br><br>• During circle time the teacher invites Stephen to sit *next to* Mark, and he does.<br><br>• While playing in the block center, DeAndre tells Susan, "Put the red block *in front of* the tower."<br><br>• During snack time the child complains, "Your quesadilla is *bigger* than mine!" |

*Key word forms in the examples are italicized.

LANGUAGE AND LITERACY

## 3.0 Grammar

| At around 48 months of age | At around 60 months of age |
|---|---|
| **Children develop age-appropriate grammar.** | **Children develop age-appropriate grammar.** |
| **3.1** Understand and use increasingly complex and longer sentences, including sentences that combine two phrases or two to three concepts to communicate ideas. | **3.1** Understand and use increasingly complex and longer sentences, including sentences that combine two to three phrases or three to four concepts to communicate ideas. |
| **Examples\*** | **Examples\*** |
| • The child demonstrates comprehension of two-, three-, and four-word requests (e.g., "please sit down," "put that over here") and sentences (e.g., "John is here," "The cat is black").<br><br>• When asked to "pick up the toys" and "take off your jacket and put it in your cubby," the child does so.<br><br>• The child produces noun phrases that include one or more descriptors (e.g., "that blue chair is mine," "the green car crashed").<br><br>• The child uses short complete sentences to comment, ask questions, and request (e.g., "Where's my baby doll?" "What's that?" and "I want a cookie"). | • The child responds with appropriate action to a statement or a request that includes multiple clauses, such as "find the girl who is sad" or "pick up the dog that fell over."<br><br>• When asked to "take off your coat, find a book, and come to the rug" or "please sit down at the table, help yourself to some crackers, and pour your juice," the child does so.<br><br>• The child uses noun phrases that include three or four descriptors (e.g., "the big red shirt is Bobby's," "I want to play with the little blue square one").<br><br>• The child produces a two-part sentence through coordination, using *and* and *but* (e.g., "I'm pushing the wagon, *and* he is pulling it!" and "It's naptime, *but* I'm not tired"). |
| **3.2** Understand and typically use age-appropriate grammar, including accepted word forms, such as subject-verb agreement, progressive tense, regular past tense, regular plurals, pronouns, and possessives. | **3.2** Understand and typically use age-appropriate grammar, including accepted word forms, such as subject-verb agreement, progressive tense, regular and irregular past tense, regular and irregular plurals, pronouns, and possessives. |
| **Examples\*** | **Examples\*** |
| Understands and uses verbs indicating present, progressive, and regular past tense.<br><br>• The child responds, "The block tower," when another child asks, "What *fell* down?" or responds appropriately to questions, such as, "Who *walked* to school today?" "Who *is drinking* juice?" or "Who *drives* the bus?" during discussion at lunch. | Understands and uses verbs indicating present, progressive, and both regular and irregular past tense (even if not always used correctly).<br><br>• While reading a picture book, the child correctly identifies "the children" and "the girl" when asked, "Who *was running* and who *fell* down?" |

\* Key word forms in the examples are italicized.

### 3.0    Grammar (Continued)

| At around 48 months of age | At around 60 months of age |
|---|---|
| *Examples (Continued)** | *Examples (Continued)** |
| • The child says, "Maria *jumps* with the rope," "Maria *is jumping* rope," or "Maria *jumped* with the rope," depending on the time when the action occurred. | • During story time, the child remarks, "The bear *ate* the fish and then he *ran* away." |
| | • Suzie tells the teacher, "He *pushed* me and I *felled*† down!" |
| Understands and applies the "s" sound at the end of words to indicate plurals (even if not always used correctly). | Understands and applies the "s" sound at the end of words to indicate plurals and understands and uses irregular plurals (even if not always used correctly). |
| • Miguel brings more than one cup to the table when the teacher requests, "Please bring me the *cups*." | • Alice points to a picture of five mice when the teacher asks, "Which is the picture of the *mice*?" |
| • The child uses plural forms of nouns, such as *socks, cups, mens,*† and *foots*† when talking about more than one sock, cup, man, or foot | • A child brings five sheep to the table after a friend says, "Now we need lots of *sheep*." |
| | • Gene exclaims, "Look at that one. He has lots of *teeths*!"*† while looking at a book about dinosaurs. |
| Understands and uses different types of pronouns, including subject (*he, she, it*), object (*him, her*), possessive (*hers, his, its*), and demonstrative (*there, here*), although usage may be incorrect and inconsistent at times. | • A child says, "Look at those *trees*; they have lots and lots of *leaves*." |
| | Understands and uses different types of pronouns, including subject (*he, she, it, they*), object (*him, her, them*), possessive (*hers, his, its, our, their*), and demonstrative (*there, here*). |
| • Lisa gives a book to the girl when an adult requests, "Please give the book to *her*," and a boy is also present, or Lisa puts the animals on the table when a friend requests, "Put *them* there, please" while gesturing toward the table. | • The child hands Maria a book when the parent volunteer says, "Please give *it* to *her*," and Juan is also present. |
| • Brandee says, "*I* have boats" during circle time, "*Him*† put that *there*" when talking with another child, or "This is *my* dolly" when in the dramatic play area. | • Darla complains to the teacher, "*This* ball is *mine* and *that* one is *his*." |
| | • The child tells a friend, "*Our* tower is bigger than *theirs*, but *they* could build *it* higher" when playing with blocks. |
| Understands and adds an "s" sound to nouns to indicate the possessive form. | • Maria responds, "Susan did. *She* gave the cookies to *them*" when asked, "Who gave the cookies to Jose and Mallika?" |
| • Richard helps find *John's coat* when asked, or Elizabeth points to *Mariella's backpack* when asked, "Which one is *Mariella's*?" | Understands and adds an "s" sound to nouns to indicate the possessive form. |
| • The child says, "I like to put on *Daddy's shoes* and walk" during a discussion about favorite pastimes, or "I brushed the *doll's hair*" when asked, "What happened?" | • Robby responds, "Those are his *mom's keys*," when an adult points to a picture and says, "The boy has *somebody's keys*. Are they his?" |
| | • The child shares, "We went to *grandma's house* because it was my *mommy's birthday*" during circle time when the children are telling what they did over the weekend. |

* Key word forms in the examples are italicized.

† Denotes common usage of an incorrect form.

# Reading

## 1.0 Concepts about Print

| *At around 48 months of age* | *At around 60 months of age* |
|---|---|
| **Children begin to recognize print conventions and understand that print carries meaning.** | **Children recognize print conventions and understand that print carries specific meaning.** |
| **1.1** Begin to display appropriate book-handling behaviors and begin to recognize print conventions. | **1.1** Display appropriate book-handling behaviors and knowledge of print conventions. |
| **Examples** | **Examples** |
| • When holding a book, the child orients it as if to read.<br>• The child can point to where the title is shown on the cover of a book.<br>• The child opens a book and turns the pages in a single direction, although not necessarily one page at a time. | • The child orients a book correctly for reading (i.e., right-side up with the front cover facing the child).<br>• The child turns the pages of a book one at a time.<br>• The child begins to track print from left to right and top to bottom (e.g., while pretending to read a story to a peer or doll).<br>• While looking through a book, the child says, "the end" after reaching the last page. |
| **1.2** Recognize print as something that can be read.* | **1.2** Understand that print is something that is read and has specific meaning.* |
| **Examples** | **Examples** |
| • The child points to letters in a book, on a sign, or on a drawing and communicates, "that says my name," although usually inaccurately.<br>• The child can indicate which part of a picture book shows the story (pictures) versus which part tells the story (text).<br>• The child "writes" something down on paper and then asks the teacher what it says (i.e., to "read" it). | • The child asks the teacher, "What does this say?" when pointing to text in a book.<br>• The child communicates, "Can you tell me what that says?" drawing attention to a sign while outside on a walk.<br>• The child asks the teacher to write down a story or note that the child dictates, and then the child "reads" it to the other children. |

\* Children can learn to recognize letters of the alphabet without being able to see conventional print. Multiple means of recognizing print include the use of tactile letters, large print, color contrast or lighting, and braille, as well as other means of representing letters.

## 2.0 Phonological Awareness

| At around 48 months of age | At around 60 months of age |
|---|---|
| | **Children develop age-appropriate phonological awareness.\*** |
| | **2.1** Orally blend and delete words and syllables without the support of pictures or objects.[†, ‡] |
| | **Examples** |
| | Orally puts together two familiar words, making a compound word. |
| | • The child plays the "What's That Word?" game while on a swing. With each push of the swing, the teacher says one part of a compound word (e.g., *sun, shine*) and then asks the child, "What's that word?" The child responds, *"Sunshine."* |
| | • While playing in the dramatic play area, the child responds, *"hairbrush"* when asked, "What word do you get when you say '*hair*' and '*brush*' together?" |
| | Orally puts together the two syllables of two-syllable words that are familiar to the child. |
| | • During mealtime conversation, the child participates in the guess-the-food game. The teacher says two-syllable words (*ta-co, su-shi, crack-er, ap-ple, but-ter*) and says each syllable distinctly. The teacher asks, "What food is this?" The child responds, *"Taco."* |
| | • The child chants, *"sister"* after singing along to, "What word do you get when you say '*sis*' and '*ter*' together?" |
| | • The child responds, *"Amit"* in unison with other classmates during circle time when the teacher says, "I'm thinking of a classmate's name that has two parts, like '*A-mit.*' Whose name is that?" |

\* "Phonological awareness" is defined for the preschool learning foundations as an oral language skill: an individual's sensitivity to the sound (or phonological) structure of spoken language. Phonological awareness is an important skill that children start to acquire during preschool and continue to build in early elementary school as they learn to read. Even though it is defined as an oral language skill, it is also an important skill for children who are deaf or hard of hearing. A teacher of the deaf should be consulted for strategies for facilitating phonological awareness in individual children who are deaf or hard of hearing.

† Some children may need assistance in holding a book or turning the pages, either through assistive technology or through the help of an adult or a peer. For example, a book can be mounted so that it does not have to be held, and sturdy tabs can be placed on the pages so that they are easier to turn. Some children may need to have an adult or a peer hold the book and turn the pages.

‡ The foundations for phonological awareness are written only for older four-year-olds because much of the initial development of phonological awareness occurs between 48 months and 60 months of age.

LANGUAGE AND LITERACY

## 2.0    Phonological Awareness (Continued)

| At around 48 months of age | At around 60 months of age |
|---|---|
| | *Examples (Continued)* |
| | Orally takes apart compound words into their component words. |
| | • The child claps out words in a compound word as part of a circle time activity. When the teacher says, "When I think of the word *'book,'* I think of clapping one time. Other words like *'bookshelf'* have two parts. So I clap two times. Let's clap out the parts for *'paintbrush.'*" |
| | • The child responds, *"table"* when asked, "What word do you get when you say *'tablecloth'* without *'cloth'*?" |
| | • The child responds, *"ball"* when asked, "What word do you get when you say *'football'* without *'foot'*?" |
| | • The child responds, *"mail"* and *"box"* when asked, "What two words make *'mailbox'*?" |
| | Orally takes apart two-syllable words into their component syllables. |
| | • The child claps out syllables in a two-syllable word as part of a circle time activity. When the teacher says, "Let's clap out how many parts we hear in the word *'cook-ie.'*" |
| | • The child responds, *"door"* when asked, "What word do you get when you say *'doorknob'* without *'knob'*?" |

LANGUAGE AND LITERACY

## 2.0    Phonological Awareness (Continued)

| At around 48 months of age | At around 60 months of age |
|---|---|
| | **2.2** Orally blend the onsets, rimes, and phonemes of words and orally delete the onsets of words, with the support of pictures or objects.* |

**Examples**

Orally blends the onsets and rimes of words with the support of pictures or objects.

- During a small group activity with several objects on the table (e.g., cat, cup, mat, bus, rat, pup), the child responds and selects the *rat* (or says *"rat"*) when a teacher asks, "Ricardo, can you find the *r—at*?"

- While playing a game of I-spy, the teacher says, "I spy a *s—un*," and the child indicates or points to the *sun* or says, *"sun."*

- While engaged in a game, the child selects the picture of a *bed* from among three or four pictures (or says, *"bed"*) when asked to put together the letter sounds *b—ed*.

Deletes the onset from a spoken word with the support of pictures or objects.

- The child selects the picture of *ants* from among three or four pictures (or says, *"ants"*) when asked to say *"pants"* without the "p" letter sound.

Orally blends individual phonemes to make a simple word with the support of pictures or objects.

- While playing a "bingo game" during small group time, the child chooses and marks pictures corresponding to the words for which the teacher sounds out the individual phonemes (e.g., *h—a—t, m—o—p, c—u—p*).

- The teacher sings, "If you think you know the word, shout it out. If you think you know the word, tell me what you've heard. If you think you know the word, shout it out . . . *s—i—t*." The child sings out *"sit"* along with the classmates.

- The child picks up the picture of a *hat* from among three or four pictures (or says, *"hat"*) when asked to put together the letter sounds *h—a—t*.

* The foundations for phonological awareness are written only for older four-year-olds because much of the initial development of phonological awareness occurs between 48 months and 60 months of age.

## 3.0   Alphabetics and Word/Print Recognition

| At around 48 months of age | At around 60 months of age |
|---|---|
| **Children begin to recognize letters of the alphabet.*** | **Children extend their recognition of letters of the alphabet.*** |

| **3.1** Recognize the first letter of own name. | **3.1** Recognize own name or other common words in print. |
|---|---|
| **Examples** | **Examples** |
| • Kavita communicates, "That's my name" while indicating the letter *K* on Karen's name card on the helper chart.<br>• Bobby indicates a word beginning with the letter *B* and says, "That's my letter."<br>• The child responds appropriately when the teacher holds up a card with the first letter of his or her name and says, "Everyone whose name begins with this letter (the first letter of the child's name), put on your jacket." | • The child recognizes his or her name on a sign-in sheet, helper chart, artwork, or name tag (e.g., name tag, label for the cubby, or place at the table).<br>• The child recognizes common or familiar words (e.g., mom or friends' names) in print. |

| **3.2** Match some letter names to their printed form. | **3.2** Match more than half of uppercase letter names and more than half of lowercase letter names to their printed form. |
|---|---|
| **Examples** | **Examples** |
| • When putting the "T" puzzle piece into the alphabet puzzle, the child says, "That's a *T.*"<br>• The child traces over sandpaper letters, saying the matching letter name for some letters.<br>• The child names some letters in storybooks, logos, or on artwork.<br>• The child says, "I want all the *A*'s," when sorting through a container of letters, picking out the *A* shapes. | • When shown an upper- or lowercase letter, the child can say its name.<br>• The child says letter names when attending to different words, such as own name, friends' names, or frequently seen signs.<br>• During circle time the child indicates or points to the correct letter on a chart when the teacher prompts with the name of the letter. |

| | **3.3** Begin to recognize that letters have sounds. |
|---|---|
| | **Examples** |
| | • The child makes the correct sound for the first letter in his name.<br>• The child says the correct letter sound while pointing to the letter in a book.<br>• The child indicates the correct picture when presented with four pictures—dog barking, car horn honking, letter *k*, and letter *n*—and asked, "Which of these make these sounds: bow-wow, honk, "k" (letter sound), "n" (letter sound)?" |

\* Children with oral motor involvement, who may have difficulty in saying words or syllables as they learn to match, synthesize, or analyze syllables and sounds, may demonstrate their knowledge by indicating yes or no in response to an adult's production of sounds or words or by identifying pictures that represent the products of these manipulations. It should be understood that children can learn letters of the alphabet and about print without being able to see typical print. Multiple means of recognizing print include the use of tactile letters, large print, color contrast or lighting, braille, and any other means of representing letters and print.

LANGUAGE AND LITERACY

## 4.0 Comprehension and Analysis of Age-Appropriate Text

| *At around 48 months of age* | *At around 60 months of age* |
|---|---|
| **Children demonstrate understanding of age-appropriate text read aloud.** | **Children demonstrate understanding of age-appropriate text read aloud.** |
| **4.1** Demonstrate knowledge of main characters or events in a familiar story (e.g., who, what, where) through answering questions (e.g., recall and simple inferencing), retelling, reenacting, or creating artwork. | **4.1** Demonstrate knowledge of details in a familiar story, including characters, events, and ordering of events through answering questions (particularly summarizing, predicting, and inferencing), retelling, reenacting, or creating artwork. |
| **Examples** | **Examples** |
| • In the dramatic play area, the child pretends to be a character from a familiar story.<br><br>• During circle time the child reminds a peer what has just happened in a story being read aloud.<br><br>• The child retells a story to peers or stuffed animals in the library center, not necessarily including all events or in the correct order.<br><br>• The child names places where Rosie walked in the book *Rosie's Walk* (e.g., chicken coop, pond).<br><br>• The child is able to label correctly a character's feelings when asked by teacher (e.g., "Critter was sad"). | • The child uses a bucket (pail of water) and step stool (the hill) to reenact the "Jack and Jill" nursery rhyme.<br><br>• The child places story picture cards or flannel board pictures in order while retelling a familiar story with peers.<br><br>• The child acts out the sequence of events in a familiar story, using props and puppets.<br><br>• The child responds to open-ended questions from teachers or other children (e.g., how, why, cause/effect, connecting events, prediction, and inferring).<br><br>• The child is able to describe the situation and feelings that led to a story character's actions (e.g., "He yelled at them because he was mad that they took his toy"). |
| **4.2** Demonstrate knowledge from informational text through labeling, describing, playing, or creating artwork. | **4.2** Use information from informational text in a variety of ways, including describing, relating, categorizing, or comparing and contrasting. |
| **Examples** | **Examples** |
| • The child demonstrates knowledge of trucks by indicating that things can be carried in the back of trucks after the teacher has read a description of jobs that trucks do.<br><br>• In the block area a group of children build an airport after being read a story about airplanes and airports.<br><br>• During outside play the child pretends to be a traffic officer by directing tricycle traffic after listening to or looking at a story about traffic officers.<br><br>• The child communicates, "I love the giraffe. Giraffes have long necks" when listening to or looking at a book about the zoo. | • The child communicates important differences and similarities of jet airplanes and propeller planes after being read a story about airplanes and airports.<br><br>• The child tells about a visit to the dentist in response to a book about getting teeth cleaned at the dentist's office.<br><br>• The child explains or demonstrates the steps of planting a seed after being read a book about gardening. |

LANGUAGE AND LITERACY

# 5.0 Literacy Interest and Response

| At around 48 months of age | At around 60 months of age |
|---|---|
| **Children demonstrate motivation for literacy activities.** | **Children demonstrate motivation for a broad range of literacy activities.** |
| **5.1** Demonstrate enjoyment of literacy and literacy-related activities. | **5.1** Demonstrate, with increasing independence, enjoyment of literacy and literacy-related activities. |
| **Examples** | **Examples** |
| • The child brings a book to an adult to share or to read together. <br><br> • The child chooses the activities in literacy or writing center (e.g., "reading" a book by oneself in the library area or pretending to write a story). <br><br> • The child displays appropriate attention while listening to a read-aloud during circle time. | • The child brings a favorite book from home to be read aloud during story time. <br><br> • The child initiates creating or obtaining appropriate written materials for dramatic play (e.g., menus for playing restaurant, lists for playing grocery store). <br><br> • The child describes a trip to the library with a family member where they selected books and checked them out to read at home. |
| **5.2** Engage in routines associated with literacy activities. | **5.2** Engage in more complex routines associated with literacy activities. |
| **Examples** | **Examples** |
| • The child listens during story time. <br><br> • The child participates in a discussion of a story. <br><br> • The child asks for help from the teacher to write something (e.g., writing a note to mother, labeling a picture, writing a story). | • The child returns books to the library shelf after independent reading. <br><br> • The child finds own journal book when entering the classroom and engages in pretend writing. <br><br> • After the reading of a book about insects during circle time, the child asks the teacher to identify other books about insects for the child to look through. |

LANGUAGE AND LITERACY

# Writing

## 1.0 Writing Strategies

| *At around 48 months of age* | *At around 60 months of age* |
|---|---|
| **Children demonstrate emergent writing skills.*** | **Children demonstrate increasing emergent writing skills.*** |
| **1.1** Experiment with grasp and body position using a variety of drawing and writing tools. | **1.1** Adjust grasp and body position for increased control in drawing and writing. |
| **Examples** | **Examples** |
| • The child holds a marker with the fist or finger grasp to draw.<br>• The child paints at an easel with fat and thin brushes.<br>• The child draws or paints with pencils, crayons, markers, brushes, or fingers. | • The child holds a pencil or pen with finger grasp to write.<br>• The child draws recognizable figures, letters, or shapes.<br>• The child child moves hand to hold paper in place while drawing or writing. |
| **1.2** Write using scribbles that are different from pictures. | **1.2** Write letters or letter-like shapes to represent words or ideas. |
| **Examples** | **Examples** |
| • The child produces scribble writing that is linear (mock cursive).<br>• The child makes scribbles of lines and circles (mock printing).<br>• The child makes scribbles that are more separated. | • The child draws a picture and writes a label (may not be readable).<br>• The child writes strings of symbols that look like letters or writes actual letters, which can vary in directionality (not necessarily left to right). |
| **1.3** Write marks to represent own name. | **1.3** Write first name nearly correctly. |
| **Examples** | **Examples** |
| • The child makes a series of circles and lines to represent name.<br>• The child writes marks and refers to them as "my name" or "this is my name." | • The child writes own name with or without mistakes, for example:<br>  – Excludes some letters (dvid).<br>  – Reverses some letters (Davib).<br>  – Uses letters that may not be written in a line. |

\* Some children may need assistance in emergent writing, either through assistive technology or through the help of an adult. Assistive technology (either low tech or high tech) may be as simple as building up the width of the marker or pencil so that it is easier to grasp, or it may be as sophisticated as using a computer. Another possibility would be for an adult or a peer to "write" for the child who would then approve or disapprove by indicating yes or no.

# Bibliographic Notes

## Listening and Speaking

### *Language Use and Conventions.*

The development of oral language is one of the most impressive accomplishments that occur during the first five years of children's lives (Genishi 1988). Oral language development results from the interaction of a variety of factors, including social, linguistic, maturational/biological, and cognitive influences, and these factors interact and modify one another (Bohannon and Bonvillian 2001). Research indicates that social factors have a prominent role on oral language development. For example, the wide variation in the rate of children's early language growth and later language outcomes is directly related to differences in maternal and other caretakers' verbal input (Baumwell, Tamis-LeMonda, and Bornstein 1997; Girolametto and Weitzman 2002; Hart and Risley 1995; Landry and others 1997; Pellegrini and others 1995; Tamis-LeMonda, Bornstein, and Baumwell 2001).

The language use and conventions substrand focuses on children's use of language for social and communicative purposes. Four aspects of language use are emphasized in the foundations: using language to communicate with others for a variety of purposes, increasing clarity of communication (i.e., phonology), developing an increasing understanding of the conventions of language use (i.e., pragmatics), and using language for narrative purposes. The first component of the foundation emphasizes the child's ability to use language for a variety of different purposes. Each time children produce language, an intention is being expressed. As children develop their language abilities during early childhood, the range of intentions they express expands. They use language not just to request, reject, and comment, but to acknowledge, to greet, to understand, to solve problems, to hypothesize, to regulate, and to describe, among other uses.

The second component centers on the ability of young children to learn to use understandable pronunciation and words. This development pertains to the articulation of specific words and the expression of specific sounds rather than to the overall way in which children speak or whether they speak with an accent. Young children may speak in ways that may contain pronunciation errors and idiosyncratic words. Usually their communication is understood by familiar adults and children. As children continue to develop, they usually speak with clear pronunciation and use common words. Their speech is usually understood by both familiar and unfamiliar adults and children.

The third component of the foundation focuses on children's increasing understanding of the conventions of communication, including conversational participation and the ability to sustain a topic over turns, and the use of appropriate verbal and nonverbal communicative behaviors, including adapting language based on communicative partners and situations.

LANGUAGE AND LITERACY

It is important to note that appropriate (or accepted) language or behavior is that which commonly occurs in the child's environment or community. For example, in some communities or environments, people make eye contact when they speak, while in other communities they do not. In the first few years of life, children are not very skilled conversationalists, only able to (typically) maintain a conversational focus for one or two turns. As children become older and near the end of the preschool years, they can maintain a conversation for several turns and take on more of the responsibility of maintaining a conversational focus. Also, as children become older, they develop an increasingly sophisticated understanding of the pragmatics of communication, or the social rules that govern the use of language and other communicative behaviors.

The fourth component of the foundation emphasizes the child's ability to use language for narrative purposes. With narrative, the child's task is, essentially, to produce an "extended monologue" as she relays an experience she had, a story she has developed, or something she wants to do in the future. Narratives include both real events (the personal narrative) as well as fictional or imagined events (the fictional narrative). There are clear developmental changes in narrative production as children mature during the preschool years (Umiker-Sebeok 1979). Children at three years of age may produce narratives organized as a series of unrelated actions or characters (e.g., "the bear, the cat, the gorilla, the end"). At around 48 months of age, children begin to organize narratives to follow a causal or temporal sequence of events (e.g., "The bear was angry because her babies woke her up. And then . . ."). The narratives of four- and five-year-old children tend to be longer and contain more information than those of three-year-olds (Curenton and Justice 2004). They contain more multiclausal sentences, more words, and a greater diversity of words. At the same time, children's narratives become more coherent as children develop and become less likely to omit key information that the listener needs to follow the events (Gutierrez-Clellen and Iglesias 1992; Peterson 1990).

Teachers can help children to develop the different aspects of conversation described previously. For instance, teachers can provide opportunities for all children to develop and apply a range of communication intentions. Teachers can develop skills in maintaining a conversational focus by repeating what children say and extending children's conversational contributions—techniques that promote children's conversational abilities (Girolametto and Weitzman 2002). Additionally, teachers can both model and promote the use of the appropriate social conventions of language. Finally, teachers can support children's narrative comprehension—which involves the ability to negotiate vocabulary, grammar, and background knowledge on the subject, to process information, to engage their phonological memory (Baddeley 1986), and when producing a narrative, to take into account the listener's needs. Teachers can elicit children's demonstration of phonological memory by requesting that children produce immediate recalls of verbally presented material (Lonigan 2004).

***Vocabulary.*** The development of vocabulary is one of the most essential, observable, and robust aspects of early language acquisition. Vocabulary knowledge is an important language tool that children use to access background knowledge, express ideas, and acquire new concepts. In addition to providing children with a tool that supports peer relationships and their interactions with adults, the size of a child's vocabulary is itself a positive influence on word learning. Children who have a larger vocabulary have an easier time acquiring new words (Nash and Donaldson 2005; Sénéchal, Thomas, and Monker 1995). They also tend to be more effective readers, mastering a wider variety of strategies to figure out the meaning of new words than less capable readers can (McKeown 1985), and are more proficient in reading comprehension (Report of the National Reading Panel 2000). On the contrary, preschool and kindergarten children who show difficulties with vocabulary exhibit relatively lower reading achievement later (Cunningham and Stanovich 1998; Share and others 1984; Stanovich, Cunningham, and Freeman 1984). The differences in vocabulary words between high and low achievers are stable over time. Vocabulary growth throughout early childhood occurs at a very rapid rate. This process continues throughout school, where children acquire from 3,000 to 5,000 new words each academic year, with about half of those words learned through reading (Nagy and Herman 1987). It is thus important to pay attention to vocabulary development from an early age. The vocabulary substrand includes three interrelated foundations: age-appropriate vocabulary, basic concepts, and vocabulary that describes relations between objects.

Vocabulary undergoes rapid growth during the preschool years. Many children enter into a period termed the "vocabulary explosion" or "word spurt" within the second year of life (Bates, Bretherton, and Snyder 1988). Vocabulary acquisition is not merely adding new words in a serial fashion to a static and established vocabulary base. Learning new vocabulary is a more complex process that involves altering and refining the semantic representation of words already in the children's vocabulary base, as well as the relationships among them (Landauer and Dumais 1997; Woodward, Markham, and Fitzsimmons 1994). Children's development of the meaning of a single word is best viewed as a gradual process in which word representations progressively develop from immature, incomplete representations to mature, accurate representations (Justice, Meier, and Walpole 2005). Children often can acquire a general representation of a new word with only a single exposure through a process called "fast mapping" (see McGregor and others 2002). This process is followed by "slow mapping," during which representations are gradually refined over time with multiple exposures (Curtis 1987). Thus, multiple experiences with words across a variety of contexts are critical for children's acquisition of a fine-grained representation of those words.

An important aspect of early vocabulary and linguistic concept development is that of "categorization" (Hoff 2005). "Vocabulary development" can be defined as the child's ongoing achievement of increasingly precise ways of representing the contents of the world. As children develop new words, those words naturally fall into different categories, such as words that describe food items, different animals, and family members. During the preschool years, as children gradually expand their use and understanding of words within a category, they also learn the "superordinate terms" (the names of the categories) by which to group these words. Examples of super-ordinate terms often acquired during the preschool years are *colors, animals, shapes, family members, friends, bugs, toys,* and *vegetables* (Owens 1999). As children grow and are exposed to a range of new experiences, they learn words from across a variety of grammatical classes and from a range of "ontological categories" (Clark 1993). These categories include objects, actions, events, relations, states and properties. Relating words and concepts within these ontological categories helps the children create meaning within their environment.

Another important element of vocabulary development is the attainment of a core group of terms that describe relations between objects. Young children's vocabulary becomes increasingly refined to show an understanding of and relay information about position and location (e.g., *in, on, under, above*), amount, and size (e.g., *small, big, huge*). For instance, three- and four-year-old children are able to produce and comprehend locational terms, such as *in, on, above, below, in front, of, next to, under, underneath,* and *beside* (see Owens 1996). During the same period, they also begin to use terms that specify amounts, such as *more, less, all,* and *none,* and physical relationships among objects on the basis of size and texture, such

as *hard/soft, big/little,* and *short/tall.* Three- and four-year-old children also begin to use the comparative *-er* and the superlative *-est* (*big, bigger, biggest; long, longer, longest*) to be discriminating about the sizes of objects. The superlative form usually emerges before the comparative form, so that children use and understand terms like *longest* and *largest* before they do the terms *longer* and *larger* (Owens 1996). Also, children's accuracy in comprehension of such terms tends to precede their use.

The development of an extensive vocabulary provides children with more sophisticated and precise ways to represent the world around them through the use of language. In the first few years of life, the language of children is developed enough to allow them to describe the immediate world—the persons, objects, and events in the immediate vicinity. Often, children's language must be contextualized, or supported by the immediate context. As their vocabulary and language concepts expand, children can be more decontextualized in their language use and comprehension. This movement from the concrete and contextualized to the abstract and decontextualized plays a critical role in the development of "academic language" (also called literate language) (see Curenton and Justice 2004) and the vocabulary used to produce and comprehend the relatively abstract content of written language. Use of an "academic language style" helps children to represent explicitly and precisely the world around them through the use of language and allows them to communicate effectively in the type of language most commonly used in school settings (Charity, Scarborough, and

Griffin 2004; Dickinson and Snow 1987; Dickinson and Tabors 1991; Snow 1983).

Children learn much of their vocabulary and basic language concepts indirectly through their interaction with others, especially adults (Cunningham and Stanovich 1998; Hayes and Ahrens 1988; Miller and Gildea 1987; Nagy and Anderson 1984; Nagy, Herman, and Anderson 1985; Nagy and Herman 1987; Sternberg 1987; Swanborn and De Glopper 1999). Children also acquire vocabulary through direct, explicit instruction. For example, Biemiller (1999) and Stahl (1999) reviewed several studies and found that children can acquire and retain two or three words a day through instruction involving contextualized introduction and explanation of new words. Other researchers have also found that direct and explicit approaches are effective in increasing children's vocabulary (see Elley 1989; Feitelson, Kita, and Goldstein 1986; Whitehurst and others 1988). With adequate instruction most children can acquire new vocabulary at rates necessary to reach "grade level" vocabulary by the middle years in elementary school (Biemiller 2001). For example, Hart and Risley (1995) found that when teachers provided 40 or more hours of rich linguistic interactions per week, children were able to perform linguistic tasks at the expected level. Similarly, Landry's study (in press) demonstrates that parents who do not frequently engage in quality conversations with their children can be coached to support their children's language and literacy skills more effectively.

***Grammar.*** During the first five years of a child's life, language acquisition develops toward an adult-like grammar. "Grammar" refers to the way in which phrases and sentences are structured to make meaning. Children seem to have an innate propensity toward learning the grammatical rules that govern their language. The grammatical rules include the organization of basic sentences (e.g., subject + verb + object: Juan drew the picture) and the joining of clauses and phrases to elaborate the basic sentence structure (e.g., subject + verb + object and subject + verb + object: Juan drew the picture and he is hanging it) (Chomsky 1957). Grammar also provides rules about the way in which nouns can be elaborated with determiners and adjectives (e.g., the big brown dog), verbs can be elaborated to share information about time (e.g., will be running), and phrases can be created for prepositions (e.g., on the table), adverbs (e.g., very, very slowly), and other parts of speech. Between the second and fifth year of life, children master virtually all the rules required for an adult-like grammar and can comprehend and produce sentences with embedded clauses (e.g., "That boy who came today is my friend"), as well as sentences with multiple subjects and predicates (e.g., "I am going and then he will get me"). The rate at which children achieve syntactic precision, however, varies from child to child (Chapman 2000). The proportion of complex sentences contained in children's language use ranges from 5 percent to 30 percent (Huttenlocher and others 2002). This variability in the rate of growth has been linked to children's experiences in hearing complex sentences from their teachers (Huttenlocher and others 2002).

The foundations are organized to emphasize the child's grammatical accomplishments at both the sentence and the word levels. Sentence-level accomplishments relate to the child's use and production of increasingly complex and longer sentences. Word-level accomplishments relate to the child's manipulation of word structure for grammatical purposes.

One foundation emphasizes children's grammatical accomplishments at the sentence level. Typically, the sentences of three-year-old children average about 3.5 words, and those of four-year-olds increase to about five words in length. (Brown 1973). While the increase in the length of sentences is not dramatic, there is a significant increase in the internal complexity of the sentences children are producing. By two years of age, children begin to produce simple sentences that include a noun + predicate (e.g., "doggy sit," "mommy work"). Later, children begin to elaborate nouns by making noun phrases (e.g., "the big brown doggy," "my mommy," "my daddy's gloves"). By four years of age, children commonly produce elaborated noun phrases that include determiners (e.g., *the, a, an, all, both, one, two*) and adjectives (e.g., *green, little, fast, angry*). This increase in complexity allows children to be highly precise in their language use (e.g., "I want that little green one over there"). A related development centers on children's ability to produce negative sentences. Children's use of basic negative sentences during the second year (e.g., "no go," "no want") becomes more precisely stated between ages three and four. Typically, these nega-

tive sentences include a fully inflected verb structure, as in, "I don't want any" and "You are not going." Some errors in negation will be seen during the preschool age (e.g., "I do want to do that!"), but these errors will become less frequent by four and five years of age as children achieve grammatical mastery (see Hoff 2004; Owens 1996).

As children near three years of age, they begin to organize phrases and clauses to produce compound sentences (e.g., "I want the cupcake and I want the cake, too") and complex sentences (e.g., "La'Kori is my friend because we go to school together"). Children typically begin producing compound sentences (conjoined with *but, so, or,* and *and*) by three years of age and then start to conjoin clauses to form complex sentences (using *if* and *because*) soon thereafter (Brown 1973).

By four years of age, most children have become skilled at both clausal embedding and clausal conjoining. "Clausal embedding" occurs when a dependent clause is embedded within an independent clause, as with, "Jose, who is two, is not yet talking" (here, the clause "who is two" is embedded into another clause). "Clausal conjoining" occurs when children link clauses, as in, "He took my toy, but I didn't want it" and "When I am four, I can chew gum." At four years up to one-third of children's sentences will be complex (Huttenlocher and others 2002), with the remainder being simple. In addition, by four years of age, children are typically able to produce complex-compound sentences that include the conjoining of two sentences using *and* or *but* as well as clauses embedded within the sentences (e.g., "I will go because she said to but I don't really want to") (Curenton and Justice 2004).

Word-level accomplishments relate to the child's manipulation of word structure for grammatical purposes. Between two and five years of age, children acquire the ability to *inflect* words to be more precise in meaning. For instance, one of the earliest word-structure achievements (by about two years of age) is inflecting verbs with the *-ing* marker to denote present progressive, as in "cat jumping" (Brown 1973). By three years of age, children are using the past tense *-ed* marker to denote events occurring in the past, as in, "I walked" (Brown 1973). As children develop their comprehension and use of these verb inflections, they tend to make errors, as in "He going" (in which the auxiliary verb *is* is omitted), "I wented," or "He hitted" (in which the *-ed* marker is added to an irregular past tense verb that does not take the *-ed*), and Carlos "walkded" (in which the *-ed* marker is added twice). Such errors are entirely commonplace and typical in early grammatical acquisition and will gradually be replaced with more accurate use (Brown 1973). By five years of age, children are quite accurate in their inflections of verbs for past tense, present progressive tense, and future tense (Brown 1973). It is important to note that some dialectical variations in the United States affect verb inflections. For instance, children who speak some variations of African-American English may omit the plural marker (e.g., two dollar) or modify the future tense (e.g., "She be mad") in ways that differ from Standard American English but are wholly appropriate to the individual's dialect (Owens 1996).

Another type of word-level achievement emphasized in the foundations is the child's development of pronouns. "Pronouns" are grammatical structures that serve in the place of nouns. They include subject pronouns (*I, you, he, she, they*), object pronouns (*me, you, him, her, them*), possessive pronouns (*hers, his, theirs*), reflexive pronouns (*myself, herself*), and demonstrative pronouns (*this, that, those*). Typically, children first develop the pronouns to refer to self (*I, me, mine, my*) between 18 and 24 months of age (see Owens 1996). Between 24 months and five years of age, children gradually master the other pronouns to include a variety of subject, object, possessive, and reflexive pronouns. Errors in usage are very common as children develop their skills with pronouns, such as, "Her did it" and "It's hims" (Owens 1996). With experience and development children will typically show few difficulties with pronouns by the end of the preschool period.

As indicated concerning the development of children's vocabulary, children's ability to use increasingly sophisticated language structures allows them to make greater use of "decontextualized language"—language that requires little reliance on the context for it to be understood. By contrast, "contextualized language" requires context to aid in understanding. For example, contrast the two sentences: "He took it" and "That boy over there took my green ball." Obviously, the latter example requires much less context for it to be understood; likewise, the latter example also places a great burden on the speaker to be linguistically precise. This level of linguistic precision, required in decontextualized situations, is referred to as "literate language" (Curenton and Justice 2004). Key markers of literate language include use of elaborated noun phrases (e.g., *my green ball*), conjunctions (*when, because*), and adverbs (*tomorrow, slowly*). As children develop literate language, they can decrease their reliance on immediate context as a tool for communication. This ability is essential in preparing young children for school, where decontextualized language is highly valued and used, and it has also proven to be an important facilitator of later reading comprehension (Dickinson and Snow 1987; Dickinson and Tabors 1991; Snow 1983).

Children's semantic (vocabulary) and syntactic (grammar) abilities become especially important in the later stages of learning to read (Bishop and Adams 1990; Bowey 1986; Demont and Gombert 1996; Gillon and Dodd 1994; Share and Silva 1987; Vellutino, Scanlon, and Tanzman 1991; Whitehurst and Lonigan 1998). These abilities are particularly relevant when children try to comprehend units of text larger than individual words (Mason 1992; Nation and Snowling 1998; Snow and others 1991; Whitehurst 1997). Thus, it is important for preschool children to continue building their semantic and syntactic abilities to facilitate their learning later in the sequence of learning to read.

## Reading

***Concepts About Print.*** An important element to the development of emergent literacy is preschool children's development of a sophisticated knowledge of how print works. Children's development of this

knowledge is enhanced by their explicit and implicit exposure to literacy practices within their homes, classrooms, and communities (Ferreiro and Teberosky 1982; Harste, Woodward, and Burke 1984; Sulzby 1987; Teale 1987). Children develop an understanding of print from television and other media exposure and from more traditional types of public literacy—like magazines, comics, newspapers, and billboards (Harste, Woodward, and Burke 1984; Holdaway 1986). Most important, children develop an awareness of concepts about print as they experience people around them using the printed word for many purposes. Children also learn about the purposes of print from labels, signs, and other kinds of print that they see around them (Neuman and Roskos 1993).

This exposure to print is key not only to developing preschool children's concepts about print, but also to providing the foundation of processes and knowledge bases that facilitate writing, reading, and reading comprehension, such as vocabulary and declarative knowledge (Adams 1990; Mason 1980; Stanovich and Cunningham 1992, 1993; West and Stanovich 1991). Children's understanding of concepts about print has been shown to be associated with later reading performance (Adams 1990; Badian 2001; Clay 1993; *Preventing Reading Difficulties in Young Children* 1998; Reutzel, Oda, and Moore 1989; Scarborough 1998; Stuart 1995; Tunmer, Herriman, and Nesdale 1988).

Central to an understanding of the nature and role of reading and writing is a child's understanding of "intentionality" (Purcell-Gates and Dahl 1991). That is, children need to recognize that print carries meaning—that a meaning or message is encoded (Purcell-Gates 1996). When a child understands intentionality, meaning and understanding become a background for all subsequent learning. Failure to develop this awareness is one characteristic of delayed reading development (Clay 1985; Purcell-Gates and Dahl 1991). Children's understanding that print carries meaning emerges between the second and fifth year of life, depending on the extent to which children interact with and are exposed to print (Mason 1980). This understanding becomes increasingly sophisticated during the preschool years (Justice and Ezell 2000). At this time, children begin to use print to communicate, to understand the way print is organized in books and other texts, to recite the alphabet, and to recognize some letters and words in print.

The first aspect of this substrand, print conventions, describes children's growing knowledge of the ways in which print is organized, including directionality and, for English orthography, the left-to-right and top-to-bottom organization of print in books or other print media (Clay 2002). Print conventions also refer to the way books are organized (e.g., front and back) and the way they should be handled (Clay 2002).

The second aspect of this substrand focuses on children's understanding that print can be read and has specific meaning. Children are beginning to understand and operate within the routines and contexts in which print is a component, and they are learning that reading and writing play a key role in various social contexts. By interacting with and observing adults using print, preschool children learn the vocabulary of reading in instructional contexts—such as read, write, draw, page, and story (Morgan cited in Weir 1989; van Kleeck 1990)—as well as the routines that govern literacy use in the classroom, home, or preschool setting, for example, reading stories, making lists, and writing letters (Elster 1988; Elster and Walker 1992).

Although natural exposure to print has a positive influence on children's awareness of concepts about print, researchers have found that adults need to deliberately and actively encourage children's engagement with print by explicitly drawing children's attention to print forms and functions (Justice and others 2005). Strategies teachers use to help young children develop print awareness skills include asking questions about print, commenting about print, tracking print when reading, and pointing to print (Justice and Ezell 2000, 2002).

***Phonological Awareness.*** "Phonological awareness" is generally defined as an individual's sensitivity to the sound (or phonological) structure of spoken language independent of meaning. Spoken language is made up of different phonological units that differ in their linguistic complexity. The phonological units include words, syllables, subsyllabic units (onsets, rimes), and individual sounds (phonemes). Phonological awareness (also called "phonological sensitivity") should be differentiated from "phonemic awareness." Phonemic awareness is the most advanced level of phonological awareness that an individual can achieve. It refers to one's ability to recognize and manipulate phonemes, which constitute the smallest units of spoken words. Phonological awareness (and phonemic awareness) should also be distinguished from phonics. "Phonics" is a method of instruction that focuses on teaching the relationships between sounds and the letters that represent them, whereas phonological awareness is an oral language skill that does not involve print.

The development of phonological awareness typically moves along a continuum in which children progress from a sensitivity to larger concrete units of sound to a sensitivity to smaller abstract units of sound (Adams 1990; Anthony and others 2002; Fox and Routh 1975; Goswami and Bryant 1990; Liberman and others 1974; Lonigan 2006; Lonigan and others 1998; Lonigan, Burgess, and Anthony 2000; MacLean, Bryant, and Bradley 1987; Treiman 1992). Typically, children's first achievements in phonological awareness are to detect and manipulate words and syllables within words and to then progress to awareness of onsets and rimes. The onset of a syllable is the first consonant or consonant cluster (e.g., the *m-* in the word *map,* the *dr-* in the word *drum*), whereas the rime of a syllable is its vowel and any ending consonants (e.g., *-ap* in the word *map, -um* in the word *drum*). Finally, children develop awareness of the smallest abstract units of sound, the phonemes. Phonemes can be represented by single letters, such as with the phonemes *c—a—t* in the word *cat,* or with two letters, such as in the *ch-* in the word *cheese*; but not all letters in a word represent a phoneme, such as the silent-*e* in the word *store.* The foundations reflect these gradations in the achievement of phonological awareness as children become gradually more

sensitive to smaller units of spoken language.

In addition to development involving the linguistic complexity of sound units, children demonstrate their phonological awareness through three types of operations—detection, synthesis, and analysis (Anthony, Lonigan, and Burgess 2003). "Detection" is the ability to match similar sounds. "Synthesis" is the ability to combine smaller segments into syllables and words. "Analysis" is the ability to segment words or syllables into smaller units. At the level of segmenting words into syllables and segmenting syllables into onset and rime, children's phonological awareness performance usually progresses from detection, to synthesis, to analysis. This development does not occur in discrete stages but instead represents overlapping abilities (Anthony, Lonigan, and Burgess 2003). That is, children do not have to completely master the earlier skill before they begin to acquire the next skill in the sequence. The foundations concurrently address the developmental levels of phonological awareness within the various performance areas, so that a progression can be seen from the ability to detect and blend words to the ability to segment at the onset-rime level.

The position of a phoneme in a word or syllable and the context in which the phoneme occurs also influence the level of difficulty of a phonological awareness task. Children are able to detect or manipulate the initial phonemes in words before they can detect or manipulate final phonemes. Additionally, children have more difficulty in identifying or manipulating a phoneme that is a part of a cluster than they do phonemes that are not in a cluster. For instance, children may be able to identify the three phonemes in *pop* but have difficulty in identifying the four phonemes in *plop* because the onset of the word contains a consonant cluster. The foundations address these variations in the level of difficulty of phonological awareness tasks by focusing the harder operations (e.g., deleting parts of words and blending phonemes) on the initial parts of words (deleting onsets rather than deleting rimes) and on simple words (blending of words that have a limited number of phonemes and do not contain clusters).

One additional source of variation relates to the amount and kind of supports provided to children so that they can perform these tasks. For example, when asking children to delete the onset of a word, the teacher can provide pictures of stimuli to reduce the level of difficulty of the task. This approach helps children to remember the different words and enhances their performance compared with having them perform this task without picture stimuli. When needed, the foundations emphasize phonological awareness performance within the context of support, and the expectation is that children will demonstrate mastery in the context of the support provided by pictures, props, objects, or other valid supportive context. This is the case for the foundations that involve the manipulation of smaller units of sound within more difficult forms of cognitive operations (e.g., deletion of a word's initial phoneme).

Phonological awareness is an important area of early and later reading instruction (Bowers 1995; Bowers and Wolf 1993; Lonigan, Burgess, and Anthony 2000; *Report of the National Reading Panel: Teaching Children to Read: An Evidence-Based Assessment of the Scientific Research Literature on Reading and Its Implications for Reading Instruction* 2000; Prather, Hendrick, and Kern 1975; Templin 1957; Wagner, Torgesen, and Rashotte 1994; Wagner and others 1997). Phonological awareness plays a key role in several of the components that help children become skilled readers, such as understanding the alphabetic principle (Burgess and Lonigan 1998; Ehri 1991, 1995), decoding printed words (Beck and Juel 1999; Bradley and Bryant 1985; Byrne and Fielding-Barnsley 1993, 1995; Demont and Gombert 1996; Tunmer, Herriman, and Nesdale 1988), spelling (Bryant and others 1990; Gentry 1982; Read 1975), and reading comprehension—although this relation with reading comprehension is not direct (Tunmer and Nesdale 1985).

Given the importance of phonological awareness to early and later literacy achievement, these foundations emphasize attention to its development for older preschool children. They do not include, however, specific indicators for younger children, as is explained next. First, evidence suggests that phonological awareness is not consistently mastered by children under four years of age (Lonigan, Burgess, and Anthony 2000), although performance at three years of age can be assessed and targeted through instruction. Second, vocabulary is highly related to children's acquisition of phonological sensitivity (Burgess and Lonigan 1998; Chaney 1992; Lonigan and others 1998; Lonigan, Burgess, and Anthony 2000). Most probably, the positive effect of vocabulary on phonological awareness is based on the fact that vocabulary development facilitates children's ability to focus their attention on parts of words, rather than on their whole, as children learn more words (see Metsala and Walley 1998), thus helping them progress in their phonological awareness from large to smaller units of sound. From these findings, Lonigan and others (Fowler 1991; Jusczyk 1995; Lonigan, Burgess, and Anthony 2000; Metsala and Walley 1998; Walley 1993) conclude that vocabulary development may provide the basis for the emergence of phonological awareness. Therefore, the foundations focus on this key precursor for three-year-olds and include phonological awareness foundations for children at around 60 months of age, because mastery of phonological awareness is more appropriate for older preschool children.

***Alphabetics and Word/Print Recognition.*** The ability to recognize letters is a basic step in the process of learning to read and write. Knowledge of the alphabet letters is a strong predictor of short- and long-term reading success. Children who have a well-developed knowledge of the letters before engaging in reading instruction make better progress than those who do not (Adams 1990; Badian 1982; Bond and Dykstra 1967; Chall 1967; Evans, Shaw, and Bell 2000; Scanlon and Vellutino 1996; Share and others 1984; Stevenson and Newman 1986; Stuart 1995; Tunmer, Herriman, and Nesdale 1988; Walsh, Price, and Gillingham, 1988). Knowing the names of letters facilitates children's ability to decode text and to apply the alphabetic principle to word recognition. For most children the name of the letters helps them connect the sounds in words and letters in print (Durrell 1980). Knowledge of letter names, then, can be conceived as a mediator in the reading process that provides children with the ability to remember the sounds associated with letters (Ehri 1979, 1998).

The order of learning the alphabet letters seems facilitated by environmental and developmental influences. An important environmental influence is exposure to the individual letters of the alphabet. Children learn first the letters that are the most familiar to them, such as the letters in their own names and the letters that occur earlier in the alphabet string (Treiman and Broderick 1998). The features of certain letters make them more amenable to learning. For instance, letters that contain their sound in a child's name, like *b* and *f*, are learned earlier than are those letters that do not, like *q* and *w* (Treiman and Broderick 1998). A developmental influence on children's learning of alphabet letters relates to the relationship between phonological development and alphabet knowledge. Children learn earlier those letters that map onto earlier-acquired phonemes, such as the "b" letter sound and the "d" letter sound, instead of letters that map onto phonemes that tend to be acquired later, such as the "r" letter sound and the "l" letter sound. (Justice and others 2006). Consequently, the focus of the foundations is on children's ability to recognize or identify familiar letters and words, such as the first letter of their name and, later, their whole first name.

As children become aware of the names of letters, they also begin to identify printed words. Ehri (1995) has defined children's development in word recognition as a series of transitions as children move from "prealphabetic readers" (learning words by sight and using salient contextual cues for word recognition), to "partial alphabetic" (applying some phonetic information, such as the sound corresponding to the first letter in a word, to recognizing the word), to "full alphabetic" (reading a word using the alphabetic principle). The word recognition skills of preschool-age children are primarily of a prealphabetic type, so that they can recognize some words, but rarely can they examine the alphabetic or phonetic structures of the word to arrive at its meaning. This is why young children are able to recognize some words in the environment (e.g., Stop, Exit, and some brand names), but they require contextual information from the environment to aid their recognition of these words. Some children who have well-developed knowledge of the alphabet and letter-sound correspondences, coupled with relatively good phonological awareness, may read at partial alphabetic levels during the preschool years. These children are able to look at some unknown words and use letters (and their corresponding sounds) to unlock the word's meaning. For instance, a child may see the word *Thomas* in a book and use some alphabetic information (e.g., the first letter *T* and its corresponding letter sound) to make a good guess as to what it says.

**Comprehension and Analysis of Age-Appropriate Text.** Reading comprehension is influenced greatly by language comprehension, and in large part they draw on the same developmental processes (Perfetti, Van Dyke, and Hart 2001). Just as children move from understanding simple phrases and directions to comprehending more detailed information, they also progress from remembering isolated aspects of simple stories to understanding parts of more complex literacy events. As children become better able to respond to complex literacy events that feature causal or temporal sequences or descriptions of nonfiction, real events, they draw on their narrative skills in particular. "Narrative" is a term that describes production and comprehension of discourse (including both written and spoken). A defining feature of narrative is its organizational cohesion, so that information is threaded over a series of utterances or sentences.

Preschool children's development of narrative thinking goes through a series of stages that ultimately help them to make sense of stories and the world around them (Paris and Paris 2003). At the early stages preschool children construct narrative scripts, which involve primitive accounts of story plots. These scripts usually focus on the description of familiar events and routine activities, such as going to a birthday party or visiting the doctor. Over time, children construct narrative schemas, which include knowledge about the main elements of stories (such as characters and settings) and about the sequence of events (such as time, order, and causal progression). In the last, and perhaps most difficult stage, preschool children come to understand and relate to characters' internal responses, such as their mental processes and experiences. This ability to understand characters' internal thinking also helps children to develop a sense of perspective by which they can empathize with the experiences and reactions of characters in a story, and it helps children develop the ability to recognize both the external and internal features of narratives.

Children's comprehension and production of narrative is an important foundation for learning to read (Burns, Griffin, and Snow 1999; Whitehurst and Lonigan 1998). Narratives are pervasive in children's language, play, and thinking and tend to be naturally supported by parents and teachers. However, narrative competence can be expanded through designed interventions (Yussen and Ozcan 1996).

Exposure to wordless picture books provides both instructional opportunities for children and a window into the process for teachers. When reading wordless picture books and books with print, preschool children use a common set of strategies to grasp meaning: they make use of prior knowledge and experiences, pay attention to intertextual cues and multiple perspectives, rely on story language and rituals, and implement active, playful behavior as a part of the reading process (Crawford and Hade 2000). Children's efforts to make sense of the pictures in wordless picture books form the foundation for the reading comprehension and meaning-making skills needed later to be successful readers (Paris and van Kraayenoord 1998). Children's narrative comprehension of wordless picture books has been shown to be an effective way to assess children's comprehension when they are still not able to decode (Paris and Paris 2003).

Storybook reading, both of wordless picture books and books with print, when combined with interactive language activities, has other benefits as well. Active discussion of stories before, during, and after shared reading has been shown to improve children's understanding and recall of oral stories (Cochran-Smith 1984; Mason and Allen 1986; Morrow 1984; Morrow and Smith 1990). Book reading also contributes to general language development, whether it is practiced at home (Chomsky 1972; Raz and Bryant 1990; Sénéchal and others 1998; Wells 1985a; Whitehurst and others 1988) or in the classroom (Dickinson 2001; Dickinson, Hao, and He 1995; Dickinson and Keebler 1989; Dickinson and Smith 1994; Martinez and Teale 1993; Teale and Martinez 1986). Within the classroom, studies conducted with preschool children have shown that intervention-enhanced teacher-child interactions have positive effects on the children's language skills (e.g., syntactic forms at the sentence level) (Arnold and Whitehurst 1994; Karweit 1989; Valdez-Menchaca and Whitehurst 1992). This enhanced development of language abilities may in turn lead to enhanced comprehension (Elley and Mangubhai 1983; Feitelson, Kita, and Goldstein 1986; Feitelson and others 1993; Morrow 1984, 1988).

Shared reading activities provide an adult with the opportunity to introduce key components of the reading task to children and to support their learning of these key issues. Research has shown that such practices as shared reading, when conducted over time, provide children with a sense of the purposes of literacy (Gee 1992; Heath 1983), the values associated with shared reading (Snow and others 1991), and the processes and skills involved in shared reading (see the preceding paragraph). While storybook reading has often been considered an introduction to literacy (Adams 1990), the practices and styles of interaction that emerge during shared reading set the foundation for the types of cognitive processing and problem solving that characterize comprehension in the elementary grades, with strategies such as self-questioning and use of mental imagery (Bauman and Bergeron 1993; Fitzgerald and Spiegel 1983). Shared reading activities also help children become familiar with the nature of written language and help preschool children realize the developmental progression from an "oral" to a "written" type of language (Purcell-Gates 1988; Sulzby 1985).

Children entering school from disadvantaged environments often have limited or minimal exposure to complex narrative texts. Shared reading, picture-book reading, and the instructional conversations are of special relevance for these children. The lack of exposure puts them at a disadvantage when they are placed in classrooms with students who have been repeatedly exposed to the language, ideas, routines, and pleasures associated with complex text (Baker, Serpell, and Sonnenschein 1995; Dahl and Freppon 1991; Marvin and Mirenda 1993; *Preventing Reading Difficulties in Young Children* 1998; Purcell-Gates and Dahl 1991). Fortunately, this exposure gap can be closed through instruction at home and in school (Clay 1979; Leppäen and others 2004; Purcell-Gates, McIntyre, and Freppon 1995). For example, adults can explicitly engage children with thinking about and responding to specific elements of texts during storybook reading interactions. They might, for instance, focus a child's attention on following the cause-and-effect sequence of a story or discussing words that occur repeatedly in a text to create coherence. It is most impor-

tant that adults who read with young children provide this structure consistently and systematically, so that they support children's engagement with certain aspects of the text (e.g., causal flow of events) that children may not be drawn to incidentally or of their own accord (Ezell and Justice 2000).

***Literacy Interest and Response.*** The comprehension of text for young children requires both skill and will, *will* usually being a precursor to *skill*. Showing an interest in books and holding a positive regard for reading are considered developmental accomplishments of three- and four-year-olds by the National Research Council (*Preventing Reading Difficulties in Young Children* 1998). Children's willing participation in such literacy activities as handling books and listening to stories is an essential precursor to their later cognitive engagement with text, in the same way that early joint attention between a caregiver and a child is an essential precursor to achievements in oral language production and comprehension. Early interest in literacy may also motivate children to persist with future challenging reading tasks (*Preventing Reading Difficulties in Young Children* 1998). Cognitive skills are necessary for children to become able readers, but to become lifelong literacy learners, children must be motivated to engage in literacy activities and persist in their engagement. As such, interest in literacy is closely linked to the issue of motivation.

Interest in and motivation toward reading describe the child's affect toward, or feelings about, literacy activities (Alexander and Filler 1976; Mathewson 1994; McKenna, Kear, and Ellsworth 1995). The beliefs, motivation, and purposes of individuals influence their decisions about which activities to do, how long to do them, and how much effort to put into them (Bandura 1997; Eccles, Wigfield, and Schiefele 1998; Pintrich and Schunk 1996). The literature on motivation makes a distinction between "intrinsic motivation," which refers to being motivated to do an activity for its own sake and out of interest and curiosity, and "extrinsic motivation," or doing an activity to receive an award or other form of recognition (Guthrie, Wigfield, and Von Secker 2000). Both intrinsic and extrinsic motivation influence the amount and frequency of children's reading. However, research has shown that intrinsic motivation is a stronger predictor of reading achievement than is extrinsic motivation (Baker and Wigfield 1999; Gottfried 1990; Schultz and Switzky 1993; Wigfield and Guthrie 1997). Motivation toward reading influences individuals' engagement with reading and literacy activities by facilitating their entry into a "psychological state of interest" (Krapp, Hidi, and Renniger 1992), in which individuals demonstrate increased attention, cognitive functioning, and persistence in different literacy tasks, as well as an increase in their affective investment (Hidi, 1990; Krapp, Hidi, and Renniger 1992). Reading in this state of interest facilitates comprehension and recall of information (see Anderson 1982; Asher 1979, 1980; Bernstein 1955; Estes and Vaughan 1973; Hidi 2001; Hidi and Baird 1986, 1988; Kintsch 1980; Schank 1979; Schraw, Bruning, and Svoboda 1995).

Studies about interest and motivation toward reading and literacy have most extensively been conducted with school-age children and college students. Nonetheless, an emerging research base shows that interest and motivation are also factors in preschool reading achievement (Scarborough and Dobrich 1994; Whitehurst and Lonigan 1998). Research with young children has confirmed that they have strong, stable, and relatively well-focused individual interests that influence their attention, recognition, and recall of information during literacy activities, such as shared storybook reading (Renninger and Wozniak 1985). In addition, children's active engagement in text-related activities, such as turning pages in a book, is related to knowledge of print concepts at four years of age (Crain-Thoresen and Dale 1992). Preschool children who are engaged and attentive during literacy activities achieve greater literacy gains in these activities (Justice and others 2003).

A positive relationship exists between children's interest in reading and their opportunities for reading at home and school. Children who are read to more frequently and from an earlier age tend to have a greater interest in literacy, exhibit superior literacy skills during the preschool and school years, choose reading more frequently, initiate reading sessions on their own, and show greater engagement during reading sessions (Lonigan 1994; Scarborough and Dobrich 1994). Guthrie and others (1996) have also reported that increasing literacy engagement and expanded reading activity are tied to increases in intrinsic motivation, whereas decreased literacy engagement is reflected in decreased intrinsic motivation. In short, adult-child storybook reading promotes children's interest in and motivation for reading, both of which lead to increased exposure, experience, and engagement with text. This engagement with text has a positive effect on overall reading ability (Bus 2001; Whitehurst and Lonigan 1998). The opposite is also true: negative attitudes toward reading, especially recreational reading, usually lead to decreased exposure to reading and reading ability (McKenna, Kear, and Ellsworth 1995).

In addition to increasing children's exposure to reading and print and their interest in literacy, early reading activities also help children learn about the context of literacy and the structure of literacy activities (Crain-Thoreson and Dale 1992), providing children with the language used at school for literacy activities (Heath 1982; Wells 1985b). Helping children become familiar with some aspects of the language (Heath 1982), participant structures (Phillips 1983), and patterns of interaction (Cazden 1986) of the classroom during the preschool years will place them in the right trajectory to be successful learners in school (*Improving Schooling for Language-Minority Children: A Research Agenda* 1997). Consequently, the foundations focus on children's engagement in literacy activities in a way that will furnish them with knowledge about the roles and routines of reading and literacy activities they are likely to experience when they enter school.

## Writing

***Writing Strategies.*** Learning to write involves cognitive, social, and physical development. From a very young age, children notice the writing in their surroundings. They begin to develop the understanding that regular signs can be used to represent ideas or concepts. At first, they may conclude that there should be some resemblance between what is being represented and the way it is represented. For example, they may say that *train* must be a very long word, while *mosquito* must be a very small one (Ferreiro and Teberosky 1982; Piaget 1962). At the same time, they begin to differentiate between writing and other kinds of visual representation (e.g., drawing) (Bissex 1980; Ferreiro and Teberosky 1982; Harste, Woodward, and Burke 1984). They accompany this realization with a differentiation between the tools for writing and those for drawing ("I need to get a pencil to write my name"). Moreover, their writing starts to look different from their drawing (Ferreiro and Teberosky 1982; Harste, Woodward, and Burke 1984), often being linear in form instead of circular.

As young children get more involved with written text by being read to, examining books, and observing others write, they begin to experiment with writing. Children's emergent writing abilities are demonstrated in the preschool classroom with such activities as pretending to write and learning to write one's name (Whitehurst and Lonigan 2001). According to some theorists, children's writing follows a developmental path. Initially, children demonstrate a global form of writing. They tend to treat writing from a pictographic perspective, which is usually demonstrated by using drawings as writing or using idiosyncratic scribble (e.g., markings that have meaning only for the child). Later, children use letter-like forms to write, usually making marks that resemble

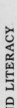

characteristics of the real writing (e.g., longer words are represented by longer strings of letter-like symbols). In the next stage children start using actual letters to write, even when there is no connection between the true spelling of what they want to write and what they produce (i.e., producing nonphonetic strings of letters) (Ferreiro and Teberosky 1982; Sulzby 1986, 1987).

This stage is followed by a period when children produce phonetic spelling, also called "invented spelling." Children use letter-like symbols to represent the parts of words that they hear and attempt to match letters to sounds or syllables, usually based on sound rather than on what is written (Ferreiro and Teberosky 1982). For example, children may recognize that to write something requires more than one or two symbols, and they may also realize that the same symbols may recur in different words and in different places in the word (Ferreiro and Teberosky 1982; Temple and others 1993), but they have not yet mastered the alphabetic principle. Nonetheless, several studies have shown that invented spelling is an effective vehicle through which many children begin to understand the alphabetic principle (Clarke 1988; Ehri 1988; Torgesen and Davis 1996).

Throughout this early stage of learning to write, children begin to realize that writing carries meaning; people should be able to read what you write (Clay 1977; Harste, Woodward, and Burke 1984; Kress 1994). They also learn that people write for different purposes (Ferreiro and Teberosky 1982; Heath 1983; Schieffelin and Cochran-Smith 1984; Taylor and Dorsey-Gaines 1988; Teale 1987). While research shows that children from different cultural and socioeconomic backgrounds have different experiences with written language, it also shows that all children have experienced written language and its purposes (McGee and Richgels 1990).

Finally, children have the physical experience of actually writing and drawing, in which they begin to develop effective (or not so effective) ways of handling writing implements. While many children handle writing implements efficiently, some children need support in learning to do so. Children who are still using scribbles and have difficulty with the basic shapes (circle, square, triangle) would benefit from informal instruction in learning to make these shapes, since they ease the transition to learning letters (Lesiak 1997).

# Glossary

**caregiver.** An adult with responsibility for children in a family child care home, or an adult who provides family, friend, or neighbor care

**contextualized language.** Language used to communicate about the "here and now," or immediate situation, with a person who may share background knowledge with the speaker and who is in the same location as are the things, actions, or events the speaker describes. (Such cues as intonation, gestures, and facial expressions may support the meaning that contextualized language conveys.)

**decontextualized language.** Language, such as that in story narratives, used to provide novel information to a listener who may share limited background knowledge with the speaker or who is not in the same location where the things or events described are located

**early childhood setting.** Any setting outside the home in which preschool children receive education and care

**family caregiver.** Mother, father, grandparent, or other adult raising the child at home

**onset.** The first consonant or consonant cluster in a syllable (e.g., the *h* in the one-syllable word *hat*, the *m* and *k* in the two syllables in the word *monkey*)

**orally blend.** To combine sound elements to make a word or syllable (e.g., combine the phonemes "k" "a" "t" to make the word *cat*)

**phoneme.** The individual unit of meaningful sound in a word or syllable

**phonemic awareness.** A subtype of phonological awareness. (Phonological awareness can refer to the detection or manipulation of large and concrete units of sounds, like words and syllables, or smaller and abstract units of sound, like onsets, rimes, and phonemes. Phonemic awareness specifically refers to the ability to manipulate or detect the smallest units of sound in the words, the phonemes.)

**phonological awareness.** The ability to detect or manipulate the sound structure of spoken words, independent of meaning. (It is an increasingly sophisticated capability that is highly predictive of, and causally related to, children's later ability to read.)

**pragmatics.** The system of social rules for using language in different communication contexts or situations. (Pragmatics includes using language for different purposes, such as greeting or requesting; changing language according to the needs of a listener or situation, such as communicating differently to a baby than to an adult; or following conversational rules, such as taking turns, making eye contact, or maintaining physical distance during a conversation. These rules vary among cultures.)

**productive language.** The process of formulating and sending a message (communicating) using language. (Speech is one form of productive or expressive language. Other means to express language include using sign language, pointing to words and pictures on a communication board, and producing written messages on a computer screen.)

**rime.** Everything left in a syllable after the onset is removed; the vowel and coda of a syllable (e.g., the *at* in the single-syllable word *hat*, the *in* in the single-syllable word *in*)

**receptive language.** The process of receiving and understanding communication through language. (Speech is one way to receive messages through language. Other means to receive language are sign language, words and pictures on a communication board, and written messages on a computer screen.)

**teacher.** An adult with responsibility for the education and care of children in a preschool program

LANGUAGE AND LITERACY

# References

Adams, M. J. 1990. *Learning to Read: Thinking and Learning About Print.* Cambridge, MA: MIT Press.

Alexander, J. E., and R. C. Filler. 1976. *Attitudes and Reading.* Newark, DE: International Reading Association.

Anderson, R. C. 1982. "Allocation of Attention During Reading," in *Discourse Processing.* Edited by A. Falmmer and W. Kintsch. New York: North-Holland.

Anthony, J. L., and others. 2002. "Structure of Preschool Phonological Sensitivity: Overlapping Sensitivity to Rhyme, Words, Syllables, and Phonemes," *Journal of Experimental Child Psychology,* Vol. 82, 65–92.

Anthony, J. L.; C. J. Lonigan; and S. R. Burgess. 2003. "Phonological Sensitivity: A Quasi-Parallel Progression of Word Structure Units and Cognitive Operations," *Reading Research Quarterly,* Vol. 38, 470–87.

Arnold, D. S., and G. J. Whitehurst. 1994. "Accelerating Language Development Through Picture Book Reading: A Summary of Dialogic Reading and Its Effects," in *Bridges to Literacy: Approaches to Supporting Child and Family Literacy.* Edited by D. K. Dickinson. Cambridge, MA: Blackwell.

Asher, S. R. 1979. "Influence of Topic Interest on Black Children's and White Children's Reading Comprehension," *Child Development,* Vol. 50, 686–90.

Asher, S. R. 1980. "Topic Interest and Children's Reading Comprehension," in *Theoretical Issues in Reading Comprehension.* Edited by R. J. Spiro; B. C. Bruce; and W. F. Brewer. Hillsdale, NJ: Erlbaum Associates.

Baddeley, A. 1986. *Working Memory.* New York: Oxford University Press.

Badian, N. A. 1982. "The Prediction of Good and Poor Reading Before Kindergarten Entry: A Four-Year Follow-Up," *The Journal of Special Education,* Vol. 16, 309–18.

Badian, N. A. 2001. "Phonological and Orthographic Processing: Their Roles in Reading Prediction," *Annals of Dyslexia,* Vol. 51, 179–202.

Baker, L., and A. Wigfield. 1999. "Dimensions of Children's Motivation for Reading and Their Relationships to Reading Activity and Reading Achievement," *Reading Research Quarterly,* Vol. 34, No. 4, 452–77.

Baker, L.; R. Serpell; and S. Sonnenschein. 1995. "Opportunities for Literacy Learning in the Homes of Urban Preschoolers," in *Family Literacy: Connections to Schools and Communities.* Edited by L. Morrow. Newark, DE: International Reading Association.

Bandura, A. 1997. *Self-Efficacy: The Exercise of Control.* New York: W. H. Freeman.

Bates, E.; I. Bretherton; and L. Snyder. 1988. *From First Words to Grammar: Individual Differences and Dissociable Mechanisms.* New York: Cambridge University Press.

Bauman, J. F., and B. S. Bergeron. 1993. "Story Map Instruction Using Children's Literature: Effects on First Graders' Comprehension of Central Narrative Elements," *Journal of Reading Behavior,* Vol. 25, 407–37.

Baumwell, L.; C. S. Tamis-LeMonda; and M. H. Bornstein. 1997. "Maternal Verbal Sensitivity and Child Language Comprehension," *Infant Behavior and Development,* Vol. 20, 247–58.

Beck, I., and C. Juel. 1999. "The Role of Decoding in Learning to Read," in *Reading Research Anthology: The Why? of Reading Instruction.* Compiled by the Consortium on Reading Excellence (CORE). Novato, CA: Arena Press.

Bernstein, M. R. 1955. "Relationship Between Interest and Reading Comprehension," *Journal of Educational Research*, Vol. 49, 283–88.

Biemiller, A. 1999. *Language and Reading Success.* Cambridge, MA: Brookline Books.

Biemiller, A. 2001. "Teaching Vocabulary: Early, Direct, and Sequential," *American Educator*, Vol. 25, 24–28.

Bishop, D. V. M., and C. Adams. 1990. "A Prospective Study of the Relationship Between Specific Language Impairment, Phonological Disorders, and Reading Retardation," *Journal of Child Psychology and Psychiatry and Allied Disciplines*, Vol. 31, 1027–50.

Bissex, G. L. 1980. "Patterns of Development in Writing: A Case Study," *Theory Into Practice*, Vol. 19, No. 3, 197–201.

Bohannon, J. N., and J. D. Bonvillian. 2001. "Theoretical Approaches to Language Acquisition," in *The Development of Language* (Fifth edition). Edited by J. B. Gleason. Boston: Allyn and Bacon.

Bond, G. L., and R. Dykstra. 1967. "The Cooperative Research Program in First-Grade Reading Instruction," *Reading Research Quarterly*, Vol. 2, No. 4, 5–142.

Bowers, P. G. 1995. "Tracing Symbol Naming Speed's Unique Contributions to Reading Disabilities Over Time," *Reading and Writing*, Vol. 7, 189–216.

Bowers, P. G., and M. Wolf. 1993. "Theoretical Links Among Naming Speed, Precise Timing Mechanisms and Orthographic Skill in Dyslexia," *Reading and Writing*, Vol. 5, 69–85.

Bowey, J. A. 1986. "Syntactic Awareness in Relation to Reading Skills and Ongoing Reading Comprehension Monitoring," *Journal of Experimental Child Psychology*, Vol. 41, 282–99.

Bradley, L., and P. Bryant. 1985. *Rhyme and Reason in Reading and Spelling.*

Ann Arbor, MI: University of Michigan Press.

Brown, R. 1973. *A First Language: The Early Stages.* Cambridge, MA: Harvard University Press.

Bryant, P. E., and others. 1990. "Rhyme and Alliteration, Phoneme Detection, and Learning to Read," *Developmental Psychology*, Vol. 26, 429–38.

Burgess, S. R., and C. J. Lonigan. 1998. "Bidirectional Relations of Phonological Sensitivity and Prereading Abilities: Evidence from a Preschool Sample," *Journal of Experimental Child Psychology*, Vol. 70, 117–41.

Burns, M. S.; P. Griffin; and C. E. Snow. 1999. *Starting Out Right.* Washington, DC: National Academies Press.

Bus, A. G. 2001. "Joint Caregiver-Child Storybook Reading: A Route to Literacy Development," in *Handbook of Early Literacy Research.* Edited by S. B. Neuman and D. K. Dickinson. New York: Guilford.

Byrne, B., and R. F. Fielding-Barnsley. 1993. "Evaluation of a Program to Teach Phonemic Awareness to Young Children: A One-Year Follow-up," *Journal of Educational Psychology*, Vol. 85 (1993), 104–11.

Byrne, B., and R. F. Fielding-Barnsley. 1995. "Evaluation of a Program to Teach Phonemic Awareness to Young Children: A Two- and Three-Year Follow-up and a New Preschool Trial," *Journal of Educational Psychology*, Vol. 87, 488–503.

Cazden, C.B. 1986. "Classroom Discourse," in *Handbook of Research on Teaching* (Third edition). Edited by M. C. Wittrock. New York: Macmillan.

Chall, J. S. 1967. *Learning to Read: The Great Debate.* New York: McGraw-Hill.

Chaney, C. 1992. "Language Development, Metalinguistic Skills, and Print Awareness in Three-Year-Old Children," *Applied Psycholinguistics*, Vol. 12, 485–514.

LANGUAGE AND LITERACY

Chapman, R. S. 2000. "Children's Language Learning: An Interactionist Perspective," *Journal of Child Psychology and Psychiatry,* Vol. 41, 33–54.

Charity, A. H.; H. S. Scarborough; and D. M. Griffin. 2004. "Familiarity with School Language in African American Children and Its Relation to Early Reading Achievement," *Child Development,* Vol. 75, No. 5, 1340–56.

Chomsky, C. 1972. "Stages in Language Development and Reading Exposure," *Harvard Educational Review,* Vol. 42, 1–33.

Chomsky, N. 1957. *Syntactic Structures.* The Hague: Mouton and Company.

Clark, E. 1993. *The Lexicon in Acquisition.* Cambridge, UK: Cambridge University Press.

Clarke, L. K. 1988. "Invented Versus Traditional Spelling in First Graders' Writings: Effects on Learning to Spell and Read," *Research in the Teaching of English,* Vol. 22, 281–309.

Clay, M. M. 1997. "Exploring with a Pencil," *Theory Into Practice,* Vol. 16, No. 5 (December, 1977), 334–41.

Clay, M. M. 1979. *Reading: The Patterning of Complex Behavior.* Auckland, NZ: Heinemann.

Clay, M. M. 1985. *The Early Detection of Reading Difficulties* (Third edition). Portsmouth, NH: Heinemann.

Clay, M. M. 1993. *Reading Recovery: A Guidebook for Teachers in Training.* Portsmouth, NH: Heinemann.

Clay, M. M. 2002. *An Observation Survey of Early Literacy Achievement* (Second edition). Portsmouth, NH: Heinemann.

Cochran-Smith, M. 1984. *The Making of a Reader.* Norwood, NJ: Ablex.

Crain-Thoreson, C., and P. S. Dale. 1992. "Do Early Talkers Become Early Readers? Linguistic Precocity, Preschool Language, and Early Literacy," *Developmental Psychology,* Vol. 28, 421–29.

Crawford, P. A., and D. D. Hade. 2000. "Inside the Picture, Outside the Frame: Semiotics and the Reading of Wordless Picture Books," *Journal of Research in Childhood Education,* Vol. 15, No. 1, 66–80.

Cunningham, A. E., and K. E. Stanovich. 1998. "What Reading Does for the Mind," *American Educator,* Vol. 22, Nos. 1-2 (Spring/Summer 1998), 8–15.

Curenton, S., and L. M. Justice. 2004. "Low-Income Preschoolers' Use of Decontextualized Discourse: Literate Language Features in Spoken Narratives," *Language, Speech, and Hearing Services in Schools,* Vol. 35, 240–53.

Curtis, M. E. 1987. "Vocabulary Testing and Instruction," in *The Nature of Vocabulary Acquisition.* Edited by M. G. McKeown and M. E. Curtis. Hillsdale, NJ: Erlbaum Associates.

Dahl, K. L., and P. A. Freppon. 1991. "Literacy Learning in Whole Language Classrooms: An Analysis of Low-Socioeconomic Urban Children Learning to Read and Write in Kindergarten," in *Learner Factors/Teacher Factors: Issues in Literacy Research and Instruction.* Edited by J. Zutell and S. McCormick. Chicago: National Reading Conference.

Demont, E., and J. E. Gombert. 1996. "Phonological Awareness as a Predictor of Recoding Skills and Syntactic Awareness as a Predictor of Comprehension Skills," *British Journal of Psychology,* Vol. 66, 315–32.

Dickinson, D. K. 2001. "Book Reading in Preschool Classrooms: Is Recommended Practice Common?" in *Beginning Literacy with Language: Young Children Learning at Home and in School.* Edited by D. K. Dickinson and P. O. Tabors. Baltimore: Brookes Publishing.

Dickinson, D. K.; W. Hao; and Z. He. 1995. "Pedagogical and Classroom Factors Related to How Teachers Read to Three- and Four-Year-Old Children," in *NRC Yearbook.* Edited by D. J. Leu. Chicago: National Research Council.

LANGUAGE AND LITERACY

Dickinson, D. K., and R. Keebler. 1989. "Variation in Preschool Teachers' Styles of Reading Books," *Discourse Processes*, Vol. 12, 353–75.

Dickinson, D. K., and M. W. Smith. 1994. "Long-term Effects of Preschool Teachers' Book Readings on Low-Income Children's Vocabulary and Story Comprehension," *Reading Research Quarterly*, Vol. 29, No. 2, 104–22.

Dickinson, D. K., and C. E. Snow. 1987. "Interrelationships Among Prereading and Oral Language Skills in Kindergartners from Two Social Classes," *Early Childhood Research Quarterly*, Vol. 2, 1–25.

Dickinson, D. K., and P. O. Tabors. 1991. "Early Literacy: Linkages Between Home, School, and Literacy Achievement at Age Five," *Journal of Research in Childhood Education*, Vol. 6, 30–46.

Durrell, D. D. 1980. "Commentary: Letter Name Values in Reading and Spelling," *Reading Research Quarterly*, Vol. 16, 159–63.

Eccles, J. S.; A. Wigfield; and U. Schiefele. 1998. "Motivation to Succeed," in *Handbook of Child Psychology* (Vol. III: *Social, Emotional, and Personality Development*). (Fifth edition). Edited by N. Eisenberg. New York: John Wiley.

Ehri, L. C. 1979. "Linguistic Insight: Threshold of Reading Acquisition," in *Reading Research: Advances in Theory and Practice* (Vol. I). Edited by T. Waller and G. E. MacKinnon. New York: Academic Press.

Ehri, L. C. 1988. "Movement in Word Reading and Spelling: How Spelling Contributes to Reading," in *Reading and Writing Connections*. Edited by J. Mason. Newton, MA: Allyn and Bacon.

Ehri, L. C. 1991. "Learning to Read and Spell Words," in *Learning to Read: Basic Research and Its Implications*. Edited by L. Rieben and C. A. Perfetti. Hillsdale, NJ: Erlbaum Associates.

Ehri, L. C. 1995. "Phases of Development in Learning to Read Words by Sight," *Journal of Research in Reading*, Vol. 18, No. 2, 116–25.

Ehri, L. C. 1998. "Grapheme-Morpheme Knowledge Is Essential for Learning to Read Words in English," in *Word Recognition in Beginning Literacy*. Edited by J. L. Metsala and L. C. Ehri. Mahwah, NJ: Erlbaum Associates.

Elley, W. B. 1989. "Vocabulary Acquisition from Listening to Stories," *Reading Research Quarterly*, Vol. 24, 174–86.

Elley, W. B., and F. Mangubhai. 1983. "The Impact of Reading on Second Language Learning," *Reading Research Quarterly*, Vol. 19, No. 1, 53–67.

Elster, C. 1988. "Collaboration and Independence: Reading in Different Classroom Settings," *Dissertation Abstracts International*, Vol. 50, No. 08, 2440 (UMI No. 8916653).

Elster, C., and C. Walker. 1992. "Flexible Scaffolds: Shared Reading and Rereading of Story Books in Head Start Classrooms," in *Literacy Research, Theory and Practice: Views from Many Perspectives, Forty-first Yearbook of the National Reading Conference*. Edited by C. Kinzer and D. Leu. Chicago: National Reading Conference.

Estes, T. H., and J. L. Vaughan. 1973. "Reading Interest Comprehension: Implications," *Reading Teacher*, Vol. 27, 149–53.

Evans, M. A.; D. Shaw; and M. Bell. 2000. "Home Literacy Activities and Their Influence on Early Literacy Skills," *Canadian Journal of Experimental Psychology*, Vol. 54, 65–75.

Ezell, H. K., and L. M. Justice. 2000. "Increasing the Print Focus of Adult-Child Shared Book Reading Through Observational Learning," *American Journal of Speech-Language Pathology*, Vol. 9, 36–47.

Feitelson, D.; B. Kita; and Z. Goldstein. 1986. "Effects of Listening to Series Stories on First-Graders' Comprehension and Use of Language," *Research*

in the Teaching of English, Vol. 20, 339–56.

Feitelson, D., and others. 1993. "Effects of Listening to Story Reading on Aspects of Literacy Acquisition in a Diagnostic Situation," *Reading Research Quarterly*, Vol. 28, 71–79.

Ferreiro, E., and A. Teberosky. 1982. *Literacy Before Schooling*. Exeter, NH: Heinemann.

Fitzgerald, J., and D. L. Spiegel. 1983. "Enhancing Children's Reading Comprehension Through Instruction in Narrative Structure," *Journal of Reading Behavior*, Vol. 15, 1–17.

Fowler, A. E. 1991. "How Early Phonological Development Might Set the Stage for Phonological Awareness," in *Phonological Processes in Literacy: A Tribute to Isabelle Y. Liberman*. Edited by S. Brady and D. Shankweiler. Hillsdale, NJ: Erlbaum.

Fox, B., and D. K. Routh. 1975. "Analyzing Spoken Language Into Words, Syllables, and Phonemes: A Developmental Study," *Journal of Psycholinguistic Research*, Vol. 4, 331–42.

Gee, J. P. 1992. *The Social Mind: Language, Ideology, and Social Practice*. New York: Bergin and Garvey.

Genishi, C. 1988. *Young Children's Oral Language Development*. http://www.comeunity.com/disability/speech/young-children.html (accessed May 20, 2005).

Gentry, J. R. 1982. "An Analysis of Developmental Spelling in GNYS AT WRK," *The Reading Teacher*, Vol. 36, 192–200.

Gillon, G., and B. J. Dodd. 1994. "A Prospective Study of the Relationship Between Phonological, Semantic, and Syntactic Skills and Specific Reading Disability," *Reading and Writing*, Vol. 6, 321–45.

Girolametto, L., and E. Weitzman. 2002. "Responsiveness of Child Care Providers in Interactions with Toddlers and Preschoolers," *Language, Speech, and Hearing Services in Schools*, Vol. 33, 268–81.

Goswami, U. C., and P. E. Bryant. 1990. *Phonological Skills and Learning to Read*. Hove, UK: Psychology Press.

Gottfried, A. 1990. "Academic Intrinsic Motivation in Young Elementary School Children," *Journal of Educational Psychology*, Vol. 82, 525–38.

Guthrie, J. T., and others. 1996. "Concept-Oriented Reading Instruction to Develop Motivational and Cognitive Aspects of Reading," in *Developing Engaged Readers in School and Home Communities*. Edited by L. Baker; P. Afflerbach; and D. Reinking. Mahwah, NJ: Erlbaum Associates.

Guthrie, J. T.; A. Wigfield; and C. Von Secker. 2000. "Effects of Integrated Instruction on Motivation and Strategy Use in Reading," *Journal of Educational Psychology*, Vol. 92, No. 2, 331–41.

Gutierrez-Clellen, V. F., and A. Iglesias. 1992. "Causal Coherence in the Oral Narratives of Spanish-Speaking Children," *Journal of Speech and Hearing Research*, Vol. 35, 363–72.

Harste, J. C.; V. A. Woodward; and C. L. Burke. 1984. "Examining Our Assumptions: A Transactional View of Literacy and Learning," *Research in the Teaching of English*, Vol. 18, No. 1, 84–108.

Hart, B., and T. Risley. 1995. *Meaningful Differences in the Everyday Experiences of Young American Children*. Baltimore: Brookes Publishing.

Hayes, D. P., and M. Ahrens. 1988. "Vocabulary Simplification for Children: A Special Case of 'Motherese'?" *Journal of Child Language*, Vol. 15, 395–410.

Heath, S. B. 1982. "What No Bedtime Story Means: Narrative Skills at Home and School," *Language in Society*, Vol. 11, 49–76.

Heath, S. B. 1983. *Ways with Words: Language, Life, and Work in Communities and Classrooms*. Cambridge, UK: Cambridge University Press.

Hidi, S. 1990. "Interest and Its Contribution as a Mental Resource for Learning," *Review of Educational Research,* Vol. 60, 549–71.

Hidi, S. 2001. "Interest, Reading, and Learning: Theoretical and Practical Considerations," *Educational Psychology Review,* Vol. 13, 191–209.

Hidi, S., and W. Baird. 1986. "Interestingness—A Neglected Variable in Discourse Processing," *Cognitive Science,* Vol. 10, 179–94.

Hidi, S., and W. Baird. 1988. "Strategies for Increasing Text-Based Interest and Students' Recall of Expository Text," *Reading Research Quarterly,* Vol. 23, 465–83.

Hoff, E. 2004. "Language Use Does Not Always Reflect Language Knowledge," Poster presented to the 18th Biennial Meeting of the International Society for Research in Behavioral Development, Ghent, Belgium, July 11–15, 2004.

Hoff, E. 2005. *Language Development* (Third edition). Belmont, CA: Wadsworth.

Holdaway, D. 1986. "Guiding a Natural Process," in *Roles in Literacy Learning.* Edited by D. R. Tovey and J. E. Kerber. Newark, DE: International Reading Association.

Huttenlocher, J., and others. 2002. "Language Input and Child Syntax," *Cognitive Psychology,* Vol. 45, No. 3, 337–74.

*Improving Schooling for Language-Minority Children: A Research Agenda.* 1997. Edited by D. August and K. Hakuta. Washington, DC: National Academies Press.

Jusczyk, P. W. 1995. "Language Acquisition: Speech Sounds and the Beginning of Phonology," in *Speech, Language, and Communication.* Edited by J. L. Miller and P. D. Eimas. San Diego: Academic Press.

Justice, L. M., and H. K. Ezell. 2000. "Stimulating Children's Print and Word Awareness Through Home-Based Parent Intervention," *American Journal of Speech-Language Pathology,* Vol. 9, 257–69.

Justice, L. M., and H. K. Ezell. 2002. "Use of Storybook Reading to Increase Print Awareness in At-Risk Children," *American Journal of Speech-Language Pathology,* Vol. 11, 17–29.

Justice, L. M.; J. Meier; and S. Walpole. 2005. "Learning New Words from Storybooks: Findings from an Intervention with At-Risk Kindergarteners," *Language, Speech, and Hearing Services in Schools,* Vol. 36, 17–32.

Justice, L. M., and others. 2003. "Emergent Literacy Intervention for Vulnerable Preschoolers: Relative Effects of Two Approaches," *American Journal of Speech-Language Pathology,* Vol. 12, 320–32.

Justice, L. M., and others. 2005. "Preschoolers, Print, and Storybooks: An Observational Study Using Eye-Gaze Analysis," *Journal of Research in Reading,* Vol. 28, No. 3, 229–43.

Justice, L. M., and others. 2006. "An Investigation of Four Hypotheses Concerning the Order by Which Four-Year-Old Children Learn the Alphabet Letters," *Early Childhood Research Quarterly,* Vol. 21, No. 3, 374–89.

Karweit, N. 1989. "The Effects of a Story-Reading Program on the Vocabulary and Story Comprehension Skills of Disadvantaged Prekindergarten and Kindergarten Students," *Early Education and Development,* Vol. 1, 105–14.

Kintsch, W. 1980. "Learning from Text, Levels of Comprehension, or: Why Anyone Would Read a Story Anyway," *Poetics,* Vol. 9, 87–89.

Krapp, A.; S. Hidi; and A. Renniger. 1992. "Interest, Learning and Development," in *The Role of Interest in Learning and Development.* Edited by R. A. Renniger; S. Hidi; and A. Krapp. Hillsdale, NJ: Erlbaum Associates.

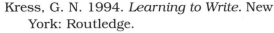

Kress, G. N. 1994. *Learning to Write.* New York: Routledge.

Landauer, T. K., and S. T. Dumais. 1997. "A Solution to Plato's Problem: The Latent Semantic Analysis Theory of Acquisition, Induction, and Representation of Knowledge," *Psychological Review,* Vol. 104, 211–40.

Landry, S. In press. *Handbook of Research and Early Literacy Development.* New York: Gilford Press.

Landry, S. H., and others. 1997. "Predicting Cognitive-Language and Social Growth Curves from Early Maternal Behaviors in Children at Varying Degrees of Biological Risk," *Developmental Psychology,* Vol. 33, 1040–53.

Leppäen, U., and others. 2004. "Development of Reading Skills Among Preschool and Primary School Pupils," *Reading Research Quarterly,* Vol. 39, No. 1, 72–93.

Lesiak, J. L. 1997. "Research-Based Answers to Questions About Emergent Literacy in Kindergarten," *Psychology in the Schools,* Vol. 34, 143–60.

Liberman, I. Y., and others. 1974. "Explicit Syllable and Phoneme Segmentation in the Young Child," *Journal of Experimental Child Psychology,* Vol. 18, 201–12.

Lonigan, C. J. 1994. "Reading to Preschoolers Exposed: Is the Emperor Really Naked?" *Developmental Review,* Vol. 14, 303–23.

Lonigan, C. J. 2004. "Family Literacy and Emergent Literacy Programs," in *Handbook on Family Literacy: Research and Services.* Edited by B. Wasik. Hillsdale, NJ: Erlbaum Associates.

Lonigan, C. 2006. "Conceptualizing Phonological Processing Skills in Pre-Readers," in *Handbook of Early Literacy Research* (Vol. II). Edited by D. Dickinson and S. B. Neuman. New York: Guilford Press.

Lonigan, C. J., and others. 1998. Development of Phonological Sensitivity in Two- to Five-Year-Old Children,"

*Journal of Educational Psychology,* Vol. 90, 294–311.

Lonigan, C. J.; S. R. Burgess; and J. L. Anthony. 2000. "Development of Emergent Literacy and Early Reading Skills in Preschool Children: Evidence from a Latent Variable Longitudinal Study," *Developmental Psychology,* Vol. 36, 596–613.

MacLean, M.; P. Bryant; and L. Bradley. 1987. "Rhymes, Nursery Rhymes, and Reading in Early Childhood," *Merrill-Palmer Quarterly,* Vol. 33, 255–82.

Martinez, M., and W. Teale. 1993. "Teacher Storybook Reading Style: A Comparison of Six Teachers," *Research in the Teaching of English,* Vol. 27, 175–99.

Marvin, C., and P. Mirenda. 1993. "Home Literacy Experiences of Preschoolers in Head Start and Special Education Programs," *Journal of Early Intervention,* Vol. 17, 351–67.

Mason, J. M. 1980. "When Children Do Begin to Read: An Exploration of Four-Year-Old Children's Letter and Word Reading Competencies," *Reading Research Quarterly,* Vol. 15, 203–27.

Mason, J. M. 1992. "Reading Stories to Preliterate Children: A Proposed Connection to Reading," in *Reading Acquisition.* Edited by P. B. Gough; L. C. Ehri; and R. Treiman. Hillsdale, NJ: Erlbaum Associates.

Mason, J. M., and J. Allen. 1986. "A Review of Emergent Literacy with Implications for Research and Practice in Reading," *Review of Research in Education,* Vol. 13, 3–38.

Mathewson, G. C. 1994. "Toward a Comprehensive Model of Affect in the Reading Process," in *Theoretical Models and Processes of Reading* (Third edition). Edited by H. Singer and R. B. Ruddell. Newark, DE: International Reading Association.

McGee, L. M., and D. J. Richgels. 1990. *Literacy's Beginnings: Supporting Young Readers and Writers,* Boston: Allyn and Bacon.

LANGUAGE AND LITERACY

McGregor, K. K., and others. 2002. "Semantic Representations and Naming in Young Children," *Journal of Speech, Language, and Hearing Research,* Vol. 45, 332–46.

McKenna, M. C.; D. J. Kear; and R. A. Ellsworth. 1995. "Children's Attitudes Toward Reading: A National Survey," *Reading Research Quarterly,* Vol. 30, No. 4, 934–55.

McKeown, M. G. 1985. "The Acquisition of Word Meaning from Context by Children of High and Low Ability," *Reading Research Quarterly,* Vol. 20, No. 4, 482–96.

Metsala, J. L., and A. C. Walley. 1998. "Spoken Vocabulary Growth and the Segmental Restructuring of Lexical Representations: Precursors to Phonemic Awareness and Early Reading Ability," in *Word Recognition in Beginning Literacy.* Edited by J. L. Metsala and L. C. Ehri. Mahwah, NJ: Erlbaum Associates.

Miller, G. A., and P. M. Gildea. 1987. "How Children Learn Words," *Scientific American,* Vol. 257, No. 3, 94–99.

Morrow, L. M. 1984. "Reading Stories to Young Children: Effects of Story Structure and Traditional Questioning Strategies on Comprehension," *Journal of Reading Behavior,* Vol. 16, 273–87.

Morrow, L. M. 1988. "Young Children's Responses to One-to-One Story Readings in School Settings," *Reading Research Quarterly,* Vol. 23, 89–106.

Morrow, L. M., and J. K. Smith. 1990. "The Effects of Group Size on Interactive Storybook Reading," *Reading Research Quarterly,* Vol. 25, 213–31.

Nagy, W. E., and R. C. Anderson. 1984. "How Many Words Are There in Printed School English?" *Reading Research Quarterly,* Vol. 19, 304–30.

Nagy, W. E., and P. A. Herman. 1987. "Breadth and Depth of Vocabulary Knowledge: Implications for Acquisition and Instruction," in *The Nature of Vocabulary Acquisition.* Edited by M. McKeown and M. Curtis. Mahwah, NJ: Erlbaum Associates.

Nagy, W. E.; P. Herman; and R. Anderson. 1985. "Learning Words from Context," *Reading Research Quarterly,* Vol. 19, 304–30.

Nash, M., and M. L. Donaldson. 2005. "Word Learning in Children with Vocabulary Deficits," *Journal of Speech, Language, and Hearing Research,* Vol. 48, 439–58.

Nation, K., and M. J. Snowling. 1998. "Semantic Processing and the Development of Word-Recognition Skills: Evidence from Children with Reading Comprehension Difficulties," *Journal of Memory and Language,* Vol. 39, 85–101.

Neuman, S. B., and K. Roskos. 1993. *Language and Literacy Learning in the Early Years.* Fort Worth, TX: Harcourt Brace.

Owens, R. E. 1996. *Language Development: An Introduction* (Fourth edition). Boston: Allyn and Bacon.

Owens, R. E. 1999. *Language Disorders: A Functional Approach to Assessment and Intervention* (Third edition). Boston: Allyn and Bacon.

Paris, A. H., and S. G. Paris. 2003. "Assessing Narrative Competence in Young Children," *Reading Research Quarterly,* Vol. 38, 36–42.

Paris, S. G., and C. E. van Kraayenoord. 1998. "Assessing Young Children's Literacy Strategies and Development," in *Global Prospects for Education: Development, Culture, and Schooling.* Edited by S. Paris and H. Wellman. Washington, DC: American Psychological Association.

Pellegrini, A. D., and others. 1995. "Joint Reading Between Mothers and Their Head Start Children: Vocabulary Development in Two Text Formats," *Discourse Processes,* Vol. 19, 441–63.

Perfetti, C. A.; J. Van Dyke; and L. Hart. 2001. "The Psycholinguistics of Basic Literacy," *Annual Review of Applied Linguistics,* Vol. 21, 127–49.

LANGUAGE AND LITERACY

Peterson, C. 1990. "The Who, When, and Where of Early Narratives," *Journal of Child Language*, Vol. 17, 433–55.

Phillips, S. U. 1983. *The Invisible Culture.* New York: Longman.

Piaget, J. 1962. *Comments on Vygotsky's Critical Remarks Concerning the Language and Thought of the Child, and Judgment and Reasoning in the Child.* Boston: MIT Press.

Pintrich, P. R., and D. H. Schunk. 1996. *Motivation in Education: Theories, Research, and Application.* Engelwood Cliffs, NJ: Merrill Prentice Hall.

Prather, E. M.; D. L. Hendrick; and C. A. Kern. 1975. "Articulation Development in Children Aged Two to Four Years," *Journal of Speech and Hearing Disorders,* Vol. 40, 179–91.

*Preventing Reading Difficulties in Young Children.* 1998. Edited by C. E. Snow; M. S. Burns; and P. Griffin. Washington, DC: National Academies Press.

Purcell-Gates, V. 1988. "Lexical and Syntactic Knowledge of Written Narrative Held by Well-Read-To Kindergartners and Second Graders," *Research in the Teaching of English*, Vol. 22, 128–60.

Purcell-Gates, V. 1996. "Stories, Coupons, and the *TV Guide:* Relationships Between Home Literacy Experience and Emergent Literacy Knowledge," *Reading Research Quarterly*, Vol. 31, 406–28.

Purcell-Gates, V., and K. L. Dahl. 1991. "Low-SES Children's Success and Failure at Early Literacy Learning in Skills-Based Classrooms," *Journal of Reading Behavior,* Vol. 23, No. 1, 1–34.

Purcell-Gates, V.; E. McIntyre; and P. A. Freppon. 1995. "Learning Written Storybook Language in School: A Comparison of Low-SES Children in Skills-Based and Whole Language Classrooms," *American Educational Research Journal,* Vol. 32, 659–85.

Raz, I. S., and P. Bryant. 1990. "Social Background, Phonological Awareness, and Children's Reading," *British Journal of Developmental Psychology,* Vol. 8, 209–25.

Read, C. 1975. *Children's Categorization of Speech Sounds in English.* Urbana, IL: National Council of Teachers of English.

Renninger, K. A., and R. H. Wozniak. 1985. "Effect of Interest on Attention Shift, Recognition, and Recall in Young Children," *Developmental Psychology,* Vol. 21, 624–32.

*Report of the National Reading Panel: Teaching Children to Read: An Evidence-Based Assessment of the Scientific Research Literature on Reading and Its Implications for Reading Instruction.* 2000. NIH Publication No. 00-4769. Washington, DC: National Institute of Child Health and Human Development.

Reutzel, D. R.; L. K. Oda; and B. H. Moore. 1989. "Developing Print Awareness: The Effects of Three Instructional Approaches on Kindergarteners' Print Awareness, Reading Readiness, and Word Reading," *Journal of Reading Behavior,* Vol. 21, 197–217.

Scanlon, D. M., and F. R. Vellutino. 1996. "Prerequisite Skills, Early Instruction, and Success in First Grade Reading: Selected Results from a Longitudinal Study," *Mental Retardation and Developmental Disabilities Research Review,* Vol. 2, 54–63.

Scarborough, H. S. 1998. "Early Identification of Children at Risk for Reading Disabilities: Phonological Awareness and Some Other Promising Predictors," in *Specific Reading Disability: A View of the Spectrum.* Edited by B. K. Shapiro; P. J. Accardo; and A. J. Capute. Timonium, MD: York Press.

Scarborough, H. S., and W. Dobrich. 1994. "On the Efficacy of Reading to Preschoolers," *Developmental Review,* Vol. 14, 245–302.

Schank, R. C. 1979. "Interestingness: Controlling Inferences," *Artificial Intelligence,* Vol. 12, 273–97.

Schiefflin, B. B., and M. Cochran-Smith. 1984. "Learning to Read Culturally: Literacy Before Schooling," in *Awakening to Literacy*. Edited by H. Goelman; A. Oberg; and F. Smith. Portsmouth, NH: Heinemann.

Schraw, G.; R. Bruning; and C. Svoboda. 1995. "Sources of Situational Interest," *Journal of Reading Behavior,* Vol. 27, 1–17.

Schultz, G. F., and H. N. Switzky. 1993. "The Development of Intrinsic Motivation in Students with Learning Problems: Instructional Implications and Options," in *Educational Psychology Annual Editions* (Seventh edition). Edited by W. Cauley; F. Linder; and J. McMillan. Guilford, CT: Dushkin Publishing Group.

Sénéchal, M., and others. 1998. "Differential Effects of Home Literacy Experiences on the Development of Oral and Written Language," *Reading Research Quarterly,* Vol. 13, 96–116.

Sénéchal, M.; E. Thomas; and J. Monker. 1995. "Individual Differences in Four-Year-Old Children's Acquisition of Vocabulary During Storybook Reading," *Journal of Educational Psychology,* Vol. 87, 218–29.

Share, D. L., and others. 1984. "Source of Individual Differences in Reading Acquisition," *Journal of Educational Psychology,* Vol. 76, 1309–24.

Share, D. L., and P. Silva. 1987. "Language Deficits and Specific Reading Retardation: Cause or Effect?" *British Journal of Disorders of Communication,* Vol. 22, 219–26.

Snow, C. E. 1983. "Literacy and Language: Relationships During the Preschool Years," *Harvard Educational Review,* Vol. 53, 165–89.

Snow, C. E., and others. 1991. *Unfulfilled Expectations: Home and School Influences on Literacy.* Cambridge, MA: Harvard University Press.

Stahl, S. A. 1999. *Vocabulary Development.* Cambridge, MA: Brookline Press.

Stanovich, K. E., and A. E. Cunningham. 1992. "Studying the Consequences of Literacy Within a Literate Society: The Cognitive Correlates of Print Exposure," *Memory and Cognition,* Vol. 20, 51–68.

Stanovich, K. E., and A. E. Cunningham. 1993. "Where Does Knowledge Come From? Specific Associations Between Print Exposure and Information Acquisition," *Journal of Educational Psychology,* Vol. 85, 211–29.

Stanovich, K. E.; A. E. Cunningham; and D. J. Freeman. 1984. "Intelligence, Cognitive Skills, and Early Reading Progress," *Reading Research Quarterly,* Vol. 19, 278–303.

Sternberg, R. J. 1987. "Most Vocabulary Is Learned from Context," in *The Nature of Vocabulary Acquisition.* Edited by M. G. McKeown and M. E. Curtis. Hillsdale, NJ: Erlbaum Associates.

Stevenson, H. W., and R. S. Newman. 1986. "Long-Term Prediction of Achievement and Attitudes in Mathematics and Reading," *Child Development,* Vol. 57, 646–59.

Stuart, M. 1995. "Prediction and Qualitative Assessment of Five- and Six-Year-Old Children's Reading: A Longitudinal Study," *British Journal of Educational Psychology,* Vol. 65, 287–96.

Sulzby, E. 1985. "Children's Emergent Abilities to Read Favorite Storybooks: A Developmental Study," *Reading Research Quarterly,* Vol. 20, 458–81.

Sulzby, E. 1986. "Writing and Reading: Signs of Oral and Written Language Organization in the Young Child," in *Emergent Literacy: Reading and Writing.* Edited by W. H. Teale and E. Sulzby. Norwood, NJ: Ablex Publishing.

Sulzby, E. 1987. "Children's Development of Prosodic Distinctions in Telling and Dictation Modes," in *Writing in Real Time: Modeling Production Processes.* Edited by A. Matsuhashi. Westport, CT: Ablex Publishing.

LANGUAGE AND LITERACY

Swanborn, M. S. L., and K. De Glopper. 1999. "Incidental Word Learning While Reading: A Meta-Analysis," *Review of Educational Research,* Vol. 69, 261–85.

Tamis-LeMonda, C. S.; M. H. Bornstein; and L. Baumwell. 2001. "Maternal Responsiveness and Children's Achievement of Language Milestones," *Child Development,* Vol. 72, No. 3, 748–67.

Taylor, D., and C. Dorsey-Gaines. 1988. *Growing Up Literate: Learning From Inner-City Families.* Portsmouth, NH: Heinemann.

Teale, W. H. 1987. "Emergent Literacy: Reading and Writing Development in Early Childhood," in *Research in Literacy: Merging Perspectives—Thirty-Sixth Yearbook of the National Reading Conference.* Edited by J. Readence and R. S. Baldwin. Rochester, NY: National Reading Conference.

Teale, W. H., and M. Martinez. 1986. "Teachers' Storybook Reading Styles: Evidence and Implications," *Reading Education in Texas,* Vol. 2, 7–16.

Temple, C., and others. 1993. *The Beginnings of Writing.* Boston: Allyn and Bacon.

Templin, M. C. 1957. *Certain Language Skills in Children: Their Development and Interrelationships.* Minneapolis: University of Minnesota Press.

Torgesen, J. K., and C. Davis. 1996. "Individual Difference Variables That Predict Response to Training in Phonological Awareness," *Journal of Experimental Child Psychology,* Vol. 63, 1–21.

Treiman, R. 1992. "The Role of Intrasyllabic Units in Learning to Read and Spell," in *Reading Acquisition.* Edited by P. B. Gough; L. C. Ehri; and R. Treiman. Hillsdale, NJ: Erlbaum Associates.

Treiman, R., and V. Broderick. 1998. "What's in a Name: Children's Knowledge About the Letters in Their Own Names," *Journal of Experimental Child Psychology,* Vol. 70, 97–116.

Tunmer, W. E.; M. L. Herriman; and A. R. Nesdale. 1988. "Metalinguistic Abilities and Beginning Reading," *Reading Research Quarterly,* Vol. 23, 134–58.

Tunmer, W. E., and A. R. Nesdale. 1985. "Phonemic Segmentation and Beginning Reading," *Journal of Educational Psychology,* Vol. 77, 418–27.

Umiker-Sebeok, D. 1979. "Preschool Children's Intraconversational Narratives," *Journal of Child Language,* Vol. 6, 91–109.

Valdez-Menchaca, M. C., and G. J. Whitehurst. 1992. "Accelerating Language Development Through Picture Book Reading: A Systematic Extension to Mexican Day-Care," *Developmental Psychology,* Vol. 28, 1106–14.

van Kleeck, A. 1990. "Emergent Literacy: Learning About Print Before Learning to Read," *Topics in Language Disorders,* Vol. 10, 25–45.

Vellutino, F. R.; D. M. Scanlon; and M. S. Tanzman. 1991. "Bridging the Gap Between Cognitive and Neuropsychological Conceptualizations of Reading Disability," *Learning and Individual Differences,* Vol. 3, 181–203.

Wagner, R. K.; J. K. Torgesen; and C. A. Rashotte. 1994. "Development of Reading-Related Phonological Processing Abilities: New Evidence of Bidirectional Causality from a Latent Variable Longitudinal Study," *Developmental Psychology,* Vol. 30, 73–87.

Wagner, R. K., and others. 1997. "Changing Relations Between Phonological Processing Abilities and Word-Level Reading as Children Develop from Beginning to Skilled Readers: A Five-Year Longitudinal Study," *Developmental Psychology,* Vol. 33, 468–79.

Walley, A. C. 1993. "The Role of Vocabulary Development in Children's Spoken Word Recognition and Segmentation Ability," *Developmental Review,* Vol. 13, 286–350.

Walsh, D. J.; G. G. Price; and M. G. Gillingham. 1988. "The Critical but

Transitory Importance of Letter-Naming," *Reading Research Quarterly,* Vol. 23, 108–22.

Weir, B. 1989. "A Research Base for Prekindergarten Literacy Programs," *The Reading Teacher,* Vol. 42, No. 7, 456–60.

Wells, G. 1985a. *Language, Learning, and Education.* Philadelphia: NFER Nelson.

Wells, G. 1985b. *Language Development in the Preschool Years.* New York: Cambridge University Press.

West, R. F., and K. E. Stanovich. 1991. "The Incidental Acquisition of Information from Reading," *Psychological Science,* Vol. 2, No. 5, 325–29.

Whitehurst, G. J. 1997. "Language Processes in Context: Language Learning in Children Reared in Poverty," in *Research on Communication and Language Disorders: Contribution to Theories of Language Development.* Edited by L. B. Adamson and M. A. Romski. Baltimore: Brookes Publishing.

Whitehurst, G. J., and others. 1988. "Accelerating Language Development Through Picture Book Reading," *Developmental Psychology,* Vol. 24, 552–59.

Whitehurst, G. J., and C. J. Lonigan. 1998. "Child Development and Emergent Literacy," *Child Development,* Vol. 69, 848–72.

Whitehurst, G. J., and C. J. Lonigan. 2001. "Emergent Literacy: Development from Prereaders to Readers," in *Handbook of Early Literacy Research.* Edited by S. B. Neuman and D. K. Dickinson. New York: Guilford Press.

Wigfield, A., and J. T. Guthrie. 1997. "Relations of Children's Motivation for Reading to the Amount and Breadth of Their Reading," *Journal of Educational Psychology,* Vol. 89, 420–32.

Woodward, A.; E. Markham; and C. Fitzsimmons. 1994. "Rapid Word Learning in 13- and 18-Month-Olds," *Developmental Psychology,* Vol. 30, 553–66.

Yussen, S., and N. M. Ozcan. 1996. "The Development of Knowledge About Narratives," *Issues in Education,* Vol. 2, 1–6.

LANGUAGE AND LITERACY

FOUNDATIONS IN
# English-Language Development

California is experiencing a dramatic increase in the number of children from birth to five years of age whose home language is not English. Currently, one in four California students—25 percent—in kindergarten through grade twelve are identified as English learners (California Department of Education [CDE] 2006a, b). The term "English learners" refers to children whose first language is not English and encompasses children learning English for the first time in the preschool setting as well as children who have developed various levels of English proficiency (Rivera and Collum 2006). For the majority of these children, Spanish is the home language, followed by Vietnamese, Cantonese, Hmong, Tagalog, Korean, and other languages (CDE 2006a). Whereas 25 percent of California children in kindergarten through grade twelve are identified as English learners, English learners represent 39 percent of children in California between three and five years of age (Children Now 2007).

Given this reality, the development of preschool learning foundations must take into consideration how young children whose home language is not English negotiate learning in all content and curricular areas. For all children, the home language is the vehicle by which they are socialized into their families and communities. Children's identity and sense of self are inextricably linked to the language they speak and the culture in which they have been socialized, which takes place in a specific family context (Crago 1988; Johnston and Wong 2002; Ochs and Schieffelin 1995; Vasquez, Pease-Alvarez, and Shannon 1994). In addition, in most families, children are first introduced to language and literacy in the home language, and those experiences provide an important foundation for success in learning literacy in English (Durgunoglu and Öney 2000; Jiménez, García, and Pearson 1995; Lanauze and Snow 1989; Lopez and Greenfield 2004).

Researchers have documented the fragility of a child's home language and cultural practices when they do not represent the mainstream or are not highly valued. Genesee, Paradis, and Crago (2004) caution that, "dual-language children are particularly at risk for both cultural and linguistic identity displacement." Loss of the home language may diminish parent-child communication, reducing a parent's ability to transmit familial values, beliefs, and understandings (Wong Fillmore 1991b), all of which form an important part of a young child's socialization and identity. Regardless of which language or languages young children are exposed to at home, they have, at best, only partially mastered the language when they enter the preschool setting (Bialystok 2001). The extent to which a child's home language and home culture can be included in the preschool classroom as a resource impacts a child's sense of self-efficacy and social and cognitive development (Chang and others 2007; Duke and Purcell-Gates 2003; Moll 1992; Riojas-Cortez 2001; *Vygotsky and Education* 1990).

The development of language and literacy skills in a child's first language is important for the development of skills in a second language and, therefore, should be considered the first step in the range of expectations for children learning English as a second language (International Reading Association and National Association for the Education of Young Children 1998). Learning by these children is not confined to one language. Children who have the skills to understand and communicate in their home language will transfer that knowledge to their learning of a second language, resulting in a more effective and efficient second-language learning process (Cummins 1979; Wong Fillmore 1991a). For example, building Spanish-speaking children's language skills in their first language directly enhances their literacy development in English (Bialystok 2001; *Childhood Bilingualism* 2006; *Preventing Reading Difficulties in Young Children* 1998). The transfer of knowledge applies to the structure of language and

early literacy skills, such as concepts about print, phonological awareness, alphabet knowledge, and writing in alphabetic script (Cárdenas-Hagan, Carlson, and Pollard-Durodola 2007; Cisero and Royer 1995; Durgunoglu 2002; Durgunoglu, Nagy, and Hancin-Bhatt 1993; Gottardo and others 2001; Mumtaz and Humphreys 2001).

Recent research suggests that the development of two languages benefits the brain through the increase in density of brain tissue in areas related to language, memory, and attention (Mechelli and others 2004). Although the brain structures of bilingual children and monolingual children are similar and process language in basically the same way, bilingual children have higher rates of engagement in particular parts of the brain (Kovelman, Baker, and Petitto 2006). This increased brain activity may have long-term positive effects (Bialystok, Craik, and Ryan 2006). In addition, it is important to acknowledge the heterogeneity of the English learner population and, in particular, the parameters of variation within the population, such as the age of the child and the amount of exposure to the home language and English; the relative dominance of each language; and the similarities and differences between the two languages. These same parameters systematically affect the language and literacy development of English learners (*Childhood Bilingualism* 2006).

The preschool learning foundations in English-language development are foundations in language and literacy for preschool children whose home language is not English. These foundations for English learners are intended for use with children who arrive at preschool functioning predominantly

ENGLISH-LANGUAGE DEVELOPMENT

in their home language, not English, and set the stage for further English-language acquisition described within the foundations. These foundations are organized to align with the content categories of California's English-language development standards, which cover kindergarten through grade twelve (K–12) and are divided into the following three categories: (1) listening and speaking; (2) reading; and (3) writing. As with the K–12 standards, the preschool learning foundations in English-language development are designed to assist classroom teachers in their understanding of children's progress toward English-language proficiency. They are meant to be used along with the language and literacy foundations, not in place of them. The foundations can be demonstrated in a variety of settings, and children will often demonstrate their language abilities when engaged in authentic, natural, child-initiated activities.

## Stages of Sequential Bilingual Language Development

Children entering a preschool program with little or no knowledge of English typically move through several stages on their journey to achieving success in the second language (Tabors 1997). Both the length of time the child remains at a stage and the level of expectation for second-language learning depend on several important characteristics of the child and the child's language environment. For example, the age of a child may help determine the child's developmental level, while the child's temperament may influence her motivation to learn a new language (Genesee, Paradis, and Crago 2004; Genishi, Yung-Chan, and

Stires 2000). The first stage for young English learners occurs when they attempt to use their home language to communicate with teachers and peers (Saville-Troike 1987; Tabors 1997). During this stage, children gradually realize they are not being understood and must adapt to their new language environment.

Over time—for some children, a matter of days; for some, months—a shift occurs, and the child begins to actively attend to the new language, observing and silently processing the features of the English language. This is considered the second stage (Ervin-Tripp 1974; Hakuta 1987, Itoh and Hatch 1978; Tabors 1997). This observational period is normal in second-language learners. The children are not shutting down; rather, they are attending to the language interactions occurring around them. Typically, the child will attempt to communicate nonverbally, using gestures, facial expressions, and often some vocalizations, such as crying or laughing.

The third stage occurs when the child is ready to "go public" with the new language. The child typically masters the rhythm and the intonation of the second language as well as some key phrases, using telegraphic and formulaic speech to communicate (Tabors 1997; Wong Fillmore 1976). "Telegraphic speech" refers to the use of a few content words without functional words or specific grammatical markers. For example, a child might use one word combined with nonverbal communication, intonation, facial expressions, and so forth to communicate different ideas. So a child saying, "Up!" while pointing at a plane in the sky might mean, "Look, there's a plane!" or a child saying, "Up?" while pointing to or otherwise indicating a toy on a shelf might mean, "Can you get me that toy? I can't reach it." Formulaic speech is a related strategy that refers to children's use of memorized chunks or phrases of language without completely understanding the function of those phrases. Sometimes children add new vocabulary as well. For example, "I want _____," is a formula that allows for a host of possibilities: "I want play." "I want doll." "I want go." Children use such formulas as a strategy to expand their communication.

In the fourth stage the child is introduced to new vocabulary words and moves into the productive language stage, at which she is able to express herself by using her own words (Tabors 1997). The child demonstrates a general understanding of the rules of English and is able to apply them more accurately to achieve increasing control over the language. However, this does not mean that the child communicates as does a native speaker of the language. The child may mispronounce words as well as make errors in vocabulary choice and grammar. Such errors are indicative of the typical process of learning a language (Genesee, Paradis, and Crago 2004).

Movement through the four stages may take anywhere from six months to two years, depending on the child and the quality of that child's language environment. The stages of second-language development should be considered when determining expectations for individual children during their preschool years.

It should be noted that full fluency (e.g., comprehension, expression, reading, and writing) in any language takes anywhere from four to ten years

(Bialystok 2001; Hakuta, Butler, and Witt 2000). In addition, the speed of acquisition is influenced by a broad range of factors (Snow 2006). Therefore, for three- and four-year-old children, it is important to provide a continuum that moves them toward a reasonable, and desirable, set of language and literacy expectations that can be achieved over the span of the one to two years that a child spends in the preschool classroom.

English learners will vary substantially in their acquisition of language competencies, depending on a number of background factors (i.e., the degree of exposure to English outside the classroom, the individual child's motivation to acquire English, and so forth). Because of the wide range of language capability found in children prior to their entering school (Ehrman, Leaver, and Oxford 2003), the use of developmental markers, such as "beginning," "middle," and "later," are used to provide for a range of expectations for performance. These markers are used in the preschool learning foundations for English-language development to designate a developmental progression for children who have made significant progress toward acquisition of the home language before beginning to acquire English (sequential bilingualism) (Genesee, Paradis, and Crago 2004).

The use of these terms should not be confused with the terms "early," "middle," and "later," as used in the resource guide *Preschool English Learners: Principles and Practices to Promote Language, Literacy, and Learning* (2007) to describe typical phases of language development for children who are monolingual speakers and children who acquire two languages from birth or sometime during the first year of life (simultaneous bilingualism).

## Structure of This Domain: A Developmental Progression

The continuum of "beginning," "middle," and "later" levels provides a framework for understanding children's second-language development in listening, speaking, reading, and writing. The first and second stages of sequential bilingual language development are combined in the "beginning" level in this domain. Young English learners may demonstrate uneven development across these foundations and may show higher levels of mastery in certain areas than in others. For example, while children may be able to understand certain words in the reading and writing areas, their productive control over grammar, pronunciation, and articulation in speaking may develop last. Related to this developmental variability across particular foundation domains is the rate of progression through the continuum of "beginning," "middle," and "later." Progression through the continuum is highly contingent on the quantity and quality of language experience in both the home and the classroom. Research on the quality of preschool environments has found that learning is influenced by a number of important classroom factors (Pianta and others 2005). Chief among them are the amount and type of verbal input provided by teachers of young children (Peisner-Feinberg and others 2001). Wong Fillmore and Snow (2000) point out that children need direct and frequent interaction with individuals who know the second language very well and can provide the English learner accurate feedback.

## Beginning Level

This is when typically developing children will have acquired age-appropriate language skills in their home language and, once introduced to English, will begin to develop receptive English abilities. Children at this level are actively processing the features of the English language, including vocabulary, grammar, phonology, and pragmatics. Most children speak little during this stage. They may be able to listen, point, match, move, draw, copy, mime, act out, choose, respond with gestures, and follow predictable routines. They will begin to develop an understanding of English based on their home language. Frequently, children will spontaneously use their home language even when not understood.

## Middle Level

Expressive language marks the middle level of early speech production in English. Children may repeat familiar phrases that have been functionally effective, such as "lookit" or "Iwant" throughout the day. It is expected that vocabulary use increases and that children will begin to combine words and phrases in English. Comprehension will continue to develop, and children will likely use telegraphic and formulaic speech in English. At the same time, they may continue to use their home language and may insert words from their home language into English-language utterances; this is known as code-switching and is a normal part of second-language acquisition. This period is analogous to the third stage of sequential bilingualism.

## Later Level

Children at the later level in the continuum will have much stronger comprehension skills. Children will begin to use English to learn different concepts across the curriculum. Their use of age-appropriate English grammar improves. They use their first and second languages to acquire new knowledge at home and at school. Although children are improving during this period, it should not be assumed that they have complete age-appropriate mastery of English; they are, however, able to engage in a majority of classroom activities in English. Errors in English usage are common at this point because children are continuing to experiment with the new language and are still learning its rules and structure.

## Categories of English-Language Development

The preschool learning foundations in English-language development describe a typical developmental progression for preschool English learners in four general categories: listening, speaking, reading, and writing. These foundations illustrate a developmental progression for children who come to preschool knowing very little, if any, English. As children move through this progression, they are developing the underlying linguistic knowledge needed to learn from a curriculum that is taught in a language they are just learning, English. As such, these foundations—especially the examples following each foundation—are intended to provide guidance to adults who are working to help preschool English learners gain the knowledge and skills necessary in all domains of the

California preschool learning foundations. The foundations are not meant to be assessment items or a checklist of behavioral indicators of the knowledge and skills that must be observed before a teacher can decide that the competency is present. Children are different from one another and will vary in the extent to which they demonstrate the behaviors described in the examples.

### Listening

Children's language development is based on active listening. For example, children's receptive control precedes their productive control of language. That is, they understand more than they can produce at the onset of language learning in both their home language (or languages) and English. When children understand, they exhibit gestures, behaviors, and nonverbal responses that indicate they understand what they have heard. Listening and understanding in English will depend on children's receptive comprehension in their home language. In other words, children's listening strategies in their home language will be applied to their strategies for learning English (Bialystok 2001). Overall, the development of early literacy foundations is built on the development of active listening, the social uses of language, and nonverbal communication (Scott-Little, Kagan, and Frelow 2005).

### Speaking

Within the classroom environment, daily routines and classroom rituals, such as organized circle time or peer-to-peer interaction on the playground, provide opportunities for English learners to use oral language in both

ENGLISH-LANGUAGE DEVELOPMENT

the home language and English (Genishi, Stires, and Yung-Chan 2001). Initially, children may use telegraphic and formulaic speech in English along with gestures, nonverbal behavior, and turn-taking. Then, the use of nonverbal communication, in combination with elaborated verbal communication, will mark their progress in learning a second language. When speaking, children may code-switch; that is, combine English with their home language to make themselves understood. In fact, the vast majority of instances of code-switching are systematic and follow the grammatical rules of the two languages (Allen and others 2002; Genesee and Sauve 2000; Köppe [in press]; Lanza 1997; Meisel 1994; Paradis, Nicoladis, and Genesee 2000; Vihman 1998).

Asking questions, responding to complex grammatical patterns, and making commentaries are indicators of later development. The creative use of language and creative expression through narrative also indicate a growing sophistication of formal language use. Research has found that narrative skills developed in the first language transfer to the second language (Miller and others 2006; Pearson 2002; Uccelli and Paez 2007). Young English learners can distinguish between their home language and the language used in the classroom, and this may be demonstrated by the children's use of either the home language or English when responding to their peers and teachers. It should be noted that the development of grammatical sequences varies among the different language populations, and this may influence their development of grammar in English (*Childhood Bilingualism* 2006; Huang and Hatch 1978; Yoshida 1978). For example, in Chinese there are no words that end with "-ing" as compared to English. In Spanish, the descriptive adjective is placed after the noun, whereas in English the adjective is placed before the noun. Furthermore, the development of oral language skills in a second language is closely tied to vocabulary expansion (Saunders and O'Brien 2006). In turn, English vocabulary development plays an important role in supporting later English literacy development (August and others 2005). The productive vocabulary of English learners is typically composed of nouns; as time passes, the vocabulary incorporates a wider variety of words, such as action verbs, adjectives, and adverbs (Jia and others 2006).

It is important to note that different languages possess different social conventions, or rules of how and when to use language, that reflect a culture's orientation toward the role of adults and children as conversational partners. In addition, social conventions guide a culture's use of verbal and nonverbal communication strategies (Rogoff 2003). Therefore, social conventions influence such things as a child's expectations to initiate during conversation, the amount of talk considered appropriate, and when and how to ask questions or interrupt during conversation (*Cultural Diversity and Early Education* 1994; Genishi, Stires, and Yung-Chan 2001). In addition, the narrative structure of discourse may vary in different cultures and language groups. In U.S. classrooms, narrative discourse focuses primarily on the communication of information; in other cultures and language groups, oral narrative stresses social engagement and the importance

ENGLISH-LANGUAGE DEVELOPMENT

of family interaction (Greenfield 1994; Heath 1983).

## Reading

Reading in the preschool classroom often begins as a social act that engages children in a meaningful language exchange. Reading is learned on the basis of need, purpose, and function. Children come to know the complexity of the act of reading by being read to, by reading with others, and by reading by themselves (Espinosa and Burns 2003; Halliday 2006). This culture is rich with environmental print, such as newspapers, books, and magazines; television; and home products, brand names, signs, and billboards. Increasingly, children may have access to print in their home language and in English. Thus, children may enter preschool with some knowledge of the written symbol system of their home language and its associations with real life. Children's oral language in both their home language and English will facilitate their ability to tell and retell stories. As their oral language develops, one of the first steps in reading is the development of an appreciation and enjoyment of reading. As children demonstrate an awareness that print carries meaning, they may begin to show progress in their knowledge of the alphabet in English, phonological awareness, and aspects of book handling and book reading (*Developing Literacy in Second-Language Learners* 2006; *Handbook of Early Literacy Research* 2006). Parents can assist their children on the path to competency in reading by reading to their children in their home language as well as by providing appropriate reading experiences in English (Hammer, Miccio, and Wagstaff 2003; Tabors and Snow 2001).

According to Scott-Little, Kagan, and Frelow (2005), early learning foundations in literacy should include book awareness and story sense, literature awareness and comprehension, and phonological and alphabetic awareness.

## Writing

Children come to know written language from their perspectives, and their conceptual interpretations are developmental in nature (Clay 2001; Ferreiro and Teberosky 1982). For example, children initially will begin to distinguish drawing from writing. Next they will progress to using facsimiles, or imitations, of letter shapes and will eventually use the symbols from their home language to represent meaning. Then they begin to use letters to represent meaning. These strings of letters are the beginning of the alphabetic principles that govern alphabetic languages, such as English and Spanish. Children's knowledge of the written language is facilitated by their engagement with letters and practice in writing their names on their own or with help from others (*Handbook of Early Literacy Research* 2006). Children will come to know that writing is used for different functions, that it is associated with oral language, that it names objects in their environments, that it is used to communicate ideas, and that it is used creatively to express their feelings, experiences, and needs. In the early childhood practice, the development of early literacy in writing begins with children understanding that the writing process is a mechanism to communicate their ideas, express themselves, and name objects in their world (Scott-Little, Kagan, and Frelow 2005).

Overall, the teacher plays a crucial role, providing opportunities for children to develop their oral language and literacy skills. For example, the teacher can foster development in the area of listening and speaking through the use of questioning strategies, language elaboration and feedback (Cazden 1988; Lyster and Ranta 1997), and the facilitation of informal peer interactions with monolingual English-speaking peers (Tabors 1997). Those opportunities will support children's literacy development as well. The teacher can also engage children in storybook reading, create a print-rich environment, structure opportunities to use writing for a variety of purposes, and provide other activities to further enhance literacy development (Dickinson and Tabors 2002; Espinosa and Burns 2003; Genishi, Stires, and Yung-Chan 2001).

ENGLISH-LANGUAGE DEVELOPMENT

# Listening*

## 1.0 Children listen with understanding.
### Focus: Beginning words

| Beginning | Middle | Later |
|---|---|---|
| **1.1** Attend to English oral language in both real and pretend activity, relying on intonation, facial expressions, or the gestures of the speaker. | **1.1** Demonstrate understanding of words in English for objects and actions as well as phrases encountered frequently in both real and pretend activity. | **1.1** Begin to demonstrate an understanding of a larger set of words in English (for objects and actions, personal pronouns, and possessives) in both real and pretend activity. |
| **Examples** | **Examples** | **Examples** |
| • Listens attentively and nods her head in response to the teacher's asking, "Is this your coat, Samantha?" while holding up a coat.<br><br>• Looks at a cup and nods or smiles when another child says, "More milk?" during snack time.<br><br>• Pays attention to the teacher during circle time, raising his hand when the teacher asks a question, but just looks and smiles when called upon.<br><br>• Focuses intently on English-speaking children while they are playing with blocks, dolls, puzzles, and so forth and conversing in English.<br><br>• Points to a picture of a dog on the page of a book when asked in English, "Where is the dog?" | • Upon hearing, "I'm finished" or "Good-bye," uses appropriate actions, such as waving good-bye to an English-speaking peer who says "Good-bye!" as she leaves at the end of the day.<br><br>• Goes to the door when the teacher says, "outside time."<br><br>• Stands up and gets a toy monkey from the shelf while his peers sing "Five Little Monkeys" during circle time.<br><br>• Reaches for a small carton of milk when asked by another child, "Pass the milk, please." | • In response to the teacher holding up a jacket and asking the child, "Does this belong to you? Or is it Lai's jacket?" as the children are getting ready to go outside, takes the jacket and gives it to his friend.<br><br>• While playing with a dollhouse and props with an English-speaking peer, puts the pants on the doll when the peer says, "Put the pants on the doll."<br><br>• In response to the teacher asking an open-ended question while holding up a photograph (e.g., "What could you do at this park?"), runs in place or hops.<br><br>• Responds by patting his chest and smiling when the teacher asks, "Whose hat is this?" (communicates possession)<br><br>• During small group outdoor play, responds to the teacher's input ("Throw the ball," "Kick the ball," "Catch the ball") with appropriate actions. |

* Any means available to the child for attending to and processing oral language information could be considered "listening." For example, a child might read lips or interpret facial expressions and other nonverbal gestures within the context of spoken language to develop understanding. This pertains to all examples in the foundations related to listening, even if attending to oral language is not explicitly stated.

## 1.0  Children listen with understanding.
### Focus: Requests and directions

| Beginning | Middle | Later |
|---|---|---|
| **1.2** Begin to follow simple directions in English, especially when there are contextual cues. | **1.2** Respond appropriately to requests involving one step when personally directed by others, which may occur with or without contextual cues. | **1.2** Follow directions that involve a one- or two-step sequence, relying less on contextual cues. |
| **Examples** | **Examples** | **Examples** |
| • Moves with other children to an activity area when the teacher ends morning circle time.<br>• Responds appropriately to simple requests, such as "Pass the napkins" at snack time or "Pick up the crayon."<br>• Washes his hands after seeing others do so and in response to the teacher's saying his name and gesturing to wash hands.<br>• Joins peers in line when she sees others do so during a practice emergency evacuation drill. | • Cleans up in an activity center when the teacher says, "Alicia, it's time to clean up."<br>• Sits by a peer when the peer says, "Come sit here," and points to a place on the carpet.<br>• Nods her head "yes" and runs to pick up a truck when asked by another child if she wants to play with the trucks.<br>• Raises his hand when the teacher asks, "Who wants more apple slices?" at snack time.<br>• Participates in a "Simon Says" game (e.g., jumps when the teacher says, "Simon says jump!"). | • Chooses a book and brings it to the teacher when the teacher says, "Go get a book and bring it to me. I'll read it with you."<br>• "Pours" something into a pot and stirs the "soup" in response to another child who says, "Put some milk in the soup. And stir, stir, stir," while in the kitchen area.<br>• Takes off her coat and places it in her cubby after the teacher says, "It's hot in here. Why don't you take off your coat and put it in your cubby?" |

## 1.0 Children listen with understanding.
### Focus: Basic and advanced concepts

| Beginning | Middle | Later |
|---|---|---|
| **1.3** Demonstrate an understanding of words related to basic and advanced concepts in the home language that are appropriate for the age (as reported by parents, teachers, assistants, or others, with the assistance of an interpreter if necessary). | **1.3** Begin to demonstrate an understanding of words in English related to basic concepts. | **1.3** Demonstrate an understanding of words in English related to more advanced concepts. |
| **Examples** | **Examples** | **Examples** |
| • Tells his grandfather in Hmong at the end of the day about the class trip to the petting zoo, talking about the baby animals, what they eat, what they like to do, and so forth (as heard by the bilingual assistant). <br><br> • During open house, tells her older sister in Farsi how she planted a seed that grew into a plant, after which her parents share with the teacher, "She's telling her sister Frough about her plant." <br><br> • Responds appropriately to directions relating spatial concepts in the home language (e.g., can identify which ball is bigger when shown two balls). | • When the teacher says, "It's your turn, Jorge. Go up the stairs and go down the slide," climbs the stairs and goes down the slide. <br><br> • Wearing a red T-shirt, leaves the circle for snack time in response to the teacher singing, "All the kids who are wearing red, wearing red, wearing red, all the kids who are wearing red, can go have snack." <br><br> • Passes several blocks to another child in response to that child communicating, "Let's use a lot of blocks for our castle! We need more!" <br><br> • Gives a peer the "big" baby in response to the peer communicating, "You have the little baby. I want the big baby," while playing in the dramatic play area. <br><br> • Communicates, "Ride bike," in response to the teacher asking, "What happened before you fell down?" | • After looking for his favorite toy lion in the zoo animal basket and not finding it, responds to the teacher's suggestion, "It's not on top. Look under the other animals," by reaching down deeper in the basket, finding the toy, and smiling. <br><br> • Responds appropriately to the directions, "First, wash your hands and then come to the table," at snack time. <br><br> • Brings the teacher the book from the previous day's "read-aloud" in response to the teacher's question, "Lai-Wan, can you bring me the book we read yesterday about fish?" <br><br> • Passes the bigger cup during water play when another child says, "Give me the bigger cup, please." <br><br> • Touches spilled juice and makes a face when a peer says, "Ooh, it's still sticky!" |

# Speaking*

## 1.0 Children use nonverbal and verbal strategies to communicate with others.
### Focus: Communication of needs

| Beginning | Middle | Later |
|---|---|---|
| **1.1** Use nonverbal communication, such as gestures or behaviors, to seek attention, request objects, or initiate a response from others. | **1.1** Combine nonverbal and some verbal communication to be understood by others (may code-switch—that is, use the home language and English—and use telegraphic and/or formulaic speech). | **1.1** Show increasing reliance on verbal communication in English to be understood by others. |
| **Examples** | **Examples** | **Examples** |
| • Uses gestures, such as extending the hand, pointing, tapping on a person's shoulder, or an intentional eye gaze, to get a person's attention.<br><br>• Uses her home language to express her wants and needs.<br><br>• Looks at the teacher and indicates or points to a toy she wants that is on a shelf.<br><br>• Cries or withdraws to show he is not sure how to express himself effectively (e.g., communicates discontent by grimacing or whimpering when an English-speaking peer picks up a crayon the child was using and had put down on the table).<br><br>• Uses props, photos, or drawings that represent an item to indicate her needs. | • Says memorized phrases, such as, "Let's go!" or "Come on!"<br><br>• Says in English and Spanish, "Want más! Más red paint!" (Want more! More red paint!) when she runs out of red while painting at an easel.<br><br>• Says in English and Mandarin Chinese,† "Diana 想 去 playground or 动物园。" (Diana wants to go to the playground or the zoo) when talking about weekend plans during circle time.<br><br>• Sings the routine song for an activity (e.g., "Clean up, clean up, everybody clean up!").<br><br>• Pulls the teacher's hand and communicates, "Come."<br><br>• Begins to string together words in English, such as "Me today yes," and "Mama doctor." | • Says, "Wanna wash my hands," after showing the teacher his fingers covered with glue, to which the teacher has responded, "What do you need?"<br><br>• Communicates to another child, "Help me?" or "How do you do that?" while trying to put a puzzle together.<br><br>• Communicates, "Move over. Move over some more," to another child who is sitting next to him during circle time.<br><br>• Learns new, more abstract words, such as "busy," "stinky," or "grouchy," from a story that has been repeated and is heard using that word.<br><br>• Communicates, "You have to share," when she wants a crayon another child is holding. |

\* Any means available to the child for communicating could be considered "speaking" English (e.g., Signed Exact English, American Sign Language, electronic communication devices). For some children, the home language may be a signed language (e.g., signed Spanish).

† For the English-language development foundation examples, all Chinese characters are written in the simplified writing system used in mainland China.

## 1.0  Children use nonverbal and verbal strategies to communicate with others.
### Focus: Vocabulary production

| Beginning | Middle | Later |
|---|---|---|
| **1.2** Use vocabulary in the home language that is age-appropriate (as reported by parents, teachers, assistants, or others and with the assistance of an interpreter if necessary). | **1.2** Begin to use English vocabulary, mainly consisting of concrete nouns and with some verbs and pronouns (telegraphic speech). | **1.2** Use new English vocabulary to share knowledge of concepts. |
| **Examples** | **Examples** | **Examples** |
| • As reported to the teacher by a parent or other family member, uses her home language to name familiar items at home and make requests (with assistance of interpreter if necessary), such as, "Tengo hambre" (I'm hungry) in Spanish. <br><br>• Uses his home language appropriately with other children in the dramatic play area (as heard by the bilingual assistant). <br><br>• Spontaneously uses her home language during unstructured school activities. <br><br>• Interacts with ease while using his home language with his parents during drop-off and pick-up times. | • Mouths "tar" after peers chorally say "star" when the teacher points to a picture of a star during circle time and asks, "What is this?" <br><br>• Says, "Me paint" and smiles in response to another child's statement, "I like your painting." <br><br>• Names many animals featured in the book *Brown Bear, Brown Bear, What Do You See?* after hearing it read aloud several times. <br><br>• Begins to refer to friends by their first name. <br><br>• Names common objects aloud in English, such as "juice," "blocks," and "music." | • Communicates, "My mommy had a baby. He cries, cries" when talking to a peer about a new baby brother. <br><br>• Says, "Bà ["Grandmother" in Vietnamese], come see the tadpoles! They have two legs now!" at the end of the day. <br><br>• Communicates, "I'm sticky," to a peer during an art activity that requires the use of glue. |

# 1.0 Children use nonverbal and verbal strategies to communicate with others.
## *Focus: Conversation**

| Beginning | Middle | Later |
|---|---|---|
| **1.3** Converse in the home language (as reported by parents, teachers, assistants, or others, with the assistance of an interpreter if necessary). | **1.3** Begin to converse with others, using English vocabulary but may code-switch (i.e., use the home language and English). | **1.3** Sustain a conversation in English about a variety of topics. |
| **Examples** | **Examples** | **Examples** |
| • Communicates, as follows, with a peer in their home language about the toys they have at home: Says, "I have a truck like this one," to which the peer responds, "I have one, too;" then asks "Is yours red?" to which the peer responds, "Yeah, mine is red." <br><br> • Describes what he did at school in detail at home, using his home language (as reported by a family member). <br><br> • Prefers to speak with teachers, peers, or other individuals who speak her home language. <br><br> • After attempting to play with others while using his home language, observes them quietly as they play and speak English. | • Says in English and Vietnamese, "My dì [maternal aunt] gave me," when a peer asks who has given the child a new backpack. <br><br> • Stays in the conversation with an English speaker by using the words "huh" or "what" and possibly combining those words with matching gestures and facial expressions. <br><br> • Says in English and Spanish, "Uh-oh! ¡Se cayó! [It fell] Blocks!" after a block tower tumbles down, and another child responds, "Yeah, uh-oh, it fell down." <br><br> • Responds, "Mommy and me" when a peer painting next to him asks, "What is that?" <br><br> • Says, "Play sand," to peer in sand play area after peer says, "I'm going to play in the sand." | • Converses, as follows, with a peer about their play situation in the block area, where they have built a bus, using large wooden blocks for seats: The peer says, "I want to be the driver;" to which the child responds, "I want to sit here;" the peer says, "OK;" and the child smiles. <br><br> • While playing outside, answers, "I jump and then run fast. We play ball," when the teacher asks, "What are you doing with your friend?" <br><br> • Communicates, "No, I be the daddy," in response to a peer who says, "You be the mommy," while in the dramatic play area. <br><br> • In response to the teacher, who asks during a family-style lunch, "What do you want to eat?" communicates, "Want juice and crackers and banana," then later communicates "Want more crackers." |

\* Children with oral motor involvement who may have difficulty saying words or syllables as they learn to match, synthesize, or analyze syllables and sounds may demonstrate their knowledge by indicating "yes" or "no" in response to an adult's production of sounds or words or by identifying pictures that represent the products of these manipulations.

## 1.0 Children use nonverbal and verbal strategies to communicate with others.
### Focus: Utterance length and complexity

| Beginning | Middle | Later |
|---|---|---|
| **1.4** Use a range of utterance lengths in the home language that is age-appropriate (as reported by parents, teachers, assistants, or others, with the assistance of an interpreter if necessary). | **1.4** Use two- and three-word utterances in English to communicate. | **1.4** Increase utterance length in English by adding appropriate possessive pronouns (e.g., *his, her*); conjunctions (e.g., and, or); or other elements (e.g., adjectives, adverbs). |
| **Examples** | **Examples** | **Examples** |
| • Communicates in Hmong, "I like to go to the park to play on the slide and the swings."<br>• Communicates in Tagalog, "We went to the shops with grandfather and we bought a cake. We had grandfather's birthday and there were lots of people." | • Communicates, "Me book," when she wants a particular book.<br>• Communicates, "No touch," when he does not want anyone to touch his toy.<br>• Communicates, "I want juice" or "I want crackers" or "I want apples" during snack time.<br>• Communicates, "I do letter A," while writing with markers at a table with other children. | • Communicates, "I give it to her" or "I like the little one better," while pointing to different props in the dramatic play area.<br>• Communicates, "My dog got hurt. So I take him to the doctor," while in the dramatic play area.<br>• Communicates, "I went to the park and had fun!" |

## 1.0 Children use nonverbal and verbal strategies to communicate with others.
### Focus: Grammar

| Beginning | Middle | Later |
|---|---|---|
| **1.5** Use age-appropriate grammar in the home language (e.g., plurals; simple past tense; use of subject, verb, object), sometimes with errors (as reported by parents, teachers, assistants, or others, with the assistance of an interpreter if necessary). | **1.5** Begin to use some English grammatical markers (e.g., *-ing* or plural *–s*) and, at times, apply the rules of grammar of the home language to English. | **1.5** Expand the use of different forms of grammar in English (e.g., plurals; simple past tense; use of subject, verb, and object), sometimes with errors. |
| **Examples** | **Examples** | **Examples** |
| • Says in Spanish, "Yo fui a la tienda con mi mamá y mi papá. Y compramos pan y leche." (I went to the store with my mom and my dad. And we bought bread and milk.)<br><br>• Says in Spanish, "Yo sabo." (I know.) (This is a common mistake for Spanish-speaking children, who often use "sabo" for "sé" when learning to conjugate the verb "saber" [to know]).<br><br>• Says in Mandarin Chinese, "爸爸已上班了。" (Daddy is already gone to work) to a peer in the dramatic play area (as reported by a bilingual assistant). | • Says in English, "I have two friends."<br><br>• Says, "He leaving," as a peer puts his jacket on to leave with his grandmother at the end of the day.<br><br>• Says, "There is two childrens," while pointing at a picture she drew.<br><br>• Says in Spanish and English, "Yo quiero el truck red." ("I want the truck red.") (In Spanish, the descriptive adjective is usually placed after the noun it describes.) | • Says, "I didn't weared that," while in the dramatic play area.<br><br>• Says, "She gave to me the cookie," at snack time.<br><br>• Says, "My pants is red" in response to the teacher saying, "The bear's pants are blue. What color are your pants?" while reading a book at circle time.<br><br>• While gesturing toward a peer, says, "Sarah don't want to play blocks," in response to the teacher saying, "Why don't you build a tower with her?"<br><br>• Responds, "We're playing house," when another child asks, "What are you doing?" |

## 1.0 Children use nonverbal and verbal strategies to communicate with others.
### Focus: Inquiry

| Beginning | Middle | Later |
|---|---|---|
| **1.6** Ask a variety of types of questions (e.g., "what," "why," "how," "when," and "where") in the home language (as reported by parents, teachers, assistants, or others, with the assistance of an interpreter if necessary. | **1.6** Begin to use "what" and "why" questions in English, sometimes with errors. | **1.6** Begin to use "what," "why," "how," "when," and "where" questions in more complete forms in English, sometimes with errors. |
| **Examples** | **Examples** | **Examples** |
| • Asks in Mandarin Chinese, "可不可以去阿姨家玩？" (Can I go to play at auntie's house?) or "你跟爸爸买的新的牙刷在哪里？" (Where is the new toothbrush that you bought with Daddy?), demonstrating the use of a variety of types of questions (as reported by parents or others). <br><br> • While going on a neighborhood walk, asks in Spanish, "¿Adónde vamos, maestra?" (Where are we going, teacher?) or "¿Por qué? ¿Por qué tengo que llevar mi chaqueta?" (Why? Why do I have to bring my jacket?) to a teacher who understands the child's home language. | • Asks, "Why no?" after hearing a peer say, "I don't want to go to the playground." <br><br> • Asks, "What you doing?" as he approaches a group of children playing in the sand box. <br><br> • Asks, "Why gone?" after noticing that the teacher is out for the day. <br><br> • Points to an item and asks, "What's that?" | • Says, "Why you did that?" to a peer who pours water from a pitcher at the water table. <br><br> • Says, "And what is for that?" pointing to a cement truck while on a walk in the neighborhood. <br><br> • Says, "How do you do this?" or "How do you make the sun?" to a peer who is painting at the easel next to him. <br><br> • Asks another child, "Where do you put this?" while holding up a pair of rain boots. <br><br> • Asks, "When do we go home?" or "When mommy coming?" toward the end of the school day. |

## 2.0 Children begin to understand and use social conventions in English.

### Focus: Social conventions

| Beginning | Middle | Later |
|---|---|---|
| **2.1** Use social conventions of the home language (as reported by teachers, parents, assistants, or others, with the assistance of an interpreter if necessary). | **2.1** Demonstrate a beginning understanding of English social conventions. | **2.1** Appropriately use words and tone of voice associated with social conventions in English. |
| **Examples** | **Examples** | **Examples** |
| • If considered a sign of respect in her culture, lowers gaze when speaking with an adult.<br><br>• If considered appropriate in his culture, stands in close proximity to others when engaged in conversation.<br><br>• Uses the formal form of his home language (e.g., Spanish, Korean, Japanese*) with unfamiliar adults and familiar form with relatives and friends. (In Spanish the familiar form uses "Tú" and the formal form uses "Usted" and the corresponding verb form. A child would say, "Buenos días, ¿Cómo estás?" [Good morning, how are you?] [informal] to a peer, but to a teacher, "Buenos días, ¿Cómo está usted, maestra?" [Good morning, how are you, teacher?] [formal]. In Japanese, the formal uses "desu," and the informal does not use it. A child says to a classmate, "Ohayoo" [good morning] [informal] but to a teacher, "Ohayoo gozaimasu" [good morning] [formal].) | • Communicates "please" and "thank you" during snack time after observing other children saying "please" to request food and "thank you" when receiving food.<br><br>• Communicates, "Hi!" or "Hello!" to greet the teacher when arriving at school.<br><br>• Responds, "Thank you," to a peer who has said, "That's pretty," while pointing to the child's painting. | • Says, "Close the door," to a peer while playing with doll-house props; follows up with, "Pleeease!" if the peer does not respond.<br><br>• Communicates, "Sorry" or "Excuse me" when she bumps into a peer.<br><br>• If another child gets hurt, asks, "Are you OK?" with a concerned tone of voice.<br><br>• Uses the slang, idioms, and colloquialisms of peers, such as, "I have to go potty." |

\* In this example, Japanese is phonologically represented in written form using the English alphabet.

### 3.0 Children use language to create oral narratives about their personal experiences.*
#### Focus: Narrative development

| Beginning | Middle | Later |
|---|---|---|
| **3.1** Create a narrative in the home language (as reported by parents, teachers, assistants, or others, with the assistance of an interpreter if necessary). | **3.1** Begin to use English to talk about personal experiences; may complete a narrative in the home language while using some English (i.e., code-switching). | **3.1** Produce simple narratives in English that are real or fictional. |
| **Examples** | **Examples** | **Examples** |
| • Talks to other children in Spanish about a family gathering: "Vino mi abuelita. Y vino mi tía. Y vino mi tío. Y comimos sopa. Y me quemé la boca. Y mi mami me dio hielo pa' que no me doliera." (My grandma came. And my aunt came. And my uncle came. And we ate soup. And I burned my mouth. And my mom gave me some ice so it wouldn't hurt) (as reported by a parent).<br><br>• Says in Mandarin Chinese, "我就去了飞机场, 坐飞机, 看奶奶。" (So I went to the airport, got on an airplane, and visited grandma.) (as reported by the bilingual assistant). | • Talks in English and Spanish about what she saw on the recent nature walk: "I see bird. I see bug, y una mariposa muy bonita. Y regresamos a la escuela." (A butterfly, really pretty. And we went back to school.)<br><br>• Draws a picture of her family and says in English and Vietnamese, "Bà (grandma), ba (dad), mẹ (mom). We go park. Lotta fun." | • Dictates a story to the teacher, gesturing with his hands, "The pony was big. The pony flew. Flew up into the sky. Really, really high!" after painting a pony sitting on a cloud.<br><br>• Draws a lizard and tells the teacher about a lizard she found outside, "I saw a lizard outside. It was a baby lizard. He didn't have a tail. He ran away."<br><br>• Tells the teacher about a conflict that came up while playing "family" with two peers, "I was the mommy and Mai was the baby. I told her to sleep and be quiet. But she not listen. I got mad at her."<br><br>• Draws a picture and tells a peer, "Look, the car goes fast. And the bus goes fast. The police say, 'Stop!'" |

* Producing narratives many vary at these ages for children who are communicating through sign language or other alternate communication systems. Teachers can support all young children's communication knowledge and skills by repeating and extending what children communicate in conversations. Teachers can also provide opportunities for children to repeat or tell stories as a way of encouraging them to produce narratives.

ENGLISH-LANGUAGE DEVELOPMENT

# Reading

## 1.0 Children demonstrate an appreciation and enjoyment of reading and literature.
### Focus: Participate in read-aloud activity

| Beginning | Middle | Later |
|---|---|---|
| **1.1** Attend to an adult reading a short storybook written in the home language or a storybook written in English if the story has been read in the home language. | **1.1** Begin to participate in reading activities, using books written in English when the language is predictable. | **1.1** Participate in reading activities, using a variety of genres that are written in English (e.g., poetry, fairy tales, concept books, and informational books). |
| **Examples** | **Examples** | **Examples** |
| • Moves closer in an attempt to see props as the teacher reviews the English vocabulary before reading a story and then reads the story aloud. <br><br> • Attends to the story and responds to questions when a storybook written in her home language is read aloud in a small group by a visiting parent who speaks the home language. <br><br> • Looks at the teacher's hand and pages in the book as teacher uses a mouse puppet during a read-aloud of a book about mice. <br><br> • Points to familiar objects and names them in the home language while the teacher reads aloud, in English, a book that she read aloud in the child's home language the day before. <br><br> • Responds in relation to the teacher and peers during a big-book read-aloud at circle time (e.g., laughs along with others). | • Responds with other children to questions in the text, using appropriate animal names during a class read-aloud of *Brown Bear, Brown Bear, What Do You See?* <br><br> • Communicates, "honk, honk, honk" when the teacher pauses after saying, "The horn on the bus goes . . . " while reading *The Wheels on the Bus.* <br><br> • Counts "one, two, three, four" with the group when the teacher counts the number of strawberries illustrated on a page. <br><br> • Participates in choral response when the teacher invites the children to participate in a class read-aloud of *There Was an Old Lady Who Swallowed a Fly* or *The Three Little Pigs.* <br><br> • Imitates the motions the teacher makes to illustrate a story read aloud in English (e.g., pretends to run like the Gingerbread Man). | • Brings a stack of books to a classroom volunteer and communicates, "First read *Rainbow Fish,* and then the ABC farm book." <br><br> • Communicates, "Humpty Dumpty is my favorite! Read that one after the egg book, OK?" during circle time. <br><br> • Calls out, "I like that one! It has black and white," pointing to the orca whale during a read-aloud of a big book about whales. <br><br> • Role-plays a simple poem about how plants grow outside after hearing the poem during circle time. <br><br> • When the teacher asks, "What does the boy see?" during a small group read-aloud, responds, "a dog!" while pointing at a picture of a dog on a page in the book. |

ENGLISH-LANGUAGE DEVELOPMENT

## 1.0 Children demonstrate an appreciation and enjoyment of reading and literature.

### Focus: Interest in books and reading

| Beginning | Middle | Later |
|---|---|---|
| **1.2** "Read" familiar books written in the home language or in English when encouraged by others and, in the home language, talk about the books. | **1.2** Choose to "read" familiar books written in the home language or in English with increasing independence and, in the home language or in English, talk about the books. | **1.2** Choose to "read" familiar books written in English with increasing independence and talk about the books in English. |
| **Examples** | **Examples** | **Examples** |
| • When playing in the block corner with cars and trucks, finds a picture book on transportation in a basket and communicates in her home language, "Look! A big truck!"<br><br>• Looks on as a peer "reads," then selects a book in her home language and sits next to the peer to "read" too.<br><br>• When asked by a bilingual assistant, "What is your favorite book?" picks up *La oruga muy hambrienta* (*The Very Hungry Caterpillar*) and asks the assistant to read it to her. | • Chooses a book about animals to "read" with another child while playing "zoo" in the block area, pretends to be an elephant, and says, "Look it. My big trunk."<br><br>• Selects a familiar book written in the home language (e.g., *Pío Peep*) from the shelf without help and sings the lyrics to a song in Spanish and in English.<br><br>• Chooses to "read" a book that was read aloud by the teacher earlier the same day or on the previous day and talks with a peer about the book in any language.<br><br>• When building a block tower, looks at a book about construction after a teacher prompts, "What a great tower! Do you think you could find a building in this book that looks like yours?" to which he responds by talking about the book in any language. | • Chooses a familiar book in English, *A Pocket for Corduroy,* settles down again on a pile of pillows, turns the pages of the book, and says, "Look, bear want pocket. Girl make pocket."<br><br>• Selects and "reads" a class book about a recent walk in the neighborhood (with photographs captioned in English) and, using English, talks about the photographs. |

## 2.0 Children show an increasing understanding of book reading.
### Focus: Personal connections to the story

| Beginning | Middle | Later |
|---|---|---|
| **2.1** Begin to identify and relate to a story from their own life experiences in the home language (as reported by parents, teachers, assistants, or others, with the assistance of an interpreter if necessary). | **2.1** Describe their own experiences related to the topic of the story, using telegraphic and/or formulaic speech in English. | **2.1** Begin to engage in extended conversations in English about stories. |
| **Examples** | **Examples** | **Examples** |
| • Tells the teacher in Spanish how the story reminds her of an experience she has had: "Mi papá dice que yo soy su princesa." (My dad says that I am his princess.)<br><br>• Brings items from home to share that are related to a storybook read aloud the previous day.<br><br>• Says to a peer in Vietnamese, "Con vuốt con chó, CôCô, môt chút xíu. Sau đó, con rửa tay với xà bông." (I pet a dog, Coco, just a little bit. After that, I washed my hands with soap.) during a read-aloud of a big book about animals (as reported by a bilingual assistant or interpreter). | • In response to hearing a book about the zoo, starts her own story with "Mommy zoo" because her mother went on a class trip to the zoo along with a small group and the teacher.<br><br>• Calls out during a read-aloud of a story about the dentist, "Me too! Me too!" while pointing at her mouth.<br><br>• Communicates, "I love cereal—not hot," after hearing the story *Goldilocks and the Three Bears*. | • After hearing *Goodnight Moon,* talks about his own house, leading to a conversation with the teacher about bedtime routines and where he lives.<br><br>• When the teacher asks, "Has anyone seen a train? What did it look like?" says, "I saw a train. I saw a big train (emphasizing "big" and using hand gestures). It was blue. I like blue," after a read-aloud of a storybook about a train ride. |

## 2.0 Children show an increasing understanding of book reading.
### Focus: Story structure

| Beginning | Middle | Later |
|---|---|---|
| **2.2** Retell a story in the home language when read or told a story in the home language (as reported by parents, teachers, assistants, or others, with the assistance of an interpreter if necessary). | **2.2** Retell a story using the home language and some English when read or told a story in English. | **2.2** Retell in English the majority of a story read or told in English. |
| **Examples** | **Examples** | **Examples** |
| • Begins to put the pictures of a simple story in sequence when told the beginning, middle, and end in the home language as part of a small group activity with a bilingual assistant; retells the story in his home language.<br><br>• Says to her mother in Spanish while looking at a book at the end of the day, "Primero, la casa de paja se cayó, después la casa de palo, y después la de ladrillo." (First, the straw house fell, next the stick house, and then the brick one.) | • Says in Spanish and English, "Se sentó en la silla de [she sat in the chair of] Papa Bear, and then Mama Bear, and then Baby Bear" to a peer in the dramatic play area.<br><br>• Participates in a whole-class reenactment of *The Little Red Hen,* using such props as a flannel board or finger puppets; retells some of story sequence primarily in his home language, using some key English phrases, such as, "'Not I,' said the duck" or "Then I will." | • Says, "First he go to the house . . . straw. Then the house . . . sticks . . . then the house . . . bricks" in a small group conversation after a read-aloud.<br><br>• Flips through the pages of a picture book of *Goldilocks and The Three Bears* and communicates, "Baby, Mama, Papa bear. Food is hot. Go outside. . . . [continues through sequence] Girl see bear and she run. The end." (This is a story the teacher has told on many occasions.) |

ENGLISH-LANGUAGE DEVELOPMENT

## 3.0 Children demonstrate an understanding of print conventions.
### Focus: Book handling*

| Beginning | Middle | Later |
|---|---|---|
| **3.1** Begin to understand that books are read in a consistent manner (e.g., in English, pages are turned from right to left and the print is read from top to bottom, left to right; this may vary in other languages). | **3.1** Continue to develop an understanding of how to read a book, sometimes applying knowledge of print conventions from the home language. | **3.1** Demonstrate an understanding that print in English is organized from left to right, top to bottom, and that pages are turned from right to left when a book is read. |
| **Examples** | **Examples** | **Examples** |
| • Rotates and flips the book over until the picture of George is right side up on the cover of *Jorge el curioso* (*Curious George*) and begins to look at the book. <br><br> • A Cantonese-speaking child picks up a book, and flips the pages from left to right, looking at the pictures (the appropriate way to read a book in Chinese). | • Turns the pages of a book and talks about illustrations in either English or his home language. <br><br> • Turns the pages of a book, although not necessarily one at a time, talking quietly to herself in Arabic; tracks the print with her finger, moving from top to bottom, right to left (the appropriate way to write and read in Arabic). <br><br> • During circle time, turns the page of a big book written in English in the appropriate direction when the teacher indicates it is time to turn the page. | • Turns an upside-down book right side up and says, "Let's start here," when sitting and "reading" with a peer in a rocking chair. <br><br> • Imitates the teacher reading to children by sitting next to a peer, holding up a book written in English that has been read aloud several times; turns the pages and points to words, tracking the print with her finger, moving from left to right and top to bottom. <br><br> • Communicates in Spanish, "Había una vez" (Once upon a time) when looking at the first page of a book, looks through the book, and communicates, "The end" when reaching the last page. |

* Some children may need assistance in holding a book or turning the pages, either through assistive technology or through the help of an adult or peer. For example, a book can be mounted so it will not have to be held, and sturdy tabs can be placed on the pages so they are easier to turn. Some children may need to have an adult or peer hold the book and turn the pages.

ENGLISH-LANGUAGE DEVELOPMENT

## 4.0 Children demonstrate awareness that print carries meaning.
### Focus: Environmental print

| Beginning | Middle | Later |
|---|---|---|
| **4.1** Begin to recognize that symbols in the environment (classroom, community, or home) carry a consistent meaning in the home language or in English. | **4.1** Recognize in the environment (classroom, community, or home) some familiar symbols, words, and print labels in the home language or in English. | **4.1** Recognize in the environment (classroom, community, or home) an increasing number of familiar symbols, words, and print labels in English. |
| **Examples** | **Examples** | **Examples** |
| • Sees the pedestrian-crossing sign at a stoplight signal (showing a green hand) and communicates in his home language, "We can go, teacher!" while on a neighborhood walk.<br><br>• During cleanup time, finds the shelf with a big block picture label and puts big blocks on the shelf or puts away musical instruments on the shelf that has a label showing musical notes.<br><br>• Recognizes logos for familiar grocery stores, restaurants, and so forth in the community (as reported by parents or others).<br><br>• Points to picture labels on a chart representing daily class routines and communicates in her home language, "book" or "blocks." | • Recognizes "stop" signs: Communicates, "Stop!" when seeing a stop sign while walking home from school (as reported by parent); stops the tricycle on the playground and raises his hand to indicate "stop" when a peer holds up a paper stop sign.<br><br>• Says in Spanish, "¡Mami, cómprame pan dulce!" (Mommy, buy me a pastry) while pointing at the sign for a Mexican bakery that has a picture of a pastry.<br><br>• Recognizes the label and picture on a package and says, "mac 'n cheese" in the kitchen play area.<br><br>• Finds more spoons for snack time in a drawer labeled with a picture of spoons and the word "spoons."<br><br>• Recognizes her own printed name on signs in the classroom (e.g., on a chart that lists how children get to school or on a label on her cubby). | • Takes a peer's jacket from the floor, finds the owner's name label on the cubby, and puts the jacket there.<br><br>• Moves toward the women's bathroom, indicates or points at the sign on the door with only the word "Women" labeled on it, and says, "This one is for girls," while visiting the public library.<br><br>• Names the exit sign or the signs for various areas, such as "library area," "science area," and so forth.<br><br>• Says, "Teacher, this is my book," and puts her book in the trunk labeled "Show and Tell" as the children gather for sharing time on the rug. |

ENGLISH-LANGUAGE DEVELOPMENT

## 5.0 Children demonstrate progress in their knowledge of the alphabet in English.
### Focus: Letter awareness

| Beginning | Middle | Later |
|---|---|---|
| **5.1** Interact with material representing the letters of the English alphabet. | **5.1** Begin to talk about the letters of the English alphabet while playing and interacting with them; may code-switch (use the home language and English). | **5.1** Begin to demonstrate understanding that the letters of the English alphabet are symbols used to make words. |
| **Examples** | **Examples** | **Examples** |
| • Plays with alphabet puzzles or magnets with a peer. <br> • Prints letters on paper, using alphabet stamps. | • Names individual letters while tracing them in the sand and says a friend's name that starts with one of the letters. <br> • Indicates or points at individual letters in an alphabet book in English and communicates, "That's my letter!" while pointing at the letter "M," the first letter in her name, Minh. <br> • Communicates, "C, O, L" as she puts letters into the appropriate spaces in the alphabet puzzle. <br> • Communicates, "A, B, C, D" to a peer while indicating or pointing to one of the piles of letters in front of him on the table during a game of ABC Bingo. <br> • Says in Spanish, "Maestra, 'T' (says letter name in English) es la mía. ¡Es mi nombre!" (Teacher, 'T' is mine. It's my name.) while pointing at the first letter of the name label for his cubby (his name is Tomás). | • Asks the teacher to write the word "tree" on his paper after drawing a tree. <br> • Asks, "What letter, teacher?" indicating or pointing at the first letter of the first word in the title of a big book during circle time. <br> • Indicates or points to words under a drawing of the sun and says, "That says 'sun'" (even if the text says something else). |

## 5.0 Children demonstrate progress in their knowledge of the alphabet in English.
### *Focus: Letter recognition*

| Beginning | Middle | Later |
|---|---|---|
| **5.2** Begin to recognize the first letter in their own name or the character for their own name in the home language or English. | **5.2** Identify some letters of the alphabet in English. | **5.2** Identify ten or more letters of the alphabet in English. |
| **Examples** | **Examples** | **Examples** |
| • Shows her parents her cubby and says in Spanish, "Mi nombre empieza con esta letra, la 'm'." (My name begins with this letter, 'm'.) (The child's name is Manuela.)<br><br>• Indicates or points to her name label written in Mandarin Chinese on her cubby and communicates to her parents in Chinese, "That's my name." | • Recognizes several letters in his classmates' names or in his parents' names.<br><br>• Identifies five letters on an alphabet poster when highlighted by the teacher.<br><br>• When looking through an "alphabet storybook" or children's illustrated alphabet book, names five or more letters. | • Identifies different letters of friends' names on a name chart.<br><br>• Names ten individual letters as a friend writes them with chalk outside. |

ENGLISH-LANGUAGE DEVELOPMENT

## 6.0 Children demonstrate phonological awareness.
### Focus: Rhyming

| Beginning | Middle | Later |
|---|---|---|
| **6.1** Listen attentively and begin to participate in simple songs, poems, and finger plays that emphasize rhyme in the home language or in English. | **6.1** Begin to repeat or recite simple songs, poems, and finger plays that emphasize rhyme in the home language or in English. | **6.1** Repeat, recite, produce, or initiate simple songs, poems, and finger plays that emphasize rhyme in English. |
| **Examples** | **Examples** | **Examples** |
| • Participates in a class chant of "Humpty Dumpty" or class sing-along of "Itsy Bitsy Spider" by making some gestures and smiling with peers.<br><br>• Imitates a frog jumping into water while listening to this rhyme in Mandarin Chinese: "一只青蛙一张嘴,两只眼睛四条腿,扑通一声跳下水。" (One frog has one mouth, two eyes, and four legs. It jumps into the water and makes a "splash" sound.) (as reported by teachers, parents, assistants, or others, with the assistance of an interpreter, if necessary). | • Sings some key words and perhaps makes some gestures for the Spanish-language songs "Pimpón" or "Aserrín, Aserrán" with a peer while playing outside (as reported by a bilingual assistant).<br><br>• Participates with a peer who is chanting "One, two buckle my shoe, three, four shut the door . . . " by joining in for the rhyming words, such as "two, shoe" and "four, door" and clapping while playing in the sandbox.<br><br>• Participates in a class sing-along of "Twinkle, Twinkle Little Star," singing rhyming words and key phrases (e.g., "Twinkle, twinkle, little star" and "what you are," but not the entire song). | • Produces a word that rhymes with the target word during chants, such as "Eddie spaghetti" or "Ana banana."<br><br>• Participates in a class sing-along of "Down by the Bay," repeating most of the song and almost all of the rhyming words in phrases (e.g., "a whale with a polka-dot tail" and "a moose kissing a goose").<br><br>• Plays a word-matching game involving rhyming (e.g., "I say no, you say go," "I say boo, you say too," or "I say cat, you say rat").<br><br>• Says, "Cindy. Bindy. They're the same!" when talking to a peer about her own name (Bindy) and her peer's name (Cindy).<br><br>• Says spontaneously to a friend, "Mother and brother sound the same—they rhyme!" while in the dramatic play area. |

## 6.0 Children demonstrate phonological awareness.
### *Focus: Onset (initial sound)*

| Beginning | Middle | Later |
|---|---|---|
| **6.2** Listen attentively and begin to participate in simple songs, poems, and finger plays in the home language or in English. | **6.2** Begin to recognize words that have a similar onset (initial sound) in the home language or in English, with support. | **6.2** Recognize and produce words that have a similar onset (initial sound) in English. |
| **Examples** | **Examples** | **Examples** |
| • Imitates motions in finger plays, following the teacher's rhythm, such as "Los elefantes" (The Elephants) in Spanish or "This Is the Way We Wash Our Hands" in English.<br><br>• Participates, using appropriate gestures only, in a class sing-along of "Where Is Thumbkin?" or the Spanish version of the song "Pulgarcito."<br><br>• Listens to the "days of the week" song in English, clapping along with peers when the current day of the week is named.<br><br>• Sings along and uses some gestures for a song in Vietnamese (as reported by parents, teachers, assistants, or others, with the assistance of an interpreter if necessary): "Kìa con bướm vàng. Kìa con bướm vàng. Xòe đôi cánh. Xòe đôi cánh. Tung cánh bay lên trên trời. Tung cánh bay lên trên trời. Em ngồi xem. Em ngồi xem." (There's the yellow butterfly. There's the yellow butterfly. Spreads its wings. Spreads its wings. Takes its flight to the sky. Takes its flight to the sky. We contemplate it. We contemplate it.) | • During a read-aloud of a big book about bugs, indicates or points to a butterfly or a beetle on a page and says "butterfly" or "beetle" in response to the teacher asking, while pointing to the corresponding images, "Which bugs start with the "b" letter sound? Butterfly, caterpillar, or beetle?"<br><br>• Cuts out pictures of things that begin with the "p" letter sound for a class book on things that begin with the "p" letter sound. The pictures include things that begin with "p" letter sound in Spanish and English (e.g., palo—stick, perro—dog, pencil). | • Says words that start with the same sound as her own name (e.g., Sara, sock, scissors).<br><br>• Draws a picture of a cat and tells a child, "That's a cat. Cat is like me. Catalina."<br><br>• Generates words that start with the same initial sound during a word game while being pushed on a swing by the teacher; for example, "m" (letter sound) "mom, man, me, mine," in response to teacher saying, "I'm thinking of a word that begins with "m" (letter sound); mouse begins with "m" (letter sound); what else begins with "m" (letter sound)? |

ENGLISH-LANGUAGE DEVELOPMENT

## 6.0 Children demonstrate phonological awareness.
### Focus: Sound differences in the home language and English

| Beginning | Middle | Later |
|---|---|---|
| **6.3** Attend to and manipulate different sounds or tones in words in the home language (as reported by parents, teachers, assistants, or others, with the assistance of an interpreter if necessary.) | **6.3** Begin to use words in English with phonemes (individual units of meaningful sound in a word or syllable) that are different from the home language. | **6.3** Begin to orally manipulate sounds (onsets, rimes, and phonemes) in words in English, with support. |
| **Examples** | **Examples** | **Examples** |
| • Repeats parts of tongue twisters in the home language, such as "Mi mamá me mima mucho" (My mom really pampers me), as reported by the grandmother, with the assistance of an interpreter. (Using tongue twisters is a common practice in Spanish-speaking families.)<br><br>• Recites parts of poems in the home language, such as "小花猫上学校，老师讲课他睡觉。左耳听，右耳冒，你说可笑不可笑。" (Little kitty goes to school, when the teacher talks he goes to sleep. Words spoken by the teacher go into his left ear, but soon come out of his right ear. Don't you think it's really silly?) as reported by the father. (Reciting poetry is a common practice in Chinese-speaking families.)<br><br>• Participates in the chant "Uno dos tres cho-, Uno dos tres co-, Uno dos tres la-, Uno dos tres te-. Cho-co-la-te, Cho-co-la-te, Bate, bate, chocolate!" (One two three cho-, one two three co-, one two three la-, one two three te. Chocolate, Chocolate, Whip, Whip the chocolate!) as observed by the teacher when an older sibling picks up the child at the end of the day. (This is a common chant in Spanish that emphasizes syllables.) | • Listens as the teacher sounds out words while writing a list on chart paper; mouths letter sounds silently, imitating the teacher.<br><br>• Utters new words with English sounds that do not exist in Mandarin Chinese or Korean, such as "uh oh" when seeing a classmate spill juice or "yum yum" when eating a favorite snack.<br><br>• Participates in activities, such as games and songs, that stress sounds in English (e.g., sings along to "The Ants Go Marching" or "This Old Man" with peers while marching outside). | • Sings along with other children during circle time to songs, such as "Willaby Wallaby Woo" or "Apples and Bananas," that emphasize the oral manipulation of sounds.<br><br>• While pointing at her untied shoelaces, says, "Teacher, tie my shoes [saying "chüz"], please," to which the teacher responds, "You want me to tie your shoes?" emphasizing the "sh" in the word "shoes," after which the child nods and responds, "Yes, my shoes [saying "shüz"]." |

# Writing

## 1.0 Children use writing to communicate their ideas.*
### Focus: Writing as communication

| Beginning | Middle | Later |
|---|---|---|
| **1.1** Begin to understand that writing can be used to communicate. | **1.1** Begin to understand that what is said in the home language or in English can be written down and read by others. | **1.1** Develop an increasing understanding that what is said in English can be written down and read by others. |
| **Examples** | **Examples** | **Examples** |
| • Makes marks (e.g., scribbles, draws lines) and, by gesturing, engages a peer to share her writing.<br><br>• Communicates "rain, rain," in the home language while painting spirals and then dots at the easel.<br><br>• Dictates, to a bilingual assistant, a simple letter in Vietnamese addressed to his dì (maternal aunt). | • Asks the teacher to write in Spanish and English, "No se toca. [Don't touch.] No touch," on a piece of paper to place in front of a block tower he has just finished building.<br><br>• Cuts a shape out of red paper that resembles a stop sign and asks the teacher to write the word "stop" on it so he can use it outside when riding tricycles.<br><br>• While playing doctor, "writes" on a paper, hands it to a peer, and communicates in Spanish, "Necesitas esta medicina." (You need this medicine.) | • Dictates a simple letter to his mother in English when he is very excited about something he was able to do.<br><br>• Pointing to the top of a painting she has just finished at the easel, says to the teacher, "I'm done! Write my name here, OK?"<br><br>• "Writes" on a paper after making a drawing, gives it to the teacher, and requests, "Read my story."<br><br>• "Writes" while saying, "Eggs. Milk. Ice Cream," while playing restaurant in the kitchen play area with other children. |

\* Some children may need assistance in emergent writing to communicate their ideas. Assistive technology may be used to facilitate "writing." This may be as simple as building up the width of a marker or pencil so it is easier to grasp or as sophisticated as using a computer. Another possibility would be for an adult or peer to "write" for a child with motor challenges, who would then agree or disagree by indicating "yes" or "no" (*Preschool English Learners* 2007).

ENGLISH-LANGUAGE DEVELOPMENT

## 1.0  Children use writing to communicate their ideas.*
### Focus: Writing to represent words or ideas

| Beginning | Middle | Later |
|---|---|---|
| **1.2** Begin to demonstrate an awareness that written language can be in the home language or in English. | **1.2** Begin to use marks or symbols to represent spoken language in the home language or in English. | **1.2** Continue to develop writing by using letters or letter-like marks to represent their ideas in English. |
| **Examples** | **Examples** | **Examples** |
| • Makes scribbles of lines and shapes that may resemble the home language.<br><br>• Gestures to a bilingual poster on the wall and asks a peer, "¿Es español o inglés?" (Is this Spanish or English?)<br><br>• Says, "That says, 'Chinese,'" in Cantonese while pointing to a calendar with Chinese characters. | • While pretend-writing with crayons and paper, communicates, "Teacher, this Korean."<br><br>• As a speaker of Ukranian, writes marks with crayons on paper and communicates, "This like Mommy writes."<br><br>• Writes marks from the bottom to the top and from right to left on a paper and communicates in English and Mandarin Chinese, "I write like my yí." (maternal aunt).<br><br>• Writes marks that resemble Chinese characters in his journal next to a picture he has drawn of a little boy with a man and says, "Me. Daddy." | • Writes a grocery list in the housekeeping center, using forms that approximate letters in English.<br><br>• Writes "blocks," with some errors, on a daily plan for center time while saying, "I am going to play with the blocks."<br><br>• Writes letter-like marks while saying "lizard" after drawing a picture of a lizard for her own page in a class book on lizards. |

\* Some children may need assistance in emergent writing either through assistive technology or through the help of an adult. Assistive technology (either low tech or high tech) may be as simple as building up the width of a marker or pencil so that it is easier to grasp or it may be as sophisticated as using a computer. Another possibility would be for an adult or peer to "write" for the child who would then approve or disapprove by indicating "yes" or "no." (*Preschool English Learners* 2007)

ENGLISH-LANGUAGE DEVELOPMENT

## 1.0 Children use writing to communicate their ideas.
### Focus: Writing their name

| Beginning | Middle | Later |
|---|---|---|
| **1.3** Write marks to represent their own name in a way that may resemble how it is written in the home language. | **1.3** Attempt to copy their own name in English or in the writing system of their home language. | **1.3** Write their first name on their own in English nearly correctly, using letters of the English alphabet to accurately represent pronunciation in their home language. |
| **Examples** | **Examples** | **Examples** |
| • Uses circles, lines, graphics, or figures that resemble the writing system for her home language to represent her own name and communicates in the home language, "That's my name!"<br><br>• "Writes" his name on a card he has made for his parent and communicates his name in the home language.<br><br>• Makes marks in the sand and communicates in her home language, "Teacher, this my name." | • Copies her name in English from her name card with some errors, using a whiteboard and markers.<br><br>• From a card with his name written in Korean by his mother, copies his name in Korean at the bottom of a picture he wants to send to his grandma, who does not speak English.<br><br>• Writes an approximation of her name in Vietnamese on the sign-in sheet when arriving at school and communicates, "I'm here!" | • Writes his name in English on a painting, with some errors.<br><br>• While outside, writes his name in English and then in Japanese next to a self-portrait, with some errors, using sidewalk chalk.<br><br>• Traces her name in English while drawing with crayons, then writes her name on her own. |

ENGLISH-LANGUAGE DEVELOPMENT

# Glossary

**chunks.** Short phrases used as units; patterned language acquired through redundant use, such as refrains and repetition phrases in stories

**code-switching.** A normal part of second-language acquisition in which the child combines English with the home language

**English learner.** Children whose first language is not English, encompassing children learning English for the first time in the preschool setting as well as children who have developed various levels of English proficiency

**formulaic speech.** The use of memorized chunks or phrases of language, without a complete understanding of their function (e.g., the formula, "I want . . . " allows for a host of possibilities, such as "I want play," "I want doll," or "I want go")

**onset.** The first consonant or consonant cluster in a syllable (e.g., the "h" in the one-syllable word "hat"; the "m" and "k" in the two syllables in the word "monkey")

**orally blend.** To combine sound elements to make a word or syllable (e.g., combining the phonemes "k" "a" "t" to make the word "cat")

**phoneme.** The individual unit of meaningful sound in a word or syllable

**phonological awareness.** The ability to detect or manipulate the sound structure of spoken words, independent of meaning. It is an increasingly sophisticated capability that is highly predictive of, and causally related to, children's later ability to read

**productive language.** The process of formulating and sending a message (communicating) using language (Speech is one form of productive or expressive language. Other means to express language include using sign language, pointing to words and pictures on a communication board, and producing written messages on a computer screen.)

**receptive language.** The process of receiving and understanding communication through language (Speech is one way to receive messages through language. Other means to receive language are sign language, words and pictures on a communication board, and written messages on a computer screen.)

**rime.** Everything left in a syllable after the onset is removed; the vowel and coda of a syllable (e.g., the "at" in the single-syllable word "hat"; the "in" in the single-syllable word "in")

**sequential bilingualism.** The process of beginning to acquire English after making significant progress toward acquisition of the home language

**simultaneous bilingualism.** The process of acquiring two languages beginning at birth or sometime during the first year of life

**social conventions.** A culture's rules for how and when to use language

**telegraphic speech.** The use of a few content words without functional words or specific grammatical markers (e.g., one word combined with nonverbal communication, intonation, or facial expressions to communicate different ideas; saying, "up!" while pointing at a plane in the sky to mean, "Look, there's a plane!")

**utterance.** Any speech sequence consisting of one or more words preceded and followed by silence. May be equivalent to a phrase or a sentence.

ENGLISH-LANGUAGE DEVELOPMENT

# References

Allen, S., and others. 2002. "Patterns of Code-Mixing in English-Inuktitut Bilinguals," in *Proceedings of the 37th Annual Meeting of Chicago Linguistics Society*, Vol. 2. Edited by M. Andronis and others. Chicago: Chicago Linguistics Society.

August, D., and others. 2005. "The Critical Role of Vocabulary Development for English Language Learners," *Learning Disabilities Research and Practice*, Vol. 20, No. 1, 50–57.

Bialystok, E. 2001. *Bilingualism in Development: Language, Literacy, and Cognition*. Cambridge, UK: Cambridge University Press.

Bialystok, E.; F. I. M. Craik; and J. Ryan. 2006. "Executive Control in a Modified Antisaccade Task: Effects of Aging and Bilingualism," *Journal of Experimental Psychology: Learning, Memory and Cognition*, Vol. 32, No. 6, 1341–54.

California Department of Education. 2006a. *Statewide English Learners by Language and Grade, 2005-06.* http://dq.cde.ca.gov/dataquest/LEPbyLang1.asp?cChoice=LepbyLang1&cYear=2005-06&cLevel=State&cTopic=LC&myTimeFrame=S&submit1=Submit (accessed February 13, 2007).

California Department of Education. 2006b. *Statewide Enrollment by Ethnicity, 2005-06.* http://dq.cde.ca.gov/dataquest/EnrollEthState.asp?Level=State&TheYear=2005-06&cChoice=EnrollEth1&p=2 (accessed February 13, 2007).

Cárdenas-Hagan, E.; C. D. Carlson; and E. D. Pollard-Durodola. 2007. The Cross-Linguistic Transfer of Early Literacy Skills: The Role of Initial L1 and L2 Skills and Language of Instruction, *Language, Speech, and Hearing Services in Schools*, Vol. 38, No. 3, 249–59.

Cazden, C. B. 1988. *Classroom Discourse: The Language of Teaching and Learning.* Portsmouth, NH: Heinemann.

Chang, F., and others. 2007. "Spanish Speaking Children's Social and Language Development in Pre-Kindergarten Classrooms," *Journal of Early Education and Development*, Vol. 18, No. 2, 243–69.

*Childhood Bilingualism: Research on Infancy Through School Age.* 2006. Edited by P. McCardle and E. Hoff. Clevedon, UK: Multilingual Matters Ltd.

Children Now. 2007. *California Report Card 2006–2007: The State of the State's Children.* http://publications.childrennow.org/publications/invest/reportcard_2007.cfm (accessed January 10, 2007).

Cisero, C. A., and J. M. Royer. 1995. "The Development of Cross-Language Transfer of Phonological Awareness," *Contemporary Educational Psychology*, Vol. 20, No. 3, 275–303.

Clay, M. 2001. *Change Over Time in Children's Literacy Development*. Auckland, New Zealand: Heinemann.

Crago, M. B. 1988. "Cultural Context in Communicative Interaction of Young Inuit Children." Montreal: McGill University (doctoral dissertation).

*Cultural Diversity and Early Education: Report of a Workshop.* 1994. Edited by D. Phillips and N. A. Crowell. Washington, DC: National Academy Press.

Cummins, J. 1979. "Linguistic Interdependence and the Educational Development of Bilingual Children," *Review of Educational Research*, Vol. 49, 222–51.

*Developing Literacy in Second-Language Learners: Report of the National Literacy Panel on Language-Minority Children and Youth.* 2006. Edited by D. August and T. Shanahan. Washington, DC: Center for Applied Linguistics.

Dickinson, D. K., and P. O. Tabors. 2002. "Fostering Language and Literacy in Classrooms and Homes," *Young Children*, Vol. 57, No. 2, 10–18.

Duke, N., and V. Purcell-Gates. 2003. "Genres at Home and at School: Bridging the Known to the New," *The Reading Teacher*, Vol. 57, No. 1, 30–37.

Durgunoglu, A. Y. 2002. "Cross-Linguistics Transfer in Literacy Development and Implications for Language Learners," *Annals of Dyslexia*, Vol. 52, 189–204.

Durgunoglu, A. Y.; W. E. Nagy; and B. J. Hancin-Bhatt. 1993. "Cross-Language Transfer of Phonological Awareness," *Journal of Educational Psychology*, Vol. 85, No. 3, 453–65.

Durgunoglu, A. Y., and B. Öney. 2000. "Literacy Development in Two Languages: Cognitive and Sociocultural Dimensions of Cross-Language Transfer." Research Symposium on High Standards in Reading for Students from Diverse Language Groups: Research, Practice, and Policy, April 19–20, 2000. Washington, DC: U.S. Department of Education, Office of Bilingual Education and Minority Language Affairs.

Ehrman, M. E.; B. L. Leaver; and R. L. Oxford. 2003. "A Brief Overview of Individual Differences in Second Language Learning," *System*, Vol. 31, No. 3, 313–30.

Ervin-Tripp, S. 1974. "Is Second Language Learning Like the First?" *TESOL Quarterly*, Vol. 8, No. 2, 111–28.

Espinosa, L. M., and M. S. Burns. 2003. "Early Literacy for Young Children and English-Language Learners," in *Teaching 4- to 8-Year-Olds: Literacy, Math, Multiculturalism and Classroom Continuity*. Edited by C. Howes. Baltimore: Brookes Publishing.

Ferreiro, E., and A. Teberosky. 1982. *Literacy Before Schooling*. Exeter, NH: Heinemann.

Genesee, F.; J. Paradis; and M. B. Crago. 2004. *Dual Language Development and Disorders: A Handbook on Bilingualism and Second Language Learning*. Baltimore: Brookes Publishing.

Genesee, F., and D. Sauve. 2000. "Grammatical Constraints on Child Bilingual Code-Mixing." Paper presented at the Annual Conference of the American Association for Applied Linguistics, Vancouver, March 2000.

Genishi, C.; S. E. Stires; and D. Yung-Chan. 2001. "Writing in an Integrated Curriculum: Prekindergarten English Language Learners as Symbol Makers," *The Elementary School Journal*, Vol. 101, No. 4, 399–411.

Genishi, C.; D. Yung-Chan; and S. Stires. 2000. "Talking Their Way into Print: English Language Learners in a Prekindergarten Classroom," in *Beginning Reading and Writing*. Edited by D. S. Strickland and L. M. Morrow. New York: Teachers College Press.

Gottardo, A., and others. 2001. "Factors Related to English Reading Performance in Children with Chinese as a First Language: More Evidence of Cross-Language Transfer of Phonological Processing," *Journal of Educational Psychology*, Vol. 93, No. 3, 530–42.

Greenfield, P. M. 1994. "Independence and Interdependence as Developmental Scripts: Implications for Theory, Research and Practice," in *Cross-Cultural Roots of Minority Child Development*. Edited by P. M. Greenfield and R. R. Cocking. Hillsdale, NJ: Lawrence Erlbaum.

Hakuta, K. 1987. "The Second Language Learner in the Context of the Study of Language Acquisition," in *Childhood Bilingualism: Aspects of Cognitive, Social and Emotional Development*. Edited by P. Homel, M. Palij, and D. Aaronson. Hillsdale, NJ: Lawrence Erlbaum.

Hakuta, K.; Y. G. Butler; and D. Witt. 2000. How Long Does It Take English Learners to Attain Proficiency? http://lmri.ucsb.edu/publications/00_hakuta.pdf (accessed February 13, 2007).

ENGLISH-LANGUAGE DEVELOPMENT

Halliday, M. A. K. 2006. *The Language of Early Childhood.* Edited by J. J. Webster. New York: Continuum International Publishing Group.

Hammer, C. S.; A. W. Miccio; and D. A. Wagstaff. 2003. "Home Literacy Experiences and Their Relationship to Bilingual Preschoolers' Developing English Literacy Abilities: An Initial Investigation," *Language, Speech, and Hearing Services in Schools,* Vol. 34, 20–30.

*Handbook of Early Literacy Research,* Vol. 2. 2006. Edited by D. K. Dickinson and S. B. Neuman. New York: Guilford Press.

Heath, S. B. 1983. *Ways with Words: Language, Life and Work in Communities and Classrooms.* Cambridge, UK: Cambridge University Press.

Huang, J., and E. Hatch. 1978. "A Chinese Child's Acquisition of English," in *Second Language Acquisition: A Book of Readings.* Edited by E. M. Hatch. Rowley, MA: Newbury House.

International Reading Association and the National Association for the Education of Young Children. 1998. "Learning to Read and Write: Developmentally Appropriate Practice for Young Children," *Young Children,* Vol. 53, No. 4, 30–46.

Itoh, H., and E. Hatch. 1978. "Second Language Acquisition: A Case Study," in *Second Language Acquisition.* Edited by E. Hatch. Rowley, MA: Newbury House.

Jia, G., and others. 2006. "Action Naming in Spanish and English by Sequential Bilingual Children and Adolescents," *Journal of Speech, Language, and Hearing Research,* Vol. 49, No. 3, 588–602.

Jiménez, R.; G. E. García; and D. Pearson. 1995. Three Children, Two Languages, and Strategic Reading: Case Studies in Bilingual/Monolingual Reading, *American Education Research Journal,* Vol. 32, 31–61.

Johnston, J., and M.-Y.A.Wong. 2002. "Cultural Differences in Beliefs and Practices Concerning Talk to Children," *Journal of Speech, Language, and Hearing Research,* Vol. 45, 916–26.

Köppe, R. In press. Is Codeswitching Acquired?in *Grammatical Theory and Bilingual Codeswitching.* Edited by J. MacSwan. Cambridge, MA: MIT Press.

Kovelman, I.; S. Baker; and L. A. Petitto. 2006. "Bilingual and Monolingual Brains Compared: An fMRI Study of a 'Neurological Signature' of Bilingualism." Paper presented at the annual meeting of the Society for Neuroscience, Atlanta, October 2006.

Lanauze, M., and C. E. Snow. 1989. "The Relation Between First- and Second-Language Skills: Evidence from Puerto Rican Elementary School Children in Bilingual Programs," *Linguistics and Education,* Vol. 1, 323–40.

Lanza, E. 1997. *Language Mixing in Infant Bilingualism: A Sociolinguistic Perspective.* Oxford, England: Clarendon Press.

Lopez, L. M., and D. B. Greenfield. 2004. "Cross-Language Transfer of Phonological Skills of Hispanic Head Start Children," *Bilingual Research Journal,* Vol. 28, No. 1, 1–18.

Lyster, R., and L. Ranta. 1997. "Corrective Feedback and Learner Uptake: Negotiation of Form in Communicative Classrooms," *Studies in Second Language Acquisition,* Vol. 19, No. 1, 37–61.

Mechelli, A., and others. 2004. "Structural Plasticity in the Bilingual Brain," *Nature,* Vol. 431, 757.

Meisel, J. M. 1994. "Code-Switching in Young Bilingual Children: The Acquisition of Grammatical Constraints," *Studies in Second Language Acquisition,* Vol. 16, 413–41.

Miller, J., and others. 2006. "Oral Language and Reading in Bilingual Children," *Learning Disabilities Research and Practice,* Vol. 21, No. 1, 30–43.

Moll, L. 1992. "Bilingual Classroom Studies and Community Analysis: Some Recent Trends." *Educational Researcher,* Vol. 21, No. 2, 20–24.

Mumtaz, S., and G. W. Humphreys. 2001. "The Effects of Bilingualism on Learning to Read English: Evidence from the

Contrast Between Urdu-English Bilingual and English Monolingual Children," *Journal of Research in Reading*, Vol. 24, No. 2, 113–34.

Ochs, E., and B. B. Schieffelin. 1995. "The Impact of Language Socialization on Grammatical Development," in *The Handbook of Child Language.* Edited by P. Fletcher and B. MacWhinney. Oxford, UK: Oxford University Press.

Paradis, J.; E. Nicoladis; and F. Genesee. 2000. "Early Emergence of Structural Constraints on Code-Mixing: Evidence from French-English Bilingual Children," in *Bilingualism: Language and Cognition.* Edited by F. Genesee. Cambridge, MA: Cambridge University Press.

Pearson, B. Z. 2002. "Narrative Competence Among Monolingual and Bilingual School Children in Miami," in *Language and Literacy in Bilingual Children.* Edited by D. K. Oller and R. E. Eilers. Clevedon, UK: Multilingual Matters Ltd.

Peisner-Feinberg, E. S., and others. 2001. "The Relation of Preschool Child Care Quality to Children's Cognitive and Social Developmental Trajectories Through Second Grade," *Child Development*, Vol. 72, No. 5, 1534–53.

Pianta, R., and others. 2005. "Features of Pre-Kindergarten Programs, Classrooms, and Teachers: Prediction of Observed Classroom Quality and Teacher-Child Interactions," *Applied Developmental Science*, Vol. 9, No. 3, 144–59.

*Preschool English Learners: Principles and Practices to Promote Language, Literacy, and Learning.* 2007. Sacramento: California Department of Education.

*Preventing Reading Difficulties in Young Children.* 1998. Edited by C. E. Snow, M. S. Burns, and P. Griffin. Washington, DC: National Academy Press.

Riojas-Cortez, M. 2001. "Preschoolers' Funds of Knowledge Displayed Through Sociodramatic Play Episodes in a Bilingual Classroom," *Early Childhood Education Journal*, Vol. 29, No. 1, 35–40.

Rivera, C., and E. Collum. 2006. *State Assessment Policy and Practice for English Language Learners: A National Perspective.* Mahwah, NJ: Lawrence Erlbaum.

Rogoff, B. 2003. *The Cultural Nature of Human Development.* New York: Oxford University Press.

Saunders, W. M., and G. O'Brien. 2006. "Oral Language," in *Educating English Language Learners: A Synthesis of Research Evidence.* Edited by F. Genesee and others. New York: Cambridge University Press.

Saville-Troike, M. 1987. "Private Speech: Second Language Learning During the 'Silent' Period," *Papers and Reports on Child Language Development*, Vol. 26, 104–15.

Scott-Little, C.; S. L. Kagan; and V. S. Frelow. 2005. *Inside the Content: The Breadth and Depth of Early Learning Standards.* Greensboro, NC: SERVE.

Snow, C. 2006. "Cross-cutting Themes and Future Directions," in *Developing Literacy in Second-Language Learners: Report of the National Literacy Panel on Language-Minority Children and Youth.* Edited by D. August and T. Shanahan. Mahwah, NJ: Lawrence Erlbaum.

Tabors, P. O. 1997. *One Child, Two Languages: A Guide for Preschool Educators of Children Learning English as a Second Language.* Baltimore: Brookes Publishing Company.

Tabors, P., and C. Snow. 2001. "Young Bilingual Children and Early Literacy Development," in *Handbook of Early Literacy Research.* Edited by S. Neuman and D. Dickinson. New York: Guilford Press.

Uccelli, P., and M. M. Paez. 2007. "Narrative and Vocabulary Development of Bilingual Children from Kindergarten to First Grade: Developmental Changes and Associations Among English and Spanish Skills," *Language, Speech and Hearing Services in Schools*, Vol. 38, No. 3, 225–36.

Vasquez, O. A.; L. Pease-Alvarez; and S. M. Shannon. 1994. *Pushing Boundaries: Language and Culture in a Mexicano Community.* New York: Cambridge University Press.

Vihman, M. 1998. "A Developmental Perspective on Codeswitching: Conversation Between a Pair of Bilingual Siblings," *International Journal of Bilingualism,* Vol. 2, 45–48.

*Vygotsky and Education: Instructional Implications and Applications of Sociohistorical Psychology.* 1990. Edited by L. C. Moll. Cambridge, UK: Cambridge University Press.

Wong Fillmore, L. 1976. "The Second Time Around: Cognitive and Social Strategies in Second Language Acquisition." Palo Alto, CA: Stanford University (doctoral dissertation).

Wong Fillmore, L. 1991a. "Second-Language Learning in Children: A Model of Language Learning in Social Context," in *Language Processing in Bilingual Children.* Edited by E. Bialystok. Cambridge, UK: Cambridge University Press.

Wong Fillmore, L. 1991b. "When Learning a Second Language Means Losing the First," *Early Childhood Research Quarterly,* Vol. 6, 323–46.

Wong Fillmore, L., and C. Snow. 2000. *What Teachers Need to Know About Language.* Washington, DC: U.S. Department of Education, Office of Educational Research and Improvement.

Yoshida, M. 1978. "The Acquisition of English Vocabulary by a Japanese-Speaking Child," in *Second Language Acquisition: A Book of Readings.* Edited by E. M. Hatch. Rowley, MA: Newbury House Publishers.

ENGLISH-LANGUAGE DEVELOPMENT

# FOUNDATIONS IN
# Mathematics

The preschool learning foundations identify for teachers and other educational stakeholders a set of behaviors in mathematics learning that are typical of children who will be ready to learn what is expected of them in kindergarten. The foundations provide age-appropriate competencies expected for *older* three-year-olds (i.e., at around 48 months of age) and for *older* four-year-olds (i.e., at around 60 months of age). That is, the preschool learning foundations represent goals to be reached by the time a three-year-old is just turning four and a four-year-old is just turning five. Focusing on the child's readiness for school in the domain of mathematics learning acknowledges that there must also be appropriate social-emotional, cognitive, and language development as well as appropriate motivation. Many such complementary and mutually supporting aspects of the child's overall development are addressed in the preschool learning foundations for other domains (e.g., social-emotional development, language and literacy, and English-language development).

These preschool learning foundations are designed with the assumption that children's learning takes place in everyday environments: through interactions, relationships, activities, and play that are part of a beneficial preschool experience. The foundations are meant to describe what is typically expected to be observed from young children in their everyday contexts, under conditions appropriate for healthy development, not as aspirational expectations under the best possible conditions. They are meant as guidelines and tools to support teaching, not as a list of items to be taught as isolated skills and not to be used for assessment.

Some mathematics foundations mention specific expectations, using exact numbers to describe a counting range (e.g., "up to three," or "up to four") at different ages or to set a minimum criterion for a particular area (e.g., "compare two groups of up to five objects"). However, some children may exhibit competencies that go beyond the level described in a particular foundation, while others may need more time to reach that level. The foundations are meant to give teachers a general idea of what is typically expected from children at around 48 or 60 months of age and are not intended to set limits on the way teachers support children's learning at different levels.

Children with special needs can demonstrate mathematical knowledge in various ways and do not necessarily need to engage in motor behavior. For example, a child might indicate to an adult or another child where to place each object in a sorting task. Or a child might ask a teacher to place objects in a particular order to make a repeating pattern. Children with visual impairments might be offered materials for counting, sorting, problem solving, and so forth that are easily distinguishable by touch. Any means of expression and engagement available to the child should be encouraged.

## Organization of the Mathematics Foundations

The California preschool learning foundations in mathematics cover five main developmental strands: Number Sense, Algebra and Functions (Classification and Patterning), Measurement, Geometry, and Mathematical Reasoning. These strands were identified after a careful review of research, the *Principles and Standards for School Mathematics* (NCTM 2000), and the California mathematics content standards for kindergarten through grade twelve (K–12).

The preschool mathematics foundations expand on the standards identified by the NCTM (2000) for the preschool age to include more detailed, age-specific expectations in the key mathematics content areas. In addition, the preschool foundations for mathematics are closely aligned with the California K–12 mathematics content standards, yet there are some particular differences in the organization of the mathematics strands. In the preschool learning foundations, Measurement and Geometry are two separate strands rather than one combined strand of Measurement and Geometry. Also, the preschool learning foundations, unlike the K–12 mathematics content standards, do not include a separate strand for statistics, data analysis, and probability. The foundations for Patterning are included in the strand for Algebra and Functions, along with the foundations for Classification.

The numbering system for the mathematics foundations follows the same numbering system used in the California K–12 mathematics content standards. The major divisions within a strand are referred to as substrands and are numbered 1.0, 2.0, and so forth. Each substrand is divided into a column for children "around 48 months of age" and a column for children "around 60 months of age" on each page. The description for younger preschool children is different from the one for older preschool children. The separate foundations are written under their substrand column by age range and are numbered sequentially. Where a substrand is numbered 1.0, the foundations under the substrand would be 1.1, 1.2, and so forth, where a substrand is numbered 2.0, the foundations under the substrand would be 2.1, 2.2, and so forth for both columns.

Immediately below each foundation, a few examples are given. The examples are meant to clarify the foundation by illustrating how the competency described in the foundation might be observed in the preschool environment. They are *not* meant to be used as a checklist of the knowledge and skills that a child must demonstrate before the teacher can decide that a competency is present.

A developmental progression by age range is articulated within each substrand. That is, the substrand description and foundations for children at around 60 months of age are written to indicate a higher level of development than the foundations for children at around 48 months of age in that same substrand. For some foundations, the change between 48- and 60-month-old children is more pronounced than for other foundations. Although there is a developmental progression from around 48 months of age to around 60 months of age within a substrand, the order in which the strands are presented is not meant to indicate any sense of developmental progression from strand to strand or from substrand to substrand within a strand.

At the end of the foundations, bibliographic notes provide a review of the research base for the foundations. Following the bibliographic notes, a list of references for the entire set of mathematics foundations is provided. Brief explanations of each strand are as follows:

*Number Sense—important aspects of counting, number relationships, and operations*

Preschool children develop an initial qualitative understanding of a quantity of small groups of objects without actually counting the objects. This understanding is referred to as visually knowing or "subitizing." It supports the ability to compare small groups of objects: to know if the groups are the same, if one group is larger (smaller), or which has more (fewer). Also developing is the ability to approach simple arithmetic-like operations on groups of objects with ideas such as "adding to," "putting together," "taking apart," "taking away," and so forth. Preschool is the time when children learn to recite the numbers in order, recognize numerals, and begin to incorporate the idea of one-to-one-correspondence and true counting. This is also a time when preschool children begin to learn about cardinality, which is the concept of knowing the last number named is the quantity of objects counted.

*Algebra and Functions (Classification and Patterning)— sorting and classifying objects; recognizing, extending, and creating patterns*

Classification involves sorting, grouping, or categorizing objects according to established criteria. Analyzing, comparing, and classifying objects provide a foundation for algebraic thinking. Although preschool children may not know how all the objects in a mixed set can be sorted or be able to say much about why some objects go together, they do begin to group like with like at around 48 months of age and will do so more completely at around 60 months of age. These foundations use the idea of sorting objects by some attribute. The term "attribute" is used here to indicate a property of objects, such as color or shape, that would be apparent to a preschooler and that the preschooler could use as a basis for grouping or sorting. A younger preschool child is expected to show some sorting of a group of objects, but not necessarily do so completely or without errors. A young preschooler might sort farm animals but remove only the cows and leave the rest ungrouped, and there may be a pig or two or a horse mixed in. But an older preschool child might make a group of all cows and a group of all pigs and a group of all horses. This competency is the precursor to many important mathematics abilities that will come later (e.g., the logic of what belongs in a set and what does not, grouping terms in an algebraic expression, data analysis, and graphing). Sorting and grouping in preschool will help prepare children for those later steps. Researchers Seo and Ginsburg (2004) point out that preschool children do not often spontaneously choose to do sorting activities on their own. Therefore, sorting is an area in which teacher facilitation and modeling across a range of situations and contexts is particularly important. The teacher should note that how a child sorts depends on the situation and the child's perception of the activity.

Thinking about patterns is another important precursor for learning mathematics in general and for learning algebra in particular (Clements 2004a). During the preschool years, children develop their abilities to recognize, identify, and duplicate patterns and to extend and create simple repeating patterns. Although less research has been conducted for preschoolers in patterning than in other areas, such as numbers and counting, recent studies (Klein and Starkey 2004; Starkey, Klein, and Wakelely 2004) provide information about the development of patterning skills. Children first learn to identify the core unit in a repeating pattern. Once they are able to identify the initial unit of a pattern, they can extend a pattern by predicting what comes next. Teacher facilitation and modeling are particularly important in introducing the notion of patterns, extending it to more aspects of the child's environment and daily activities, and encouraging the child's attempts to create patterns.

## Measurement—comparing and ordering objects by length, weight, or capacity; precursors of measurement

Measuring is assigning a number of units to some property, such as length, area, or weight, of an object. Although much more learning will take place later as children become increasingly competent with core measurement concepts, preschool is when children gain many of the precursors to this kind of understanding about comparing, ordering, and measuring things. For example, young preschool children are becoming aware that objects can be compared by weight, height, or length and use such words as "heavier," "taller," or "longer" to make comparisons. They begin to compare objects directly to find out which is heavier, taller, and so forth. They can compare length by placing objects side by side and order three or more objects by size. By the time children are around 60 months old, they develop the understanding that measuring length involves repeating equal-size units and counting the number of units. They may start measuring length by laying multiple copies of same-size units end to end (Clements 2004a).

## Geometry—properties of objects (shape, size, position) and the relation of objects in space

Geometry is a tool for understanding relations among shapes and spatial properties mathematically. Preschool children learn to recognize and name two-dimensional shapes, such as a circle, square, rectangle, triangle, and other shapes. At first, they recognize geometric shapes by their overall holistic physical appearance. As they gain more experience comparing, sorting, and analyzing shapes, children learn to attend to individual attributes and characteristics of different shapes. Younger preschool children use shapes in isolation, while older preschool children use shapes to create images of things they know and may combine shapes into new shapes (Clements 2004a, 2004b). In the early preschool years, children also develop spatial reasoning. They can visualize shapes in different positions and learn to describe the direction, distance, and location of objects in space. Teachers can facilitate children's development of geometry and spatial thinking by offering many opportunities to explore attributes of different shapes and to use vocabulary words about the position of objects in space.

*Mathematical Reasoning—using mathematical thinking to solve problems in play and everyday activities*

Children in preschool encounter situations in play and everyday activities that require them to adapt and change their course of action. Although they may not realize it, some situations call for mathematical reasoning—to determine a quantity (e.g., how many spoons?) or to reason geometrically (e.g., what shape will fit?). Other situations require general reasoning. For preschoolers, when the context is familiar and comfortable enough, a simple strategy may be applied to solve an immediate problem—even something as simple as counting the number of objects held in the hand or carrying a block over to see if there are others like it. A young preschool child may begin this process by trying a strategy that is not always effective. An older preschool child may try several strategies, finally finding one that works. The important point is that both younger and older preschool children learn through reasoning mathematically. As the above examples suggest, encouraging young children to engage in mathematical reasoning is not only beneficial in itself, it also opens the door to children's exploration of the other mathematics foundations, such as geometric shapes, counting, and classification.

# Number Sense*

| At around 48 months of age | At around 60 months of age |
|---|---|
| **1.0 Children begin to understand numbers and quantities in their everyday environment.** | **1.0 Children expand their understanding of numbers and quantities in their everyday environment.** |
| **1.1** Recite numbers in order to ten with increasing accuracy.[†] | **1.1** Recite numbers in order to twenty with increasing accuracy.[†] |
| **Examples** | **Examples** |
| • Recites one to ten incompletely or with errors while playing (e.g., "one, two, three, four, five, seven, ten").<br>• Recites one to ten while walking.<br>• Recites one to ten while singing. | • Recites one to twenty incompletely or with errors (e.g., "one, two, three, four, five, . . . nine, ten, eleven, twelve, thirteen, fifteen , seventeen, eighteen, twenty").<br>• Chants one to twenty in order while swinging.<br>• Recites one to twenty to show her friend how high she can count. |
| **1.2** Begin to recognize and name a few written numerals. | **1.2** Recognize and know the name of some written numerals. |
| **Examples** | **Examples** |
| • Communicates, "That's a one," when playing with magnetic numerals.<br>• Indicates or points to the numerals on a cube and names, "three, two, five."<br>• Identifies the numeral 3 on the page of the *Five Little Speckled Frogs* book while sitting with a teacher. | • Names some numerals found in books or during a game.<br>• Points to numerals in a number puzzle as the teacher names them. |

---

\* Throughout these mathematics foundations many examples describe the child manipulating objects. Children with motor impairments may need assistance from an adult or peer to manipulate objects in order to do things such as count, sort, compare, order, measure, create patterns, or solve problems. A child might also use adaptive materials (e.g., large manipulatives that are easy to grasp). Alternately, a child might demonstrate knowledge in these areas without directly manipulating objects. For example, a child might direct a peer or teacher to place several objects in order from smallest to largest. Children with visual impairments might be offered materials for counting, sorting, or problem solving that are easily distinguishable by touch. Their engagement is also facilitated by using containers, trays, and so forth that contain their materials and clearly define their work space.

[†] Some children may not be able to count by either saying the numbers or signing them. Any means available to the child for demonstrating knowledge of numbers in order should be encouraged. For example, a child may indicate or touch number cards or might respond yes or no when an adult counts.

| At around 48 months of age | At around 60 months of age |
|---|---|
| **1.3** Identify, without counting, the number of objects in a collection of up to three objects (i.e., subitize). | **1.3** Identify, without counting, the number of objects in a collection of up to four objects (i.e., subitize). |
| **Examples** | **Examples** |
| • Perceives directly (visually, tactilely, or auditorily) the number of objects in a small group without needing to count them.<br>• Indicates or points to a pile of blocks and communicates, "Three of them."<br>• Attends to the child next to her at snack time and communicates, "Clovey has two."<br>• Looks briefly at a picture with three cats and immediately communicates the quantity by saying "three" or showing three fingers. | • Perceives directly (visually, tactilely, or auditorily) the number of objects in a small group without needing to count them.<br>• Looks briefly at a picture of four frogs and immediately communicates the quantity four.<br>• During storytime, puts her hand on the picture of four ladybugs and communicates, "Four ladybugs."<br>• Correctly points out, "That's three cars there." |
| **1.4** Count up to five objects, using one-to-one correspondence (one object for each number word) with increasing accuracy.* | **1.4** Count up to ten objects, using one-to-one correspondence (one object for each number word) with increasing accuracy.* |
| **Examples** | **Examples** |
| • After building a block tower, counts the number of blocks by pointing to the first block and communicating "one," then pointing to the next block and communicating "two." The child counts up to five blocks.<br>• Indicates or points to each toy in a line while communicating, "One, two, three, four, five." | • Indicates or points to a flower in the garden and communicates, "one," then points to another flower and communicates, "two." The child counts up to seven different flowers.<br>• Counts ten children by identifying them one by one during circle time.<br>• Counts the blocks in a pile, keeping track of which blocks have already been counted.<br>• Counts out eight napkins in preparation for snack time. |

* Children with motor disabilities may need assistance manipulating objects in order to count them. Children may also demonstrate knowledge of object counting by using eye-pointing or by counting while an adult or another child touches or moves the objects.

MATHEMATICS

| At around 48 months of age | At around 60 months of age |
|---|---|
| **1.5** Use the number name of the last object counted to answer the question, "How many . . . ?" | **1.5** Understand, when counting, that the number name of the last object counted represents the total number of objects in the group (i.e., cardinality). |
| **Examples** | **Examples** |
| • Counts the number of sticks in her hand, communicating, "one, two, three, four, five." The teacher asks, "How many sticks do you have?" and the child communicates "five." | • After giving away some bears, counts the remaining bears to find out how many are left and communicates, "I now have six bears." |
| • When asked, "How many cars do you have?" counts, "one, two three, four" and communicates, "four." | • Lines up cars on a track and counts, then communicates, "My train has seven cars!" |
| • Counts the beads in her necklace, communicating, "one, two, three, four, five, six." A friend asks, "How many beads do you have?" and the child replies, "six." | • Counts dolls, "one, two, three, four" and communicates, "There are four dolls." |
| | • Counts her sticks and communicates, "I have five," when the teacher asks during an activity, "Does everyone have five sticks?" |
| | • Counts five apple slices and recognizes there is one slice of apple for each of the five children around the table. |

| At around 48 months of age | At around 60 months of age |
|---|---|
| **2.0 Children begin to understand number relationships and operations in their everyday environment.** | **2.0 Children expand their understanding of number relationships and operations in their everyday environment.** |
| **2.1** Compare visually (with or without counting) two groups of objects that are obviously equal or nonequal and communicate, "more" or "same."* | **2.1** Compare, by counting or matching, two groups of up to five objects and communicate, "more," "same as," or "fewer" (or "less").* |
| **Examples** | **Examples** |
| • Examines two groups of counting bears, one with two bears and the other with six bears, and indicates or points to the group of six bears when asked which group has more.<br>• Communicates, "I want more—she's got more stamps than me" during a small group activity.<br>• Communicates, "We have the same," when referring to apple slices during snack time. | • Counts the number of rocks he has and the number a friend has and communicates, "Five and five, you have the same as me."<br>• Compares a group of four bears to a group of five bears and communicates, "This one has less."<br>• Counts her own sand toys, then counts a friend's and communicates, "You have more." |
| **2.2** Understand that adding to (or taking away) one or more objects from a group will increase (or decrease) the number of objects in the group. | **2.2** Understand that adding one or taking away one changes the number in a small group of objects by exactly one. |
| **Examples** | **Examples** |
| • Has three beads, takes another, and communicates, "Now I have more beads."<br>• When the teacher adds more cats on the flannel board, indicates that there are now more cats.<br>• While playing bakery, communicates that after selling some bagels there are now fewer bagels in the bakery shop.<br>• Gives away two dolls and communicates that now she has fewer. | • Adds another car to a pile of five to have six, just like his friend.<br>• Removes one animal from a collection of eight animals and communicates, "She has seven now."<br>• Correctly predicts that if one more car is added to a group of four cars, there will be five. |

*Comparison may be done visually, tactilely, or auditorily.

**MATHEMATICS**

| At around 48 months of age | At around 60 months of age |
|---|---|
| **2.3** Understand that putting two groups of objects together will make a bigger group. | **2.3** Understand that putting two groups of objects together will make a bigger group and that a group of objects can be taken apart into smaller groups. |

| Examples | Examples |
|---|---|
| • Combines his blocks with a pile of his friend's blocks and communicates, "Now we have more." <br> • Puts together crayons from two separate boxes to have more. <br> • Puts together the red bears and the yellow bears to have a bigger group of bears. | • Refers to a collection of six balloons and communicates, "Three red balloons for me and three green ones for you." <br> • Indicates seven by holding up five fingers on one hand and two fingers on another. <br> • Removes three (of five) ducks from the flannel board, communicating, "Three left, and only two stay" when acting a story. |

| At around 48 months of age | At around 60 months of age |
|---|---|
| **2.4** Solve simple addition and subtraction problems nonverbally (and often verbally) with a very small number of objects (sums up to 4 or 5). | **2.4** Solve simple addition and subtraction problems with a small number of objects (sums up to 10), usually by counting. |

| Examples | Examples |
|---|---|
| • Recognizes that one ball together with another one makes a total of two balls. The child may create a matching collection or say or indicate "two." <br> • Adds one car to a train with two cars and indicates the total number of cars in train by showing three fingers. <br> • Recognizes that only two bananas are left after giving away one of three bananas to a friend. <br> • Takes away one flower from a group of four flowers on the flannel board, while acting out a story, and communicates that only three flowers are left. | • During a small group activity, count oranges on the flannel board and communicate, "There are six oranges." The teacher puts one more orange on the board and asks, "How many oranges do we have now?" Some say seven; others first count, "One, two three, four, five, six, seven" and then say seven. <br> • Adds two more cups to a group of two, says that there are four cups. <br> • Takes two boats away from a group of five boats and communicates, "One, two, three—three boats left" while playing with friends. <br> • Watches a friend connect a train with three cars to a second train with three cars. Counts the cars and communicates, "Now our train has six cars." <br> • Builds a stack of five blocks and adds two more saying, "One, two, three, four, five, six, seven. I have seven blocks now." |

# Algebra and Functions
## (Classification and Patterning)*

| At around 48 months of age | At around 60 months of age |
|---|---|
| **1.0  Children begin to sort and classify objects in their everyday environment.** | **1.0  Children expand their understanding of sorting and classifying objects in their everyday environment.** |
| **1.1**  Sort and classify objects by *one* attribute into two or more groups, with increasing accuracy. | **1.1**  Sort and classify objects by *one or more* attributes, into two or more groups, with increasing accuracy (e.g., may sort first by one attribute and then by another attribute).† |
| **Examples** | **Examples** |
| • Selects some red cars for himself and some green cars for his friend, leaving the rest of the cars unsorted.<br>• Chooses the blue plates from a variety of plates to set the table in the kitchen play area.<br>• Sorts through laundry in the basket and takes out all the socks.<br>• Places all the square tiles in one bucket and all the round tiles in another bucket.<br>• Attempts to arrange blocks by size and communicates, "I put all the big blocks here and all the small ones there." | • Sorts the large blue beads into one container and the small red beads in another.<br>• Puts black beans, red kidney beans, and pinto beans into separate bowls during a cooking activity.<br>• Arranges blocks on the shelf according to shape.<br>• Sorts a variety of animal photographs into two groups: those that fly and those that swim.<br>• Sorts buttons first by size and then each subgroup by color into muffin tin cups. |

* Throughout these mathematics foundations many examples describe the child manipulating objects. Children with motor impairments may need assistance from an adult or peer to manipulate objects in order to do things such as count, sort, compare, order, measure, create patterns, or solve problems. A child might also use adaptive materials (e.g., large manipulatives that are easy to grasp). Alternately, a child might demonstrate knowledge in these areas without directly manipulating objects. For example, a child might direct a peer or teacher to place several objects in order from smallest to largest. Children with visual impairments might be offered materials for counting, sorting, or problem solving that are easily distinguishable by touch. Their engagement is also facilitated by using containers, trays, and so forth that contain their materials and clearly define their work space.

† Attributes include, but are not limited to, size, shape, or color.

MATHEMATICS

| At around 48 months of age | At around 60 months of age |
|---|---|
| **2.0 Children begin to recognize simple, repeating patterns.*** | **2.0 Children expand their understanding of simple, repeating patterns.*** |
| **2.1** Begin to identify or recognize a simple repeating pattern. | **2.1** Recognize and duplicate simple repeating patterns. |
| **Examples** | **Examples** |
| • Recognizes a simple repeating pattern made with interlocking cubes, such as yellow, green, yellow, green.<br>• Sings, moves, or claps through part of a pattern song (e.g., the teacher begins a "clap-pat-clap-pat" pattern, and the child repeats with guidance).<br>• Anticipates a repeating pattern in a storybook, with support. | • Fills in an item missing from a pattern (e.g., apple, pear, apple, pear), with guidance.<br>• Copies simple repeating patterns, using the same kind of objects as the original pattern.<br>• Attempts to sing, sign, move, or clap through a pattern song, trying to maintain the pattern. |
| **2.2** Attempt to create a simple repeating pattern or participate in making one. | **2.2** Begin to extend and create simple repeating patterns. |
| **Examples** | **Examples** |
| • Puts together connecting blocks in alternating colors to form a repeating pattern, with guidance.<br>• Demonstrates a pattern of claps, signs, or movements, with guidance.<br>• Lines up pretzel sticks and cheese slices to make patterns at snack time. | • Adds a red bead and then a blue bead in a red-blue-red-blue pattern to complete a bead necklace.<br>• Alternates short and tall blocks to make a fence around a farm.<br>• Makes up a clapping or action pattern, "clap, clap, hop, hop" in rhythm to a song.<br>• Uses different materials such as buttons, beads, or sequins to create patterns. |

* A simple repeating pattern has two repeating elements. Examples are as follows: A-B-A-B (e.g., red-blue-red-blue); A-A-B-B (e.g., dog-dog-cat-cat); A-B-B-A-B-B (e.g., clap-stomp-stomp-clap-stomp-stomp); and so forth.

# Measurement*

| At around 48 months of age | At around 60 months of age |
|---|---|
| **1.0  Children begin to compare and order objects.** | **1.0  Children expand their understanding of comparing, ordering, and measuring objects.** |
| **1.1** Demonstrate awareness that objects can be compared by length, weight, or capacity, by noting gross differences, using words such as *bigger, longer, heavier,* or *taller,* or by placing objects side by side to compare length. | **1.1** Compare two objects by length, weight, or capacity directly (e.g., putting objects side by side) or indirectly (e.g., using a third object). |
| **Examples** | **Examples** |
| • Communicates, "I'm big like my daddy." <br><br> • Communicates, "This one's heavier" when choosing from a variety of beanbags in a basket. <br><br> • Communicates, "He has more clay than me." <br><br> • Communicates, "Mine is longer than yours" when placing trains side by side to check which is longer. <br><br> • Builds a tower beside another child, attempting to make her tower taller. | • Tries to determine if he is taller than another child by standing next to the child. <br><br> • Uses a balance scale to find out which of two rocks is heavier. <br><br> • Pours water into different size containers at the water table to find out which one holds more. <br><br> • Shows that the blue pencil is longer than the red pencil by placing them side by side. <br><br> • Compares the length of two tables by using a string to represent the length of one table and then laying the string against the second table. <br><br> • Uses a paper strip to mark the distance from knee to foot and compares it to the distance from elbow to fingertip. |

* Throughout these mathematics foundations many examples describe the child manipulating objects. Children with motor impairments may need assistance from an adult or peer to manipulate objects in order to do things such as count, sort, compare, order, measure, create patterns, or solve problems. A child might also use adaptive materials (e.g., large manipulatives that are easy to grasp). Alternately, a child might demonstrate knowledge in these areas without directly manipulating objects. For example, a child might direct a peer or teacher to place several objects in order from smallest to largest. Children with visual impairments might be offered materials for counting, sorting, or problem solving that are easily distinguishable by touch. Their engagement is also facilitated by using containers, trays, and so forth that contain their materials and clearly define their work space.

MATHEMATICS

| At around 48 months of age | At around 60 months of age |
|---|---|
| **1.2** Order three objects by size. | **1.2** Order four or more objects by size. |
| **Examples** | **Examples** |
| • Sets bowls by size in dramatic play area, the biggest bowl for daddy bear, the medium bowl for mommy bear, and the smallest bowl for baby bear.<br><br>• Lines up three animal figures by size.<br><br>• Attempts to arrange nesting cups or ring stackers in correct order by size. | • Arranges four dolls from smallest to largest in pretend play with dolls.<br><br>• In sandbox, lines up buckets by size, from the bucket that holds the most sand to one that holds the least.<br><br>• On a playground, orders different kinds of balls (e.g., beach ball, basketball, soccer ball, tennis ball) by size. |
| | **1.3** Measure length using multiple duplicates of the same-size concrete units laid end to end.* |
| | **Examples** |
| | • Uses paper clips laid end to end to measure the length of different size blocks, with adult guidance.<br><br>• Measures the length of a rug by laying same-size block units end to end and communicating, "The rug is ten blocks long," with adult guidance.<br><br>• Measures the length of a table using inch "worms," with adult guidance.<br><br>• Measures the distance from the reading area to the block area by using meter sticks, with adult guidance. |

* A foundation for measurement is written only for children at around 60 months of age, because the development of the ability to use same-size units to measure quantity typically occurs between 48 months and 60 months of age.

# Geometry*

| At around 48 months of age | At around 60 months of age |
|---|---|
| **1.0 Children begin to identify and use common shapes in their everyday environment.** | **1.0 Children identify and use a variety of shapes in their everyday environment.** |
| **1.1** Identify simple two-dimensional shapes, such as a circle and square. | **1.1** Identify, describe, and construct a variety of different shapes, including variations of a circle, triangle, rectangle, square, and other shapes. |

| Examples | Examples |
|---|---|
| • When playing a matching game, communicates, "This is a circle." <br><br> • While playing shape bingo, indicates or points to the correct shape. <br><br> • Indicates a shape block and communicates, "This is a square." <br><br> • Sorts shape manipulatives of varying sizes into different shape groups (e.g., points to the group of triangles and communicates, "Here are the triangles: big, small, and very small triangles"). | • While playing the "I Spy the Shape" game, communicates, "I see a circle—the clock." Later, says, "I see a rectangle—the table." <br><br> • Correctly identifies shapes as the teacher calls them out in a game of shape bingo. <br><br> • Uses play dough to construct rectangles of different sizes and orientations. <br><br> • Sorts manipulatives of different sizes and orientations by shape and explains why a particular shape does or does not belong in a group. <br><br> • Tears paper shape and communicates, "Look! A triangle" while making a collage. |

| **1.2** Use individual shapes to represent different elements of a picture or design. | **1.2** Combine different shapes to create a picture or design. |
|---|---|

| Examples | Examples |
|---|---|
| • Uses a circle for a sun and a square for a house in a picture. <br><br> • Puts together a foam shape puzzle in which each shape is outlined. <br><br> • Creates a design by putting shape tiles together. | • Uses a variety of shapes to construct different parts of a building. <br><br> • Uses flannel pieces of different shapes to create a design. <br><br> • Creates a house, from different shapes, using a computer program. |

\* Throughout these mathematics foundations many examples describe the child manipulating objects. Children with motor impairments may need assistance from an adult or peer to manipulate objects in order to do things such as count, sort, compare, order, measure, create patterns, or solve problems. A child might also use adaptive materials (e.g., large manipulatives that are easy to grasp). Alternately, a child might demonstrate knowledge in these areas without directly manipulating objects. For example, a child might direct a peer or teacher to place several objects in order from smallest to largest. Children with visual impairments might be offered materials for counting, sorting, or problem solving that are easily distinguishable by touch. Their engagement is also facilitated by using containers, trays, and so forth that contain their materials and clearly define their work space.

MATHEMATICS

| At around 48 months of age | At around 60 months of age |
|---|---|
| **2.0** **Children begin to understand positions in space.** | **2.0** **Children expand their understanding of positions in space.** |
| **2.1** Identify positions of objects and people in space, such as in/on/under, up/down, and inside/outside. | **2.1** Identify positions of objects and people in space, including in/on/under, up/down, inside/outside, beside/between, and in front/behind. |
| **Examples** | **Examples** |
| • Goes under the table when the teacher communicates, " Pick up the cup. It's under the table."<br>• Communicates to another child in the playhouse, "Put the pan on the stove."<br>• Requests that another child put the balls inside the box.<br>• Looks up when the teacher says, "If you look up, you'll see your coat." | • During a treasure hunt, gives or follows directions to find something behind the doll bed or under the mat.<br>• Follows directions when asked by the teacher to stand in front of or behind another child.<br>• Communicates, "Where's my book?" A friend says, "It's over there on the table." She finds the book.<br>• Follows along with the directions during a game of "Simon Says" (e.g., "Put your hands in front of your legs"). |

# Mathematical Reasoning*

| *At around 48 months of age* | *At around 60 months of age* |
|---|---|
| **1.0 Children use mathematical thinking to solve problems that arise in their everyday environment.** | **1.0 Children expand the use of mathematical thinking to solve problems that arise in their everyday environment.** |
| **1.1** Begin to apply simple mathematical strategies to solve problems in their environment. | **1.1** Identify and apply a variety of mathematical strategies to solve problems in their environment. |

| **Examples** | **Examples** |
|---|---|
| <ul><li>Reconfigures blocks to build a balanced, tall tower by placing the rectangular blocks at the bottom and triangular blocks at the top.</li><li>Asks for one more paintbrush so he can put one brush in each paint cup while helping to set up an easel for painting.</li><li>Gives a friend two flowers and keeps two for himself, so they both have the same number of flowers.</li><li>Compares the length of her shoe to her friend's shoe by placing them side by side to check who has a longer shoe.</li><li>Classifies objects according to whether they can roll or not.</li><li>Pours sand from a big bucket to a smaller bucket and realizes that not all the sand can fit. The child looks for a bigger bucket.</li></ul> | <ul><li>After placing plates and napkins around the snack table, recognizes that he needs one more napkin for the last place and asks the teacher for another napkin.</li><li>Following a discussion about the size of the room, works with other children to measure the length of the room using block units, lay blocks of the same size along the wall end to end, and count the number of blocks.</li><li>Predicts the number of small balls in a closed box and then communicates, "Let's count."</li><li>Has run out of long blocks to complete a road and solves the problem by using two smaller blocks to "fill in" for a longer block.</li><li>When in need of six cones to set up an obstacle course but having only four, communicates, "I need two more cones."</li><li>Sorts the animal figures into two groups, wild animals for him and pets for his friend, when asked to share the animal figures with a friend.</li></ul> |

* Throughout these mathematics foundations many examples describe the child manipulating objects. Children with motor impairments may need assistance from an adult or peer to manipulate objects in order to do things such as count, sort, compare, order, measure, create patterns, or solve problems. A child might also use adaptive materials (e.g., large manipulatives that are easy to grasp). Alternately, a child might demonstrate knowledge in these areas without directly manipulating objects. For example, a child might direct a peer or teacher to place several objects in order from smallest to largest. Children with visual impairments might be offered materials for counting, sorting, or problem solving that are easily distinguishable by touch. Their engagement is also facilitated by using containers, trays, and so forth that contain their materials and clearly define their work space.

# Bibliographic Notes

## Number Sense

Research suggests that children start developing number sense in early infancy (Feigenson, Dehaene, and Spelke 2004). Much of what preschool children know about number is closely related to and depends on their understanding and mastery of counting (*Adding It Up* 2001). Counting builds a foundation for children's future understanding of mathematics, and this basic skill becomes the reference point as children learn to manipulate larger quantities in the future.

Children's understanding of numbers is initially qualitative, as they gain an understanding of "number-ness" (e.g., three-ness, four-ness) with small quantities, using subitizing: visually knowing "how many" are in a set without actually counting them (Clements 2004a; Fuson 1988, 1992a). Counting is a natural activity for young children as their everyday contexts often involve numbers and quantities, although it requires them to have a sophisticated set of skills based on many experiences to be able to count accurately.

Literature suggests that the three major basic building blocks for counting are learning of (1) the sequence of number words, (2) one-to-one correspondence, and (3) cardinality (knowing that the last number assigned to the last object counted gives the total number in the set) (*Adding It Up* 2001; Becker 1989; Clements 2004a; Fuson 1988, 1992a, 1992b; Hiebert and others 1997; Sophian 1988). Children are likely to experience the aspects of counting at different times and in different contexts. As they gain more experience, they start to connect and coordinate these individual concepts and develop skill in counting with fluency. The specific ways in which these different aspects of counting develop depend largely on individual children and their experiences. Research, however, is in agreement that very young children (ages up to three) may be able to handle small quantities first (groups of two to three), and as they grow older, they are more likely to be able to manage larger sets (by age five, groups of 10). Cardinality is typically developed between the ages of three and four years (Fuson 1988). The preschool years are a critical time for children to master the art of counting small numbers of objects.

Young children's understanding of quantities and numbers is largely related to counting, as noted in the previous section. Another important factor in children's development of number sense is early experience with number operations (*Adding It Up* 2001; Clements 2004a; Hiebert and others 1997; *Principles and Standards for School Mathematics* 2000). Research shows that counting and number operations are related and that children as young as three years are able to understand simple visual number patterns that involve number operations such as, "two fingers and two fingers make four" (Fuson 1988, 1992a). When children enter elementary schools, much of their engagement with mathematics will be devoted to learning how quantitative and logical relationships work in the world, and number operations hold a key to such learning (*Adding It Up* 2001; *Principles and Standards for School Mathematics* 2000). Although standard mathematical and abstract symbols (e.g., +, =) are absent from those early experiences with math operations, informal and early mathematics experience becomes the foundation for children's later learning in this area. Children generally use a diverse range of strategies to make sense of mathematical situations around them, and this diversity of thinking usually becomes a feature of their subsequent mathematical development (*Adding It Up* 2001).

Young children initially understand a quantity as an aggregate of single units (Fuson 1988, 1992a, 1992b; Carpenter and Moser 1988; Hiebert and others 1997; Geary 1994). Thus, when asked to combine two sets of objects, they count the two different sets starting from "one" to determine the answer (the counting-all strategy); therefore, the development of number operations is closely related to the way they learn to count. As children gain experiences, they gradually develop more sophisticated methods by abstracting the quantity of one of the two groups (one of the addends) and starting to count on (or count up, in subtraction) from that number. Children eventually become adept at decomposing numbers into smaller chunks for the purpose of adding and subtracting, although this method is usually not formally taught in U.S. classrooms (Fuson, 1992a). Nevertheless, preschool children's first experiences with the concept of decomposition of a number into smaller groups of

numbers is the beginning of an important development in mathematical reasoning. Learning the concept that groups or chunks of numbers make up larger numbers supports the understanding of arithmetic operations. For example, children's emerging understanding of different ways the number 10 can be decomposed into groups (e.g., 5 + 5, 4 + 6) contributes to their future learning of multidigit addition and subtraction (i.e., the operation of making 10 and moving it to the next position to the left of a multidigit number).

## Algebra and Functions

During the preschool years children develop beginning algebraic concepts as they sort and classify objects, observe patterns in their environment, and begin to predict what comes next based on a recognized pattern. Sorting items, classifying them, and working with patterns help children to bring order, organization, and predictability to their world. Classification and the analysis of patterns provide a foundation for algebraic thinking as children develop the ability to recognize relationships, form generalizations, and see the connection between common underlying structures (*Principles and Standards for School Mathematics* 2000; Clements 2004a).

Classification is the systematic arrangement of objects into groups according to established criteria and involves sorting, grouping, and categorizing. Classification is at the heart of identifying what is *invariant* across groups of mathematical objects or mathematical processes. Clements (2004a) suggests that analyzing, comparing, and classifying objects help create new knowledge of objects and their relationships; in *Developmental Guidelines for Geometry,* he recommends a classification activity in which four-year-olds match shapes to identify congruent and noncongruent two-dimensional shapes. Certainly, identifying triangles from within a set of figures that include examples and nonexamples of triangles is essentially a classification exercise. But classification should not be reserved solely for work with shapes; rather, it should be included in young children's mathematical activities as it also facilitates work with patterns and data analysis. The developmental continuum for data analysis starts with classification and counting and evolves into data representation (e.g., graphing).

Seo and Ginsburg (2004) were interested in how frequently four- and five-year-olds engaged in mathematical activities during play. Interestingly enough, after studying 90 of these children the researchers report that classification activities were the least frequently occurring of the mathematical activities observed. Only 2 percent of the mathematical activities observed could be categorized as classification activities.

Patterns help children learn to find order, cohesion, and predictability in seemingly disorganized situations. The recognition and analysis of patterns clearly provide a foundation for the development of algebraic thinking (Clements 2004a). Identifying and extending patterns are important preschool activities. For example, Ginsburg, Inoue, and Seo (1999) report that the detection, prediction, and creation of patterns with shapes are the most frequent mathematical activities in preschool. However,

compared with counting, little is known about young children's knowledge of patterns.

Patterns involve replication, completion, prediction, extension, and description or generalization (Greenes 1999). In preschool years, young children gradually develop the concept of patterns that includes recognizing a pattern, describing a pattern, creating a pattern, and extending a pattern. To understand a pattern, children should be able to identify similarities and differences among elements of a pattern, note the number of elements in the repeatable group, identify when the first group of elements begins to replicate itself, and make predictions about the order of elements based on given information.

Klein and Starkey (2004) report that young children experience difficulty at the beginning of the year with a fundamental property of repeating patterns: identifying the core unit of the pattern. However, experiences can have a positive impact on young children's knowledge of duplication and extension of patterns (Klein and Starkey 2004; Starkey, Klein, and Wakeley 2004).

In a study about the kinds of mathematical activities in which young children engage during play, Seo and Ginsburg (2004) found that four- and five-year-old children most often engage in "pattern and shape" activities, which the authors describe as ". . . identifying or creating patterns or shapes or exploring geometric properties and relationships. For example, Jennie makes a bead necklace, putting plastic beads into a string one by one. She uses only yellow and red beads for her necklace and makes a yellow-red color pattern" (Seo and Ginsburg 2004, 94).

These researchers provide some evidence that young children, when engaged in play, do generate their own repeating patterns. In preschool settings, teachers can encourage children to share their patterns created with objects, bodies, and sounds in relation to music, art, and movement (Smith 2001). Although the cited work is invaluable to the education of young children and the development of preschool learning foundations, much research remains to be done.

The developmental trajectory of patterns has been characterized as evolving from three-year-old children's ability to identify repeating pattern to four-year-old children's ability to engage in pattern duplication and pattern extension (Klein and Starkey 2004). The perception of the initial unit plays a fundamental role in both the duplication and extension of patterns.

## Measurement

Measurement is defined as a mathematical process that involves assigning numbers to a set of continuous quantities (Clements and Stephen 2004). Technically, measurement is a number that indicates a comparison between the attribute of the object being measured and the same attribute of a given unit of measure. To understand the concept of measurement, children must be able to decide on the attribute of objects to measure, select the units to measure the attribute, and use measuring skills and tools to compare the units (Clements 2004a; Van de Walle 2001). To accomplish this task, children should understand the different units that are assigned to physical quantities such as length, height, weight, volume, and nonphysical quantities such as time, and temperature (Smith 2001).

Measurement is one of the main real-world applications of mathematics. Shaw and Blake (1998) note that in children's mathematics curricula, measurement is an integration of number operation and geometry in everyday mathematical experiences. A typical developmental trajectory involves children first learning to use words that represent quantities or magnitude of a certain attribute. Then, children begin to demonstrate an ability to compare two objects directly and recognize equality or inequality. For example, they may compare two objects to determine which is longer or heavier. After comparing two items, children develop the ability to compare three or more objects and to order them by size (e.g. from shortest to longest) or by other attributes. Finally, children learn to measure, connecting numbers to attributes of objects, such as length, weight, amount, and area (Clements 2004a; Ginsburg, Inoue, and Seo 1999).

This theoretical sequence establishes the basis for the measurement strand. Children's familiarity with the language required to describe measurement relationships—such as longer, taller, shorter, the same length, holds less, holds the same amount—is an important foundation for the concept of measurement (Greenes 1999) that should be directly addressed in preschool and, thus, is incorporated as part of the mathematics foundations for children at around 48 months of age. Young preschoolers learn to use words that describe measurement relationships as they compare two objects directly to determine equality or inequality, and as they order three or more objects by size. Older preschool children begin to make progress in reasoning about measuring quantities with less dependence on perceptual cues (Clements 2004a, Clements and Stephen 2004). Children start to compare the length of objects, indirectly, using transitive reasoning, and to measure the length of objects often by using nonstandard units. They develop the ability to think of the length of a small unit (i.e., a block) as part of the length of the object being measured and to place the smaller unit repeatedly along the length of the larger object.

## Geometry

Geometry is the study of space and shape (Clements 1999). Geometry and spatial reasoning offer a way to describe, interpret, and imagine the world. They also provide an important tool for the study of mathematics and science. The research literature shows that young children bring to kindergarten a great deal of knowledge about shapes. This finding is important because teachers and curriculum writers seem to underestimate the knowledge about geometric figures that students bring to school. This underestimation and teachers' lack of confidence in their own geometry knowledge usually result in teachers' minimizing the time dedicated to teaching geometry concepts to children (Clements 2004a; Lehrer, Jenkins, and Osana 1998).

The literature recommends that young children be given the opportunity to work with many varied examples of a particular shape and many "nonexamples" of a particular shape (Clements 2004a). For example, children need to experience examples of triangles that are not just isosceles triangles. They need to experience triangles that are skewed—that is, a triangle where the "top" is not "in the middle," as in an isosceles triangle. They need also to experience triangles with a varying *aspect ratio*—the ratio of height to base. Without the opportunity to experience a wide range of triangles, children may come to "expect" triangles to have an aspect ratio that is close to 1 and, consequently, often reject appropriate examples of triangles because they are too "pointy" or too "flat." In addition, children need to experience nonexamples of triangles so that they can develop a robust and explicit sense of the properties of a triangle.

In 1959, Van Hiele developed a hierarchy of ways of understanding spatial ideas (Van Hiele 1986). The hierarchy consists of the following levels: 1—Visualization, 2—Analysis, 3—Abstraction, 4—Deduction, and 5—Rigor. Van Hiele's theory has become the most influential factor in geometry curricula. Recently, researchers have suggested a level of geometric thinking that exists before the visual level: a "precognition" level in which children cannot yet reliably identify circles, triangles, and squares (Clements 2004b; Clements and others 1999).

Shape knowledge involves not only recognition and naming but also an understanding of shape characteristics and properties. One way in which children demonstrate this understanding is through their ability to put together shapes into new shapes (Clements

2004a). The developmental trajectory for the composition of geometric figures evolves as children begin to use shapes individually to represent objects, progress to covering an outline with shapes, and eventually be able to combine shapes without an outline and make shape units (i.e., smaller shapes that make up a larger shape that is itself a part of a larger picture) (Clements 2004a; Clements and Sarama 2000).

Developing a sense of space is as important as developing spatial sense. Spatial sense allows people to get around in the world and know the relative positions of artifacts in the physical environment (Smith 2001). Spatial reasoning involves location, direction, distance, and identification of objects (Clements 1999). Very young children do develop an initial spatial sense to get around in the world. For example, young preschoolers learn to navigate their way around their school and classroom, and this ability suggests that they have created a mental map of those places. In the beginning stages of spatial reasoning, children use their own position as a point of reference for locating positions and orientations of objects in space, such as in/out and above/below. Then, children develop the ability to relate positions of two objects external to themselves or in themselves such as in front/in back, forward/backward, near/far, close to/far from (Greenes 1999). There is evidence that even preschool children develop mapping skills. They can build maps using familiar objects and as they get older, build imagery maps in familiar classroom settings (Blaut and Stea 1974; Gouteux and Spelke 2004; Rieser, Garing, and Young 1994).

Children's growth in understanding and knowledge about shape and space is thought to develop through education and experience rather than merely through maturational factors. Therefore, it is important not only to create a foundation for addressing this mathematics area, but also to encourage preschool programs to provide children with plenty of rich and varied opportunities to engage with various aspects of geometry. Engagement should be done in such a way that it grounds young children's experiences with shapes in action. As a result, the preschool foundations tend to de-emphasize the "naming" of shapes in this foundation; rather, they focus on children's ability to identify shapes, whether verbally or nonverbally.

## Mathematical Reasoning

Mathematical proficiency entails strategic competence, adaptive reasoning, conceptual understanding, productive disposition, and procedural fluency (*Adding It Up* 2001). Each of these competencies sets the foundation for what is often called problem solving or mathematical reasoning.

Most preschool children by at least three years of age show that they can solve problems involving simple addition and subtraction, often by modeling with real objects or thinking about sets of objects. In a study by Huttenlocher, Jordan, and Levine (1994), preschoolers were presented with a set of objects of a given size that were then hidden in a box, followed by another set of objects that were also placed in the box. The children were asked to produce a set of objects corresponding to the total number of objects contained in the box. The majority of three-year-olds were able to solve these types of problems when they involved adding or subtracting a single item, but their performance decreased rapidly as the size of the second set increased.

Preschoolers demonstrate the conceptual understanding and procedural fluency necessary for them to solve simple word problems (Fuson 1992b). Simple word problems are thought to be easier for preschool children to solve than number problems that are not cast in a context (Carpenter and others 1993). All ages of problem-solvers are influenced by the context of the problem and tend to perform better with more contextual information (Wason and Johnson-Laird 1972; Shannon 1999). However, preschool children tend to be more heavily influenced by the context of the problem than do older children and adults, thus limiting their ability to solve number problems that are not presented in context.

Alexander, White, and Daugherty (1997) propose three conditions for reasoning in young children: the children must have a sufficient knowledge base, the task must be understandable and motivating, and the context of the task must be familiar and comfortable to the problem-solver. These conditions probably apply to all ages of problem-

solvers (Wason and Johnson-Laird 1972; Shannon 1999).

Researchers indicate that four- and five-year-olds engage in advanced mathematical explorations spontaneously in their play (Ginsburg, Inoue, and Seo 1999; Seo and Ginsburg 2004). In their everyday activities, young children spontaneously engage in a variety of mathematical explorations and applications such as pattern analysis, change and transformation, comparison of magnitude, and estimations. Any logical thinking that children exhibit to solve real-life problems could potentially be considered beginning mathematical reasoning. For example, children distributing the same (or almost same) amount of snack to classmates or using strategies to solve immediate situations in play are situations in which children begin to demonstrate their ability to solve mathematical problems. Thus, it is crucial for teachers to be attuned to the fact that mathematical reasoning happens all the time in children's lives, and teachers would do well to use those occasions to nurture children's mathematical thinking skills. The examples illustrate the authentic problems that occur in preschoolers' everyday activities and all the different skills involved in mathematical reasoning and problem solving.

# Glossary

**attribute.** A property or characteristic of an object or a person; attributes such as size, color, or shape would be apparent to a preschool child and would be used in grouping or sorting

**cardinality.** The concept that the number name applied to the last object counted represents the total number of objects in the group (the quantity of objects counted)

**classification.** The sorting, grouping, or categorizing of objects according to established criteria

**one-to-one correspondence.** One and only one number word is used for each object in the array of objects being counted

**simple repeating pattern.** A pattern with two repeating elements: A-B-A-B, A-A-B-B, A-B-B-A-B-B

**subitize.** The ability to quickly and accurately determine the quantity of objects in a small group (of up to five objects) without actually counting the objects

# References

*Adding It Up: Helping Children Learn Mathematics.* 2001. Edited by J. Kilpatrick, J. J. Swafford, and B. Findell. Washington, DC: National Academy Press.

Alexander, P. A.; C. S. White; and M. Daughterty. 1997. "Analogical Reasoning and Early Mathematics Learning," in *Mathematical Reasoning: Analogies, Metaphors, and Images.* Edited by L. D. English. Mahwah, NJ: Lawrence Erlbaum Associates.

Becker, J. 1989. "Preschoolers' Use of Number Words to Denote One-to-One Correspondence," *Child Development,* Vol. 60, 1147–57.

Baroody, A. J. 1992. "The Development of Preschooler's Counting Skills and Principles," in *Pathways to Number: Children's Developing Numerical Abilities.* Edited by J. Bideaud, C. Meljac, and J. P. Fischer. Hillsdale, NJ: Erlbaum.

Baroody, A. J. 2004. "The Developmental Bases for Early Childhood Number and Operations Standards" in *Engaging Young Children in Mathematics: Standards for Early Childhood Mathematics Education.* Edited by D. H. Clements, J. Sarama, and A. M. DiBiase. Mahwah, NJ: Erlbaum.

Blaut, J. M., and D. Stea. 1974. "Mapping at the Age of Three," *Journal of Geography,* Vol. 73, No. 7, 5–9.

Brush, L. R. 1978. "Preschool Children's Knowledge of Addition and Subtraction," *Journal of Research in Mathematics Education,* Vol. 9, 44–54.

Carpenter, T. P., and others. 1993. "Models of Problem Solving: A Study of Kindergarten Children's Problem-Solving Processes, *Journal for Research in Mathematics Education,* Vol. 24, 428–41.

Carpenter, T. P., and J. M. Moser. 1982. "The Development of Addition and Subtraction Problem-Solving Skills," in *Addition and Subtraction: A Cognitive Perspective.* Edited by T. P. Carpenter, J. M. Moser, and T. A. Romberg. Hillsdale, NJ: Erlbaum.

Clements, D. H. 1999. "Geometric and Spatial Thinking in Young Children," in *Mathematics in the Early Years.* Edited by J. V. Copley. Reston, Va.: National Council of Teachers of Mathematics.

Clements, D. H. 2004a. "Major Themes and Recommendations," in *Engaging Young Children in Mathematics: Standards for Early Childhood Mathematics Education.* Edited by D. H. Clements, J. Sarama, and A. M. DiBiase. Mahwah, NJ: Erlbaum.

Clements, D. H. 2004b. "Geometric and Spatial Thinking in Early Childhood Education," in *Engaging Young Children in Mathematics: Standards for Early Childhood Mathematics Education.* Edited by D. H. Clements, J. Sarama, and A. M. DiBiase. Mahwah, NJ: Erlbaum.

Clements, D. H., and J. Sarama. 2000. "Young Children's Ideas About Geometric Shapes," *Teaching Children Mathematics,* Vol. 6, 482-88.

Clements, D. H., and others. 1999. "Young Children's Concepts of Shape," *Journal of Research in Mathematics Education,* Vol. 30, 192–212.

Clements, D. H., and M. Stephan. 2004. "Measurement in Pre-K to Grade 2 Mathematics," in *Engaging Young Children in Mathematics: Standards for Early Childhood Mathematics Education.* Edited by D. H. Clements, J. Sarama, and A. M. DiBiase. Mahwah, NJ: Erlbaum.

Cooper, R. G. 1984. "Early Number Development: Discovering Number Space with Addition and Subtraction," in *Origins of Cognitive Skills.* Edited by C. Hillsdale, NJ: Erlbaum.

Copeland, R. W. 1984. *How Children Learn Mathematics* (Fourth edition). New York: Macmillan.

Copley, J. 2001. *The Young Child and Mathematics.* Washington, DC: National Association for the Education of Young Children.

Devlin, K. 1988. *The Math Gene: How Mathematical Thinking Evolved and Why Numbers Are Like Gossip.* New York: Basic Books.

Fayol, M. 1992. "From Number to Numbers in Use: Solving Arithmetic Problems," in *Pathways to Number: Children's Developing Numerical Abilities.* Edited by J. Bideaud, C. Meljac, and J. P. Fischer. Hillsdale, NJ: Erlbaum.

Feigenson, L.; S. Dehaene; and E. Spelke. 2004. "Core Systems of Number," *Trends in Cognitive Sciences,* Vol. 8, 307–14.

Fischer, J. P. 1992. "The Discontinuity After Three," in *Pathways to Number: Children's Developing Numerical Abilities.* Edited by J. Bideaud, C. Meljac, and J. P. Fischer. Hillsdale, NJ: Erlbaum.

Freund, L. S.; L. Baker; and S. Sonnenschein. 1990. "Developmental Changes in Strategic Approaches to Classification," *Journal of Experimental Child Psychology,* Vol. 49, 342–62.

Friedman, W. J. 1989. "The Development of Children's Knowledge of Temporal Structure," *Child Development,* Vol. 57, 1386–1400.

Friedman, W. J. 1990. "Children's Representations of the Pattern of Daily Activities," *Child Development,* Vol. 61, 1399–1412.

Friedman, W. J. 1992. "The Development of Children's Representations of Temporal Structure," in *Time, Action, and Cognition: Towards Bridging the Gap.* Edited by F. Macar, V. Pouthas, and W. J. Friedman. Dordrecht, The Netherlands: Kulwer Academic Publishers.

*From Neurons to Neighborhoods: The Science of Early Childhood Development.* 2000. Edited by J. P. Shonkoff and D. A. Phillips. Washington, DC: National Academy Press.

Fuson, K. C. 1988. *Children's Counting and Concepts of Number.* New York: Springer-Verlag.

Fuson, K. C. 1992a. "Relationships between Counting and Cardinality from Age 2 to Age 8," in *Pathways to Number: Children's Developing Numerical Abilities.* Edited by J. Bideau, C. Meljac, and J. P. Fischer. Hillsdale, NJ: Lawrence Erlbaum.

Fuson, K. C. 1992b. "Research on Whole Number Addition and Subtraction," in *Handbook of Research on Mathematics Teaching and Learning.* Edited by D. Grouws. New York: Macmillan.

Fuson, K. C. 2004. "Pre-K to Grade 2 Goals and Standards: Achieving 21st-Century Mastery for All, " in *Engaging Young Children in Mathematics: Standards for Early Childhood Mathematics Education.* Edited by D. Clements, J. Sarama; and A. M. DiBiase. Mahwah, NJ: Erlbaum.

Fuson, K. C., and Y. Kwon. 1992. "Korean Children's Single-Digit Addition and Subtraction: Numbers Structured by Ten," *Journal for Research in Mathematics Education,* Vol. 23, 148–65.

Fuson, K. C., and others. 2000. "Blending the Best of the Twentieth Century to Achieve a Mathematics Equity Pedagogy in the Twenty-First Century," in *Learning Mathematics for a New Century* (2000 Yearbook of the National Council of Teachers of Mathematics). Edited by M. J. Burke. Reston, VA: National Council of Teachers of Mathematics.

Fuson, K.; J. Richards; and D. J. Briars. 1982. "The Acquisition and Elaboration of the Number Word Sequence," in *Progress in Cognitive Development: Children's Logical and Mathematical Cognition* (Vol. 1). Edited by C. Brainerd. New York: Springer-Verlag.

Geary, D. C. 1994. *Children's Mathematical Development: Research and Practical Applications.* Washington, DC: American Psychological Association,

Gelman, R., and C. R. Gallistel. 1978. *The Child's Understanding of Number.* Cambridge, MA: Harvard University Press.

Ginsburg, H. P.; N. Inoue; and K. H. Seo. 1999. "Young Children Doing Mathematics: Observations of Everyday Activities," in *Mathematics in the Early Years.* Edited by J. V. Cooper. Reston, VA: National Council of Teachers of Mathematics.

Ginsburg, H. P.; A. Klein; and P. Starkey. 1998. "The Development of Children's Mathematical Thinking: Connecting Research with Practice," in *Handbook of Child Psychology: Vol. 4. Child Psychology in Practice* (Fifth edition). Edited by W. Damon (Series Ed.), J. E. Sigel, and A. Renninger (Vol. Eds.), New York: Wiley.

Ginsburg, H. P., and others. 2006. "Mathematical Thinking and Learning," in *Blackwell Handbook of Early Childhood Development.* Edited by K. McCartney and D. Phillips. Malden, MA: Blackwell Publishing.

Ginsburg, H. P., and S. Opper. 1988. *Piaget's Theory of Intellectual Development.* Englewood Cliffs, NJ: Prentice Hall.

Gouteux, S., and E. Spelke. 2004. "Children's Use of Geometry and Landmarks to Reorient in an Open Space," *Cognition,* Vol. 81, No. 2, 119–48.

Greenes, C. 1999. "Ready to Learn," in *Mathematics in the Early Years.* Edited by J. V. Cooper. Reston, VA: National Council of Teachers of Mathematics.

Hatano, G. 1988. "Social and Motivational Basis for Mathematical Understanding," *New Directions for Child Development,* Vol. 41, 55–70.

Hiebert, J., and others. 1997. *Making Sense: Teaching and Learning Mathematics with Understanding.* Portsmouth, NH: Heinemann.

Hughes, M. 1986. *Children and Number: Difficulties in Learning Mathematics.* New York: Basil Blackwell.

Huttenlocher, J.; N. C. Jordan; and S. C. Levine. 1994. "A Mental Model for Early Arithmetic," *Journal of Experimental Psychology,* Vol. 123, 284–96.

Inhelder, B., and J. Piaget. 1969. *The Early Growth of Logic in the Child.* New York: W.W. Norton & Company.

Klein, A., and P. J. Starkey. 2004. "Fostering Preschool Children's Mathematical Knowledge: Findings from the Berkeley Math Readiness Project," in *Engaging Young Children in Mathematics: Standards for Early Childhood Mathematics Education.* Edited by D. H. Clements and J. Samara. Hillsdale, NJ: Lawrence Erlbaum.

Lehrer, R.; M. Jenkins; and H. Osana. 1998. "Longitudinal Study of Children's Reasoning about Space and Geometry," in *Designing Learning Environments for Developing Understanding of Geometry and Space.* Edited by R. Lehrer and D. Chazen. Mahwah, NJ: Erlbaum.

Long, K., and C. Kamii. 2001. "The Measurement of Time: Children's Construction of Transitivity, Unit Iteration, and Conservation of Speed," *School Science and Mathematics,* Vol. 101, No. 3, 125–32.

Marvin, C. A. 1995. "The Family Car as a 'Vehicle' for Children's Use of Distant Time Referents," *Early Childhood Research Quarterly,* Vol. 10, 185–203.

Matsushita, K. 1994. "Acquiring Mathematical Knowledge through Semantic and Pragmatic Problem Solving," *Human Development,* Vol. 37, 220–32.

Murata, A. 2004. "Paths to Learning Ten-Structured Understanding of Teen Sums: Addition Solution Methods of Japanese Grade 1 Students," *Cognition and Instruction,* Vol. 22, 185–218.

National Association for the Education of Young Children (NAEYC) and National

Council for Teachers of Mathematics (NCTM). 2002. *Joint Position Statement, Early Childhood Mathematics: Promoting Good Beginnings.*

National Council of Teachers of Mathematics (NCTM). 2000. *Principles and Standards for School Mathematics.* Reston, VA: Author.

Piaget, J., and B. Inhelder. 1967. *The Child's Conception of Space.* New York: Norton.

Piaget, J.; B. Inhelder; and A. Szeminka. 1960. *The Child's Conception of Geometry.* New York: Basic Books.

Pieraut-Le Bonniec, G. 1982. "From Rhythm to Reversibility," in *Action and Thought: From Sensorimotor Schemes to Symbolic Operations.* Edited by G. E. Forman. London: Academic Press.

*Principles and Standards for School Mathematics.* Reston, VA: National Council of Teachers of Mathematics (NCTM). 2000.

*A Research Companion to Principles and Standards for School Mathematics.* Reston, VA: National Council of Teachers of Mathematics (NCTM). 2003.

Rieser, J. J.; A. E. Garing; and M. F. Young. 1994. "Imagery, Action, and Young Children's Spatial Orientation: It's Not Being There That Counts, It's What One Has in Mind," *Child Development,* Vol. 65, No. 5, 1272–78.

Scott, C. 1997. "The Acquisition of Some Conversational Time Concepts by Preschool Children." Paper presented at the Annual Meeting of the American Educational Research Association. Chicago, Illinois, March.

Seo, K., and H. P. Ginsburg. 2004. "What Is Developmentally Appropriate in Early Childhood Mathematics Education? Lessons from New Research," in *Engaging Young Children in Mathematics: Standards for Early Childhood Mathematics Education.* Edited by D. H. Clements, J. Sarama, and A. M. DiBiase. Hillsdale, NJ: Lawrence Erlbaum.

Shannon, A. 1999. *Keeping Score.* Washington, DC: National Academy Press.

Shaw, J. M., and S. S. Blake. 1998. *Mathematics for Young Children.* Upper Saddle River, NJ: Prentice-Hall.

Siegler, R. S., and M. Robinson. 1982. "The Development of Numerical Understandings," in *Advances in Child Development and Behavior,* Vol. 16. Edited by H. W. Reese and L. P. Lipsitt. New York: Academic Press.

Smith, S. S. 2001. *Early Childhood Mathematics.* Boston, MA: Allyn and Bacon.

Sophian, C. 1996. *Children's Numbers.* Boulder, CO: Westview Press.

Sophian, C. 1998. "Early Developments in Children's Understanding of Number: Inferences about Numeracy and One-to-One Correspondence," *Child Development,* Vol. 59, 1397–1414.

Sophian, C., and N. Adams. 1987. "Infants' Understanding of Numerical Transformations," *British Journal of Developmental Psychology,* Vol. 5, 257–64.

Starkey, P. 1992. "The Early Development of Numerical Reasoning," *Cognition,* Vol. 43, 93–126.

Starkey, P., and R. G. Cooper. 1995. "The Development of Subitizing in Young Children," *British Journal of Developmental Psychology,* Vol. 13, 399–420.

Starkey, P.; A. Klein; and A. 2004. Wakeley. "Enhancing Young Children's Mathematical Knowledge Through a Pre-Kindergarten Mathematics Intervention," *Early Childhood Research Quarterly,* Vol. 19, 99–120.

Steen, L. A. 1990. *On the Shoulders of Giants: New Approaches to Numeracy.* Washington, DC: National Academy Press.

Stigler, J. 1984. "Mental Abacus: The Effect of Abacus Training on Chinese Children's Mental Calculation," *Cognitive Psychology,* Vol. 16, 145–76.

Van de Walle, J. A. 2001. *Elementary and Middle School Mathematics: Teaching Developmentally* (Fourth edition). New York: Longman.

Van Hiele, P. M. *Structure and Insight: A Theory of Mathematics Education.* Orlando, FL: Academic Press, 1986.

Wagner, S. H., and J. Walters. 1982. "A Longitudinal Analysis of Early Number Concepts: From Numbers to Number," in *Action and Thought: from Sensorimotor Schemes to Symbolic Operations.* Edited by G. E. Forman. New York: Academic Press.

Wason. P. C., and P. N. Johnson-Laird. 1972. *Psychology of Reasoning: Structure and Content.* Cambridge, MA: Harvard University Press.

# The Foundations

## Social-Emotional Development

### Self

#### 1.0 Self-Awareness

| *At around 48 months of age* | *At around 60 months of age* |
|---|---|
| 1.1 Describe their physical characteristics, behavior, and abilities positively. | 1.1 Compare their characteristics with those of others and display a growing awareness of their psychological characteristics, such as thoughts and feelings. |

#### 2.0 Self-Regulation

| | |
|---|---|
| 2.1 Need adult guidance in managing their attention, feelings, and impulses and show some effort at self-control. | 2.1 Regulate their attention, thoughts, feelings, and impulses more consistently, although adult guidance is sometimes necessary. |

#### 3.0 Social and Emotional Understanding

| | |
|---|---|
| 3.1 Seek to understand people's feelings and behavior, notice diversity in human characteristics, and are interested in how people are similar and different. | 3.1 Begin to comprehend the mental and psychological reasons people act as they do and how they contribute to differences between people. |

#### 4.0 Empathy and Caring

| | |
|---|---|
| 4.1 Demonstrate concern for the needs of others and people in distress. | 4.1 Respond to another's distress and needs with sympathetic caring and are more likely to assist. |

#### 5.0 Initiative in Learning

| | |
|---|---|
| 5.1 Enjoy learning and are confident in their abilities to make new discoveries although may not persist at solving difficult problems. | 5.1 Take greater initiative in making new discoveries, identifying new solutions, and persisting in trying to figure things out. |

# Social Interaction

## 1.0   Interactions with Familiar Adults

| *At around 48 months of age* | *At around 60 months of age* |
|---|---|
| 1.1   Interact with familiar adults comfortably and competently, especially in familiar settings. | 1.1   Participate in longer and more reciprocal interactions with familiar adults and take greater initiative in social interaction. |

## 2.0   Interactions with Peers

| | |
|---|---|
| 2.1   Interact easily with peers in shared activities that occasionally become cooperative efforts. | 2.1   More actively and intentionally cooperate with each other. |
| 2.2   Participate in simple sequences of pretend play. | 2.2   Create more complex sequences of pretend play that involve planning, coordination of roles, and cooperation. |
| 2.3   Seek assistance in resolving peer conflict, especially when disagreements have escalated into physical aggression. | 2.3   Negotiate with each other, seeking adult assistance when needed, and increasingly use words to respond to conflict. Disagreements may be expressed with verbal taunting in addition to physical aggression. |

## 3.0   Group Participation

| | |
|---|---|
| 3.1   Participate in group activities and are beginning to understand and cooperate with social expectations, group rules, and roles. | 3.1   Participate positively and cooperatively as group members. |

## 4.0   Cooperation and Responsibility

| | |
|---|---|
| 4.1   Seek to cooperate with adult instructions but their capacities for self-control are limited, especially when they are frustrated or upset. | 4.1   Have growing capacities for self-control and are motivated to cooperate in order to receive adult approval and think approvingly of themselves. |

# Relationships

## 1.0    Attachments to Parents

| *At around 48 months of age* | *At around 60 months of age* |
|---|---|
| 1.1  Seek security and support from their primary family attachment figures. | 1.1  Take greater initiative in seeking support from their primary family attachment figures. |
| 1.2  Contribute to maintaining positive relationships with their primary family attachment figures. | 1.2  Contribute to positive mutual cooperation with their primary family attachment figures. |
| 1.3  After experience with out-of-home care, manage departures and separations from primary family attachment figures with the teacher's assistance. | 1.3  After experience with out-of-home care, comfortably depart from their primary family attachment figures. Also maintain well-being while apart from primary family attachment figures during the day. |

## 2.0    Close Relationships with Teachers and Caregivers

| | |
|---|---|
| 2.1  Seek security and support from their primary teachers and caregivers. | 2.1  Take greater initiative in seeking the support of their primary teachers and caregivers. |
| 2.2  Contribute to maintaining positive relationships with their primary teachers and caregivers. | 2.2  Contribute to positive mutual cooperation with their primary teachers and caregivers. |

## 3.0    Friendships

| | |
|---|---|
| 3.1  Choose to play with one or two special peers whom they identify as friends. | 3.1  Friendships are more reciprocal, exclusive, and enduring. |

# Language and Literacy

## Listening and Speaking

### 1.0  Language Use and Conventions

| *At around 48 months of age* | *At around 60 months of age* |
|---|---|
| 1.1  Use language to communicate with others in familiar social situations for a variety of basic purposes, including describing, requesting, commenting, acknowledging, greeting, and rejecting. | 1.1  Use language to communicate with others in both familiar and unfamiliar social situations for a variety of basic and advanced purposes, including reasoning, predicting, problem solving, and seeking new information. |
| 1.2  Speak clearly enough to be understood by familiar adults and children. | 1.2  Speak clearly enough to be understood by both familiar and unfamiliar adults and children. |
| 1.3  Use accepted language and style during communication with familiar adults and children. | 1.3  Use accepted language and style during communication with both familiar and unfamiliar adults and children. |
| 1.4  Use language to construct short narratives that are real or fictional. | 1.4  Use language to construct extended narratives that are real or fictional. |

### 2.0  Vocabulary

| | |
|---|---|
| 2.1  Understand and use accepted words for objects, actions, and attributes encountered frequently in both real and symbolic contexts. | 2.1  Understand and use an increasing variety and specificity of accepted words for objects, actions, and attributes encountered in both real and symbolic contexts. |
| 2.2  Understand and use accepted words for categories of objects encountered and used frequently in everyday life. | 2.2  Understand and use accepted words for categories of objects encountered in everyday life. |
| 2.3  Understand and use simple words that describe the relations between objects. | 2.3  Understand and use both simple and complex words that describe the relations between objects. |

## 3.0  Grammar

| *At around 48 months of age* | *At around 60 months of age* |
|---|---|
| 3.1  Understand and use increasingly complex and longer sentences, including sentences that combine two phrases or two to three concepts to communicate ideas. | 3.1  Understand and use increasingly complex and longer sentences, including sentences that combine two to three phrases or three to four concepts to communicate ideas. |
| 3.2  Understand and typically use age-appropriate grammar, including accepted word forms, such as subject-verb agreement, progressive tense, regular past tense, regular plurals, pronouns, and possessives. | 3.2  Understand and typically use age-appropriate grammar, including accepted word forms, such as subject-verb agreement, progressive tense, regular and irregular past tense, regular and irregular plurals, pronouns, and possessives. |

# Reading

## 1.0    Concepts about Print

| *At around 48 months of age* | *At around 60 months of age* |
|---|---|
| 1.1  Begin to display appropriate book-handling behaviors and begin to recognize print conventions. | 1.1  Display appropriate book-handling behaviors and knowledge of print conventions. |
| 1.2  Recognize print as something that can be read. | 1.2  Understand that print is something that is read and has specific meaning. |

## 2.0    Phonological Awareness

|  | *At around 60 months of age* |
|---|---|
|  | 2.1  Orally blend and delete words and syllables without the support of pictures or objects. |
|  | 2.2  Orally blend the onsets, rimes, and phonemes of words and orally delete the onsets of words, <u>with</u> the support of pictures or objects. |

### 3.0    Alphabetics and Word/Print Recognition

| *At around 48 months of age* | *At around 60 months of age* |
|---|---|
| 3.1  Recognize the first letter of own name. | 3.1  Recognize own name or other common words in print. |
| 3.2  Match some letter names to their printed form. | 3.2  Match more than half of uppercase letter names and more than half of lowercase letter names to their printed form. |
|  | 3.3  Begin to recognize that letters have sounds. |

### 4.0    Comprehension and Analysis of Age-Appropriate Text

| | |
|---|---|
| 4.1  Demonstrate knowledge of main characters or events in a familiar story (e.g., who, what, where) through answering questions (e.g., recall and simple inferencing), retelling, reenacting, or creating artwork. | 4.1  Demonstrate knowledge of details in a familiar story, including characters, events, and ordering of events through answering questions (particularly summarizing, predicting, and inferencing), retelling, reenacting, or creating artwork. |
| 4.2  Demonstrate knowledge from informational text through labeling, describing, playing, or creating artwork. | 4.2  Use information from informational text in a variety of ways, including describing, relating, categorizing, or comparing and contrasting. |

### 5.0    Literacy Interest and Response

| | |
|---|---|
| 5.1  Demonstrate enjoyment of literacy and literacy-related activities. | 5.1  Demonstrate, with increasing independence, enjoyment of literacy and literacy-related activities. |
| 5.2  Engage in routines associated with literacy activities. | 5.2  Engage in more complex routines associated with literacy activities. |

# Writing

## 1.0    Writing Strategies

| At around 48 months of age | At around 60 months of age |
|---|---|
| 1.1  Experiment with grasp and body position using a variety of drawing and writing tools. | 1.1  Adjust grasp and body position for increased control in drawing and writing. |
| 1.2  Write using scribbles that are different from pictures. | 1.2  Write letters or letter-like shapes to represent words or ideas. |
| 1.3  Write marks to represent own name. | 1.3  Write first name nearly correctly. |

# English-Language Development

## Listening

### 1.0   Children listen with understanding.

#### *Focus: Beginning words*

| Beginning | Middle | Later |
|---|---|---|
| 1.1 Attend to English oral language in both real and pretend activity, relying on intonation, facial expressions, or the gestures of the speaker. | 1.1 Demonstrate understanding of words in English for objects and actions as well as phrases encountered frequently in both real and pretend activity. | 1.1 Begin to demonstrate an understanding of a larger set of words in English (for objects and actions, personal pronouns, and possessives) in both real and pretend activity. |

#### *Focus: Requests and directions*

| | | |
|---|---|---|
| 1.2 Begin to follow simple directions in English, especially when there are contextual cues. | 1.2 Respond appropriately to requests involving one step when personally directed by others, which may occur with or without contextual cues. | 1.2 Follow directions that involve a one- or two-step sequence, relying less on contextual cues. |

#### *Focus: Basic and advanced concepts*

| | | |
|---|---|---|
| 1.3 Demonstrate an understanding of words related to basic and advanced concepts in the home language that are appropriate for the age (as reported by parents, teachers, assistants, or others, with the assistance of an interpreter if necessary). | 1.3 Begin to demonstrate an understanding of words in English related to basic concepts. | 1.3 Demonstrate an understanding of words in English related to more advanced concepts. |

# Speaking

## 1.0 Children use nonverbal and verbal strategies to communicate with others.

### Focus: Communication of needs

| Beginning | Middle | Later |
|---|---|---|
| 1.1 Use nonverbal communication, such as gestures or behaviors, to seek attention, request objects, or initiate a response from others. | 1.1 Combine nonverbal and some verbal communication to be understood by others (may code-switch—that is, use the home language and English—and use telegraphic and/or formulaic speech). | 1.1 Show increasing reliance on verbal communication in English to be understood by others. |

### Focus: Vocabulary production

| Beginning | Middle | Later |
|---|---|---|
| 1.2 Use vocabulary in the home language that is age-appropriate (as reported by parents, teachers, assistants, or others and with the assistance of an interpreter if necessary). | 1.2 Begin to use English vocabulary, mainly consisting of concrete nouns and with some verbs and pronouns (telegraphic speech). | 1.2 Use new English vocabulary to share knowledge of concepts. |

### Focus: Conversation

| Beginning | Middle | Later |
|---|---|---|
| 1.3 Converse in the home language (as reported by parents, teachers, assistants, or others, with the assistance of an interpreter if necessary). | 1.3 Begin to converse with others, using English vocabulary but may code-switch (i.e., use the home language and English). | 1.3 Sustain a conversation in English about a variety of topics. |

## 1.0 Children use nonverbal and verbal strategies to communicate with others.

### Focus: Utterance length and complexity

| Beginning | Middle | Later |
|---|---|---|
| 1.4 Use a range of utterance lengths in the home language that is age-appropriate (as reported by parents, teachers, assistants, or others, with the assistance of an interpreter if necessary). | 1.4 Use two- and three-word utterances in English to communicate. | 1.4 Increase utterance length in English by adding appropriate possessive pronouns (e.g., his, her); conjunctions (e.g., and, or); or other elements (e.g., adjectives, adverbs). |

### Focus: Grammar

| Beginning | Middle | Later |
|---|---|---|
| 1.5 Use age-appropriate grammar in the home language (e.g., plurals; simple past tense; use of subject, verb, object), sometimes with errors (as reported by parents, teachers, assistants, or others, with the assistance of an interpreter if necessary). | 1.5 Begin to use some English grammatical markers (e.g., -ing or plural –s) and, at times, apply the rules of grammar of the home language to English. | 1.5 Expand the use of different forms of grammar in English (e.g., plurals; simple past tense; use of subject, verb and object), sometimes with errors. |

### Focus: Inquiry

| Beginning | Middle | Later |
|---|---|---|
| 1.6 Ask a variety of types of questions (e.g., "what," "why," "how," "when," and "where") in the home language (as reported by parents, teachers, assistants, or others, with the assistance of an interpreter if necessary. | 1.6 Begin to use "what" and "why" questions in English, sometimes with errors. | 1.6 Begin to use "what," "why," "how," "when," and "where" questions in more complete forms in English, sometimes with errors. |

## 2.0 Children begin to understand and use social conventions in English.

### Focus: Social conventions

| Beginning | Middle | Later |
|---|---|---|
| 2.1 Use social conventions of the home language (as reported by teachers, parents, assistants, or others, with the assistance of an interpreter if necessary). | 2.1 Demonstrate a beginning understanding of English social conventions. | 2.1 Appropriately use words and tone of voice associated with social conventions in English. |

## 3.0 Children use language to create oral narratives about their personal experiences.

### Focus: Narrative development

| Beginning | Middle | Later |
|---|---|---|
| 3.1 Create a narrative in the home language (as reported by parents, teachers, assistants, or others, with the assistance of an interpreter if necessary). | 3.1 Begin to use English to talk about personal experiences; may complete a narrative in the home language while using some English (i.e., code-switching). | 3.1 Produce simple narratives in English that are real or fictional. |

# Reading

## 1.0  Children demonstrate an appreciation and enjoyment of reading and literature.

### Focus: Participate in read-aloud activity

| Beginning | Middle | Later |
|---|---|---|
| 1.1  Attend to an adult reading a short storybook written in the home language or a storybook written in English if the story has been read in the home language. | 1.1  Begin to participate in reading activities, using books written in English when the language is predictable. | 1.1  Participate in reading activities, using a variety of genres that are written in English (e.g., poetry, fairy tales, concept books, and informational books). |

### Focus: Interest in books and reading

| Beginning | Middle | Later |
|---|---|---|
| 1.2  "Read" familiar books written in the home language or in English when encouraged by others and, in the home language, talk about the books. | 1.2  Choose to "read" familiar books written in the home language or in English with increasing independence and, in the home language or in English, talk about the books. | 1.2  Choose to "read" familiar books written in English with increasing independence and talk about the books in English. |

## 2.0 Children show an increasing understanding of book reading.

### Focus: Personal connections to the story

| Beginning | Middle | Later |
| --- | --- | --- |
| 2.1 Begin to identify and relate to a story from their own life experiences in the home language (as reported by parents, teachers, assistants, or others, with the assistance of an interpreter if necessary). | 2.1 Describe their own experiences related to the topic of the story, using telegraphic and/or formulaic speech in English. | 2.1 Begin to engage in extended conversations in English about stories. |

### Focus: Story structure

| Beginning | Middle | Later |
| --- | --- | --- |
| 2.2 Retell a story in the home language when read or told a story in the home language (as reported by parents, teachers, assistants, or others, with the assistance of an interpreter if necessary). | 2.2 Retell a story using the home language and some English when read or told a story in English. | 2.2 Retell in English the majority of a story read or told in English. |

## 3.0 Children demonstrate an understanding of print conventions.

### Focus: Book handling

| Beginning | Middle | Later |
| --- | --- | --- |
| 3.1 Begin to understand that books are read in a consistent manner (e.g., in English, pages are turned from right to left and the print is read from top to bottom, left to right; this may vary in other languages). | 3.1 Continue to develop an understanding of how to read a book, sometimes applying knowledge of print conventions from the home language. | 3.1 Demonstrate an understanding that print in English is organized from left to right, top to bottom, and that pages are turned from right to left when a book is read. |

## 4.0 Children demonstrate awareness that print carries meaning.

### Focus: Environmental print

| Beginning | Middle | Later |
|---|---|---|
| 4.1 Begin to recognize that symbols in the environment (classroom, community, or home) carry a consistent meaning in the home language or in English. | 4.1 Recognize in the environment (classroom, community, or home) some familiar symbols, words, and print labels in the home language or in English. | 4.1 Recognize in the environment (classroom, community, or home) an increasing number of familiar symbols, words, and print labels in English. |

## 5.0 Children demonstrate progress in their knowledge of the alphabet in English.

### Focus: Letter awareness

| | | |
|---|---|---|
| 5.1 Interact with material representing the letters of the English alphabet. | 5.1 Begin to talk about the letters of the English alphabet while playing and interacting with them; may code-switch (use the home language and English). | 5.1 Begin to demonstrate understanding that the letters of the English alphabet are symbols used to make words. |

### Focus: Letter recognition

| | | |
|---|---|---|
| 5.2 Begin to recognize the first letter in their own name or the character for their own name in the home language or English. | 5.2 Identify some letters of the alphabet in English. | 5.2 Identify ten or more letters of the alphabet in English. |

## 6.0 Children demonstrate phonological awareness.

### *Focus: Rhyming*

| Beginning | Middle | Later |
|---|---|---|
| 6.1 Listen attentively and begin to participate in simple songs, poems, and finger plays that emphasize rhyme in the home language or in English. | 6.1 Begin to repeat or recite simple songs, poems, and finger plays that emphasize rhyme in the home language or in English. | 6.1 Repeat, recite, produce, or initiate simple songs, poems, and finger plays that emphasize rhyme in English. |

### *Focus: Onset (initial sound)*

| | | |
|---|---|---|
| 6.2 Listen attentively and begin to participate in simple songs, poems, and finger plays in the home language or in English. | 6.2 Begin to recognize words that have a similar onset (initial sound) in the home language or in English, with support. | 6.2 Recognize and produce words that have a similar onset (initial sound) in English. |

### *Focus: Sound differences in the home language and English*

| | | |
|---|---|---|
| 6.3 Attend to and manipulate different sounds or tones in words in the home language (as reported by parents, teachers, assistants, or others, with the assistance of an interpreter if necessary.) | 6.3 Begin to use words in English with phonemes (individual units of meaningful sound in a word or syllable) that are different from the home language. | 6.3 Begin to orally manipulate sounds (onsets, rimes, and phonemes) in words in English, with support. |

# Writing

## 1.0    Children use writing to communicate their ideas.

### Focus: Writing as communication

| Beginning | Middle | Later |
|---|---|---|
| 1.1  Begin to understand that writing can be used to communicate. | 1.1  Begin to understand that what is said in the home language or in English can be written down and read by others. | 1.1  Develop an increasing understanding that what is said in English can be written down and read by others. |

### Focus: Writing to represent words or ideas

| | | |
|---|---|---|
| 1.2  Begin to demonstrate an awareness that written language can be in the home language or in English. | 1.2  Begin to use marks or symbols to represent spoken language in the home language or in English. | 1.2  Continue to develop writing by using letters or letter-like marks to represent their ideas in English. |

### Focus: Writing their name

| | | |
|---|---|---|
| 1.3  Write marks to represent their own name in a way that may resemble how it is written in the home language. | 1.3  Attempt to copy their own name in English or in the writing system of their home language. | 1.3  Write their first name on their own in English nearly correctly, using letters of the English alphabet to accurately represent pronunciation in their home language. |

# Mathematics

## Number Sense

| *At around 48 months of age* | *At around 60 months of age* |
|---|---|
| **1.0  Children begin to understand numbers and quantities in their everyday environment.** | **1.0  Children expand their understanding of numbers and quantities in their everyday environment.** |
| 1.1  Recite numbers in order to ten with increasing accuracy. | 1.1  Recite numbers in order to twenty with increasing accuracy. |
| 1.2  Begin to recognize and name a few written numerals. | 1.2  Recognize and know the name of some written numerals. |
| 1.3  Identify, without counting, the number of objects in a collection of up to three objects (i.e., subitize). | 1.3  Identify, without counting, the number of objects in a collection of up to four objects (i.e., subitize). |
| 1.4  Count up to five objects, using one-to-one correspondence (one object for each number word) with increasing accuracy. | 1.4  Count up to ten objects, using one-to-one correspondence (one object for each number word) with increasing accuracy. |
| 1.5  Use the number name of the last object counted to answer the question, "How many . . . ?" | 1.5  Understand, when counting, that the number name of the last object counted represents the total number of objects in the group (i.e., cardinality). |
| **2.0  Children begin to understand number relationships and operations in their everyday environment.** | **2.0  Children expand their understanding of number relationships and operations in their everyday environment.** |
| 2.1  Compare visually (with or without counting) two groups of objects that are obviously equal or nonequal and communicate, "more" or "same." | 2.1  Compare, by counting or matching, two groups of up to five objects and communicate, "more," "same as," or "fewer" (or "less"). |
| 2.2  Understand that adding to (or taking away) one or more objects from a group will increase (or decrease) the number of objects in the group. | 2.2  Understand that adding one or taking away one changes the number in a small group of objects by exactly one. |

| At around 48 months of age | At around 60 months of age |
|---|---|
| 2.3 Understand that putting two groups of objects together will make a bigger group. | 2.3 Understand that putting two groups of objects together will make a bigger group and that a group of objects can be taken apart into smaller groups. |
| 2.4 Solve simple addition and subtraction problems nonverbally (and often verbally) with a very small number of objects (sums up to 4 or 5). | 2.4 Solve simple addition and subtraction problems with a small number of objects (sums up to 10), usually by counting. |

# Algebra and Functions
## (Classification and Patterning)

| At around 48 months of age | At around 60 months of age |
|---|---|
| **1.0 Children begin to sort and classify objects in their everyday environment.** | **1.0 Children expand their understanding of sorting and classifying objects in their everyday environment.** |
| 1.1 Sort and classify objects by one attribute into two or more groups, with increasing accuracy. | 1.1 Sort and classify objects by one or more attributes, into two or more groups, with increasing accuracy (e.g., may sort first by one attribute and then by another attribute). |
| **2.0 Children begin to recognize simple, repeating patterns.** | **2.0 Children expand their understanding of simple, repeating patterns.** |
| 2.1 Begin to identify or recognize a simple, repeating pattern. | 2.1 Recognize and duplicate simple, repeating patterns. |
| 2.2 Attempt to create a simple, repeating pattern or participate in making one. | 2.2 Begin to extend and create simple, repeating patterns. |

# Measurement

| At around 48 months of age | At around 60 months of age |
|---|---|
| **1.0  Children begin to compare and order objects.** | **1.0  Children expand their understanding of comparing, ordering, and measuring objects.** |
| 1.1  Demonstrate awareness that objects can be compared by length, weight, or capacity, by noting gross differences, using words such as *bigger, longer, heavier,* or *taller,* or by placing objects side by side to compare length. | 1.1  Compare two objects by length, weight, or capacity directly (e.g., putting objects side by side) or indirectly (e.g., using a third object). |
| 1.2  Order three objects by size. | 1.2  Order four or more objects by size. |
|  | 1.3  Measure length using multiple duplicates of the same-size concrete units laid end to end. |

# Geometry

| At around 48 months of age | At around 60 months of age |
|---|---|
| **1.0  Children begin to identify and use common shapes in their everyday environment.** | **1.0  Children identify and use a variety of shapes in their everyday environment.** |
| 1.1  Identify simple two-dimensional shapes, such as a circle and square. | 1.1  Identify, describe, and construct a variety of different shapes, including variations of a circle, triangle, rectangle, square, and other shapes. |
| 1.2  Use individual shapes to represent different elements of a picture or design. | 1.2  Combine different shapes to create a picture or design. |
| **2.0  Children begin to understand positions in space.** | **2.0  Children expand their understanding of positions in space.** |
| 2.1  Identify positions of objects and people in space, such as in/on/under, up/down, and inside/outside. | 2.1  Identify positions of objects and people in space, including in/on/under, up/down, inside/outside, beside/between, and in front/behind. |

# Mathematical Reasoning

| At around 48 months of age | At around 60 months of age |
|---|---|
| **1.0 Children use mathematical thinking to solve problems that arise in their everyday environment.** | **1.0 Children expand the use of mathematical thinking to solve problems that arise in their everyday environment.** |
| 1.1 Begin to apply simple mathematical strategies to solve problems in their environment. | 1.1 Identify and apply a variety of mathematical strategies to solve problems in their environment. |

R16-009  PR16-0016  4-17  10M

OSP 17 142718